SPYMASTER

SPYMASTER

Startling Cold War Revelations
of a Soviet KGB Chief

Tennent H. Bagley

Skyhorse Publishing

Copyright © 2013 by Tennent H. Bagley

Skyhorse Publishing books may be purchased in bulk at special discounts for sales promotion, corporate gifts, fund-raising, or educational purposes. Special editions can also be created to specifications. For details, contact the Special Sales Department, Skyhorse Publishing, 307 West 36th Street, 11th Floor, New York, NY 10018 or info@skyhorsepublishing.com.

Skyhorse® and Skyhorse Publishing® are registered trademarks of Skyhorse Publishing, Inc.®, a Delaware corporation.

Visit our website at www.skyhorsepublishing.com.

10 9 8 7 6 5 4 3 2 1

Library of Congress Cataloging-in-Publication Data is available on file.

ISBN: 978-1-62636-065-5

Printed in the United States of America

Contents

Preface

THIS VOYAGE BACK into the darker regions of the Cold War began in a little country inn in eastern Germany.

As I walked into the sunny breakfast room, the sparkle of silverware on an undisturbed sea of white tablecloths showed me I was early. But not the earliest: a thin and bespectacled man sat alone at a corner table. I recognized him as another participant in the TV production that had brought me to the inn so I walked up to him.

"May I join you?" I asked.

"Please do," he replied with a welcoming gesture toward the seat to his right.

We introduced ourselves, but he evidently knew me already just as I knew him. In fact, this man and I had probably known of each other for more than thirty years. He was Sergey Kondrashev, one of the KGB's most influential figures during the Cold War years, when on the other side I had been supervising CIA's work against his service.

Having long grappled with Soviet deception operations, I was about to breakfast with a man who had run them.

Over orange juice and toast, we talked amicably of our past in the spy game. Kondrashev mentioned that his career in foreign intelligence operations had not started there, but in the KGB's internal-counterintelligence directorate where, in the late 1940s and into the 1950s, he had worked against the American Embassy in Moscow.

That grabbed my interest; I knew that some unsolved mysteries had originated there and then. Old questions rushed to my head. Did I dare ask them of this familiar stranger? Why not? "Tell me, then," I said without preamble or explanation, "something that has been bothering me for a long time. Why ever did Kovshuk make that trip to Washington?"

My breakfast companion had no trouble translating my reference. Vladislav Kovshuk, while heading the KGB's work against American Embassy personnel in Moscow, had travelled to the United States under a pseudonym in early 1957 on a trip that had somehow helped the KGB uncover America's most important spy in the Soviet Union.

Kondrashev could have deflected the question or pretended ignorance, but instead he answered matter-of-factly and right away, "Oh, that was to meet an important agent." After a brief pause he added, "One who was never uncovered."

Just ten minutes into our acquaintance, the great Soviet spymaster had thrown out a morsel that convinced me this could be a fruitful relationship. I nodded. "Yes, I've long thought so" (as indeed I had), then dropped the subject. To dig for the identity of that still-hidden spy would surely force him to pull back. We smiled at each other, knowing how exceptional our exchange had been.

This astonishing start to a first meeting between former enemies was to set the tone of a relationship that ended only with Kondrashev's death thirteen years later, a tone of affinity, cordiality, mutual respect, and growing confidence between two old professionals.

We were breakfasting there north of Berlin in what had been forbidden territory for me until the recent end of the Cold War. We were not just inside former Communist East Germany, but in the very heart of the once tightly-patrolled Wandlitz area where the Party bigwigs had their summer homes. In this roadside inn in the village of Prenden, we practically sat atop the huge, once-secret underground bunker that would have protected them in case of atomic war.

It was March 1994. A Franco-German TV company had invited retired spy-service veterans, two from the East and two from the West, to chat together about our Cold War in front of the cameras. Along with Kondrashev, the East was represented by the fabled East German intelligence chief Markus Wolf, who had offered the use of his *dacha* here in Prenden for the occasion. I had already been introduced to Wolf a year earlier in his East Berlin apartment, and we had hit it off well. Later I learned that one reason Kondrashev had been so open with me was that "Mischa" Wolf, his long-time colleague and friend, had already assured him he could talk confidently with me.

After breakfast I joined the other Western participant, Constantin Melnik, who had overseen the intelligence and security services of France, to walk the few hundred yards along the narrow road to Wolf's *dacha*. At the gate we introduced ourselves through a speaker-phone and were cheerfully admitted. As we walked the forty yards up to the A-frame cottage set in the forest greenery, I wondered how many Eastern spymasters must have enjoyed Wolf's hospitality here during the Cold War to plot against my country and my service.

We talked for two days in fine spring weather, our "round table" being a rough-hewn outdoor garden table whenever we were not

The team who made *La Guerre des Loups* [War of the Wolves] at its first broadcast, Paris, September 1994. L. to R.: Sergey Kondrashev, Tennent H. Bagley, producer Daniel Leconte, Constantin Melnik, author J. M. Meurisse, Markus Wolf, author Maurice Najman.

on the terrace sipping drinks, or inside dining on the *pelmeni* dumplings that were Mischa's culinary specialty.[1]

Later that year we reassembled in Paris for the first TV broadcast of the film documenting our talks.[2] Its positive reception encouraged further TV "round table" projects. The next year we found ourselves together again, this time in Berlin to talk about Cold War spying in that area. And later that year, when those talks were broadcast on French TV, we met again in Paris.[3] Finally, we came together in 1996 in Sochi, Russia, where our public exchange was one event of an international film festival.

Each of these five occasions provided opportunities for long, informal talks with Kondrashev, often about family and other personal matters. He was moved, as he put it after Sochi, by "our good personal contact and mutual understanding."

During this same period in the mid-1990s, a series of joint East-West research projects brought out more of the secret history of the just-ended Cold War. Under an arrangement with the American publisher Random House, the Russian Foreign Intelligence Service made selected KGB file materials accessible to its veterans who cooperated with Westerners bringing documents from their own side, to shed fresh light on major espionage episodes. From this project books emerged on the undersides of the Cuban Missile Crisis, on Soviet atom-bomb espionage in America, on the activities of certain Soviet undercover operatives, and on the long KGB-CIA confrontation in Berlin. In the latter project, Sergey Kondrashev, the former head of the KGB's German Department, collaborated with my colleague and friend David E. Murphy, former CIA chief in Berlin and head of its Soviet Bloc Division, in a years-long effort that produced the book *Battleground Berlin*.[4]

Seeing that his own service was willing to release some previously secret information, Kondrashev decided to follow the example of other KGB veterans and write his memoirs. However, to earn a reasonable amount of hard currency, his story would have to be published in the West as *Battleground Berlin* had been and, as Sergey put it, "in the English vernacular." He asked David Murphy to help him, but wearied by long, frustrating efforts to spring useful material from KGB files for their Berlin book, Murphy did not want to take on this new project. He suggested that Kondrashev turn to me.

Having gained confidence in my goodwill and discretion over the previous five years, having recommendations from Murphy and Wolf, and knowing I had already written a book on the KGB, Kondrashev asked me in 1999 if I would assist him in writing his story. He knew that my familiarity with the KGB would spare him the need to provide the context for his recollections and could even contribute to their substance.

I readily accepted, thus beginning a unique relationship. There have been a lot of contacts between KGB and CIA veterans since the end of the Cold War but none, I think, in which a top-level, still-loyal KGB veteran permitted—indeed, invited—an experienced Cold War enemy to delve for year after year into the details of his personal and professional life. And because I was being asked not just to write "in the English vernacular" what Kondrashev chose to recount, but also to choose the topics and shape his telling of his life story, I could ask whatever questions I wanted.

Thus, long after retiring from the CIA, where I had grappled with subtle and deceptive Soviet operations, I was given the undreamed-of opportunity to dig back into them with an expert insider.

I considered it a stroke of fortune. To some it might seem curious that I would want to associate with veterans of the KGB, the prime executor of the longest and cruellest repression of modern times, a system that I had dedicated my career to combating. But I knew that behind the blood-spattered walls of that Cheka-OGPU-NKVD-KGB lay the answers to questions never resolved—involving ongoing threats to the security of my country—and only their veterans knew those answers. Though I had retired and severed contact with the CIA more than thirty years earlier, I still felt the responsibility and the attractions of my old job, and I was still nagged by those questions.

For about seven years, Sergey Kondrashev and I worked on his autobiography, inevitably exploring ever deeper the field of deception where he had played a leading role. From 2000 through 2006, we met about twice a year for two or three weeks at a time in Brussels, the city where I had retired to, and for shorter periods

Kondrashev with the author at a conference in Germany and at work in the author's study.

at European conferences. In Brussels we worked in my personal study where my elaborate library on Soviet Bloc espionage, organized and catalogued, offered immediate reference to details and reminders of the past. He either stayed as our house guest or in Russian Embassy-provided quarters not far away. Between working sessions, we relaxed during forest walks and tourist outings. And when not together, we exchanged drafts and comments via mail, email, and telephone between Brussels and Moscow.

The renamed KGB (now SVR for its foreign intelligence operations and FSB for its internal counterintelligence and security work) were fully aware of who I was and what we were doing. Indeed, Kondrashev went out of his way to minimize Moscow suspicions that he might be sharing too much with this former adversary. He arranged that some of our correspondence and drafts passed through the SVR's Press Bureau. He made no secret of our Brussels meetings; on some mornings, the local Russian counterintelligence chief even drove him to my apartment building.

As we completed chapters, Sergey would routinely submit them for clearance for publication. The SVR objected to only a few passages, but later, when we had nearly completed the manuscript, they required Kondrashev to translate my English-language original into Russian for final review by "a special committee of leading personalities of the service."

Then, abruptly, the situation changed.

Perhaps SVR people saw more clearly how sensitive the matters were that Kondrashev was planning to divulge. And with security tightening under Putin's regime, the FSB had entered the scene, apparatchiks who took a wider view of what might constitute a secret. In April 2007 the SVR revoked all earlier chapter clearances. They told Kondrashev that his manuscript would be circulated inside the SVR for the orientation of their officers, but they refused to release any part of it for publication.

From that forbidden manuscript, which will now enlighten Russian spymasters, I have taken much of the present book.

It is not surprising that Moscow might judge our revelations as too sensitive to publish. Sergey Kondrashev was not just any senior KGB veteran, but one of a mere handful who knew many of its deepest secrets. During his half-century of active KGB service (1944–1992), he had worked in some of its darkest corners:

- In a case of colossal importance that vaulted his career, Kondrashev had personally recruited in Moscow an American Embassy code clerk whose betrayal allowed the KGB to break American military ciphers. This traitor was never uncovered.
- He personally handled the earlier defection of another American Embassy military code clerk in Moscow.
- He handled a historically-important mole inside British Intelligence, the MI6 officer George Blake.
- He headed two of the most important KGB stations abroad, those in London and Vienna.
- He was chief of the KGB's German-Austrian Department, overseeing its penetrations of the West German government and other clandestine actions in that area of prime Soviet concern.
- He led the KGB's Service A ("active measures"), the element tasked to weaken, mislead, and confuse Western governments and their intelligence services.
- He worked directly with the Politburo inside its premises while it coped with the Prague Spring crisis of 1968.
- He was deputy head of the KGB's worldwide clandestine operations, specifically overseeing its deception operations, among others. In that capacity, he was one of only two foreign-intel-

ligence (FCD) officers briefed on the tightest-held operations abroad of the SCD (internal-counterintelligence directorate).

- He commanded the secret intelligence operations of Soviet border troops along their vast frontiers in northern Europe, Central Asia, China, and the northern Pacific.
- As Chief Senior Consultant to four KGB Chairman for more than a dozen years, he helped supervise the most sensitive intelligence operations abroad and prepared the Chairman's participation in meetings of the nation's high command, the Politburo.

To bring out stories from such depths, while remaining steadfastly loyal to his country and his service, Kondrashev had to tread an unmarked path between those things he could safely reveal and those he could not. Sometimes when our talks got too close to the edge, he shifted into generalities or deftly changed the subject or pretended not to hear a certain question. He would (unconvincingly) deny knowledge of certain matters. But I could discern the truth from the consistency in his accounts of the same events related months or even years apart and from my growing familiarity with his character and manner. Sergey Kondrashev wanted to present for posterity as true and complete a picture as he could of his life and motivation. He did not exaggerate his role or achievements nor, to the best of my knowledge, did he fabricate any part of his story, even its most trivial incidents.

Throughout all our time together he was aware—we in fact discussed it—that I was composing a book of my own on the subject of KGB deception operations, one that centered on the case of the putative KGB defector Yuri Nosenko whom, as he knew, I had handled for CIA.[5] Some of the questions I put to Kondrashev pertained more to my own interests than to his life story. Sometimes he would answer them without recognizing their pertinence. At other times he would smilingly reproach me: "Pete, that question was for your book, not mine!" When I admitted it with a rueful grin, he would shrug and answer it anyway.

To clarify a forgotten detail, he would sometimes go back and question former colleagues in Moscow. On at least one occasion, he did so on my behalf, getting from one of Nosenko's former associates some details about Nosenko's KGB career that were quite different from what Nosenko had fed to CIA.

Kondrashev inevitably strayed off that unmarked path from time to time, ever more frequently as our friendly understanding ripened throughout the years. Outside our working sessions, as we relaxed over a meal or drink or strolled in the woods, he told me things that he would never publish and that his Moscow reviewers would never clear.

I asked Kondrashev what might be the consequences if I were indiscreetly to publish in my book sensitive facts attributable to him. After a moment's reflection, he said it might cost him his (very modest) pension, but more important to him was his status in his community. He would be discredited among his former colleagues in the semi-official KGB retirees' circle. It would also compromise his continued association with the SVR itself, which still consulted him and provided him services, such as special telephones, a car and driver when necessary, and file information for his writings and contributions to historical seminars. So I refrained from using any details that might point to Sergey as a source in my book *Spy Wars*.

In 2007, Sergey Kondrashev died of long-standing heart troubles. He can no longer be harmed by these revelations, and his family has agreed to my publishing his story in the West with my own input to make his contribution to the history of the secret Cold War more accessible to the Western reader.

What follows, then, is an account that even today Russian intelligence doesn't want you to read. It offers new insights into famous episodes of the Cold War and exposes others for the first time—like that of the American traitor who helped launch the Korean War.

One: Breaking American Ciphers—
and Starting a War

THE ALL-POWERFUL HEAD of Soviet State Security reached toward the corner of his wide desk and picked up the little pile of hand-written and amateurishly-typed papers, knocked them together, and stuffed them into a large envelope. With his pen, he wrote on the envelope, "File closed. To be opened only with the handwritten authority of the Minister of State Security" and signed, "Viktor S. Abakumov." He dropped the envelope into his own safe, perhaps the closest-guarded of all archives in this secret center of a secretive regime.

In that thin sheaf of papers was the entire written record to the present day of a spy story that deserves volumes. It told how the KGB (then MGB) had recruited an American code clerk in Moscow, enabling it to break America's military ciphers at a critical moment of the Cold War.

There was more paper on this triumph elsewhere, of course, somewhere inside the secret realms of the cipher-breakers: calculations and work sheets, lists of machine key settings, steps in reconstructing the American cipher machine, and heaps of deciphered American military communications. But those other papers gave no hint of what was in Abakumov's envelope: who the source was and where and when and how he had been recruited and handled. Aside from Minister Abakumov, only seven people in the world knew these things and at the same time knew of the cipher break—aside from the recruiter himself.

The recruiter was Sergey Kondrashev.[1]

Fewer still, and never anyone in the West, became aware of the impact this KGB operation had on Josef Stalin. Abakumov, who was probably closer to Stalin's innermost secrets than anyone alive, personally carried to him the transcripts of these deciphered American military messages along with the KGB's analysis of them. Stalin had confided to Abakumov that they were swaying him. These authentic insights into American thinking, Abakumov told Kondrashev when later rewarding him, had been "especially persuasive for Stalin at this particular moment."

"At this particular moment" the Americans had withdrawn their military forces from Korea. Secretary of State Dean Acheson had publicly enunciated a new defense perimeter in the Pacific "from the Ryukyus to the Philippine Islands,"[2] which excluded Korea. North Korean leader Kim Il-Sung had long pleaded with Stalin to support—in effect, permit—a military invasion and takeover of South Korea, but Stalin, fearing American military intervention, continued to rebuff him. Now, Abakumov told Kondrashev, these deciphered high-level American communications conveyed to Stalin the impression that there would be little danger of direct conflict with the United States even if the USSR gave massive aid to the North Korean venture. That was why Stalin finally removed his objection to the North Koreans' long-standing plans to invade.[3]

This American code clerk may thus have inadvertently touched off the Korean War. But the KGB had kept the secret well. Until now that traitor's role has remained unknown.

• • •

THE SPY HAD GIVEN the Soviets what every government most wants and, having obtained, then most needs to hide: the ability to read the secret communications of its rivals and potential enemies. To preserve such a rare advantage, of the sort the Allies had in the Second World War after mastering the Nazi German cipher machine Enigma, almost any cost is warranted. Many lives had been sacrificed to protect the "Enigma" secret. So well had it been kept, that thirty years passed after the war's end, an entire generation, before the public became aware of it and historians were obliged to rewrite parts of the war's history.

The Soviets broke that record of secret-keeping. More than sixty years have elapsed since the cipher-break, and only now is this first public account of the spy who triggered the Korean War published. He died undiscovered, as far as I know, and the US government presumably remained unaware that during those early days of the Cold War evolving and a hot war threatening, the Soviets possessed the war-winning capability of reading America's secret military communications.

● ● ●

As THE YEARS WENT by, here and there within the KGB, one or another part of the story—but never both—became known or suspected. Some insiders attributed Kondrashev's unusually fast rise in KGB ranks to a major operational success. Others independently got wind of the recruitment of an unidentified American code clerk in Moscow at some unspecified time after the war. Then at the end of 1961, the first hint leaked to the West when KGB officer Anatoly Golitsyn defected to the Americans. Golitsyn had learned of several recruitments of American and other Western code clerks, two quite recent, but at least one from the early postwar years. Of the latter, he had learned only the code name of an American, "Jack," which was indeed the code name of Kondrashev's recruit. But thanks to Abakumov's precautions, American counterintelligence would be forced to do some painstaking investigating to identify "Jack."

To throw those American investigators off the track opened by Golitsyn to this and the other code clerks, the KGB put to work its time-tested practice of deception (as described in Chapter 14). It succeeded: As far as I or Kondrashev know, the Americans failed to pin down the identity of "Jack" or any of the other code clerks Golitsyn had pointed to. Even to this day, the American Government may believe its ciphers remained secure back in those earlier times.

When Kondrashev embarked on writing his memoirs, he could not fail to mention these events that had so fundamentally influenced his life and career. Accordingly, here is the first public exposure of one of the Cold War's most dangerous spies.

• • •

THE STORY BEGAN ONE morning in the early spring of 1948, the year before "Jack" entered the picture. Members of KGB section 2b-1, the one working against the American Embassy in Moscow (described in Chapter 3) of which Sergey Kondrashev was deputy chief, assembled for a routine staff meeting. Each member was watching one or another group of Americans in or close to the Embassy to detect any spying—and to spot individuals whom the KGB might induce or coerce into becoming spies.

Roman Markov, whose target was the Military Attaché's office, spoke up. "*Naruzhka*[4] has observed an American sergeant repeatedly seeing a Russian girl. Maybe he's a code clerk."

That was big news! Code clerks were the KGB's most desired recruitment targets in the American Embassy, but at the same time the least accessible. They lived and worked under tight restrictions and observed special precautions whenever they moved outside American-controlled buildings and met foreigners. Now perhaps they had found a bridge to one of them.

"Do we know the girl?" asked section chief Mikhail Levin.

"No, nothing on her, no file, no contact. We know nothing about her."

"Check her out."

After Markov met her to get a feel for the situation, his report was favorable. This was no one-night stand; the "stompers" had stumbled onto a real love affair. "Valya" (as Kondrashev chose to call her) told Markov of her deep affection for the American soldier "Mac"—Sergeant James M. McMillin—and she felt sure that he genuinely loved her, too. Markov told her that Soviet authorities had no objection and in fact hoped she would develop the relationship further.[5]

Levin reported this encouraging development to the American Department (2b) chief, Anatoly Kholevo. Coming back, he told Kondrashev, "You get ready to handle this. You speak the best English." The two of them went to the office of the overall chief of counterintelligence, Yevgeniy Pitovranov, who, after consulting with Minister Abakumov, concurred. If things worked out, it would be Sergey, along with Pitovranov's deputy Leonid Raikhman, who would talk with Mac.

Kondrashev went with Markov to meet Valya and assured her they would do everything possible to help them stay together, but she and Mac must not tell anyone about their relationship. If any Americans heard, the two would be ripped apart. She agreed to follow their directions.

As the weeks went by, Mac and Valya continued to meet in parks, coffeehouses, and at the flat where she lived with her parents. Kondrashev and Markov met her regularly to keep abreast of developments. The "stompers" stayed on the job to see if anything might be amiss, but with a strict injunction to break off if there was the slightest chance of Mac's spotting them. It would spoil everything if he were to get the idea that the KGB was sponsoring their friendship. The surveillance also served as a sort of protection for Mac: "Relations between our countries were so tense that we feared someone might attack him," Kondrashev told me.

Then one day Valya told Kondrashev that Mac had decided to stay with her at any price and make their future lives together in Russia.

"Down the drain went our hopes to recruit a source inside American communications," Kondrashev lamented, "but at least we would get details of the Embassy code room."

At Kondrashev's suggestion, Valya told Mac she knew "people who could help them," and he readily agreed to meet them. "We gave them the address of a safe apartment near Pushkin Square," Kondrashev recalled, and when they arrived one summer afternoon, Raikhman and Sergey were waiting to meet them.

An impressive, gray-haired man then in his late fifties, Raikhman spoke in a fatherly manner. He promised Mac a job and an apartment in Moscow if he was serious about his intentions, but added "we would want to know about certain matters." Mac expected this quid pro quo, and after only a slight pause, said he would help as well as he could.

Now all Mac had to do, Kondrashev told him, is go back to the quarters he shared with other Military Attaché personnel to get his personal belongings. "Take only what you really need, and only small things," Kondrashev said, "We'll give you whatever you need. Just don't let anyone wonder what you're doing."

Off he went. Raikhman and Sergey's nerves were on edge, asking themselves, "Will he really come back?" But even in their agitated state they both noticed that Valya remained calm. She obviously had no doubt.

After what seemed a long wait, a phone call brought welcome news from the stakeout near Mac's quarters. He had been spotted emerging alone with a package and heading in the right direction without being followed.

Mac and Valya stayed there for a few days before moving to a two-room safe apartment that had been stocked with food and drink so they could stay indoors.

Soon the American Embassy asked the Foreign Ministry about the missing soldier. After a few days they replied that he was well but had decided to leave American service and stay in the Soviet Union. "We turned down their request to interview him, too," Kondrashev added. "We weren't sure then that he could have withstood the pressure."

[But six months later—when their son was born—Sergey came to realize that Mac would indeed have withstood pressure and why Valya had remained so calm.]

Kondrashev began questioning Mac about the code room. "He told us how the cipher machines worked—how the rotors were installed and their position alternated according to a key list—and how they would be destroyed in an emergency," Sergey told me. Mac told of the daily routines and personalities of the other code clerks, but as a junior code clerk he didn't know much and had not brought any key lists. "Already after four or five sessions I realized that we had reached the limit. We had made a step forward, but we couldn't break the ciphers."

If they were ever to do that, Kondrashev realized, the Section would have to recruit a code clerk in place.

Someone in the Section proposed that McMillin's defection be publicized to gain a propaganda point against the United States. Kondrashev squelched the idea. To exploit the affair publicly would ensure that other American officials, knowing they might be used that way, would not come over to the Soviet side. "My caution proved fruitful, I think. If there'd been publicity about this case I doubt we'd ever have recruited 'Jack.'"

• • •

THE HOPED-FOR OPPORTUNITY AROSE within months. Roman Markov reported another observation by foot surveillants of an American code clerk spending the night with a Russian girl.

Markov knew he was a code clerk; by now, thanks to McMillin's defection, this KGB section was familiar with the layout and procedures of the American Embassy's code room and was giving its personnel special attention.

"Get on it, right away!" said Section Chief Levin.

They did, and received some surprises. A check of the files showed that the KGB already knew this street address and even the girl's name, and that they had an earlier relationship with her. "Nadya" (as Kondrashev chose to call her) had briefly cooperated with another part of the KGB, but the contact had lapsed. It now became evident that Nadya had gone out on her own and obtained a job in the American Embassy. For more than a year she had worked there in contact with a lot of Embassy people, but the KGB, confident that they already had enough sources inside, hadn't even bothered to check her out. Their embarrassment redoubled when they now found that two or three of their inside sources had known that Nadya was flirting with the American soldier. Clearly, *naruzhka* had saved the KGB from missing a rare opportunity.

Nadya, who was rather attractive, was still single, though over thirty. Outside her apartment of two small rooms off Gorky Street, the "stompers" began a stakeout and saw the code clerk come frequently and stay late.

Markov visited Nadya and told her the affair was known, but far from discouraging it, the authorities wanted her to develop it. In fact, a colleague might be able to help them. Markov introduced Kondrashev, who began to direct her relationship with the code clerk, to whom the section now gave the code name "Jack."[6]

To Kondrashev it looked promising. Nadya dreamed of getting married and, like many Soviet women of her time, of living abroad. She saw Jack as her chance for both, and Jack looked susceptible — both to her and to Kondrashev: He was a bit younger than Nadya, by no means tall or handsome, and beginning to lose his hair.

As Kondrashev was soon to learn, Jack was also unscrupulous and greedy for money. When they began laying plans to marry and leave for America, he told Nadya he hoped somehow to get enough to make their life rich and bright. Jack liked drinking so much that Kondrashev imagined his highest ambition might be to own a bar of his own, but even for that they would need a lot more money than he could ever accumulate in the Army. Kondrashev told Nadya to push Jack to think about ways to get more.

Having nourished their greed, Kondrashev then told Nadya to tell Jack that she had a relative (or family friend, Sergey no longer remembered) who might pay good money for information. Jack jumped at the opportunity. He suggested to her that she invite the man to meet him at her place.

Kondrashev stayed only a few minutes on this initial visit, talking only in general terms about the Embassy to avoid scaring Jack off. But he left Nadya with an envelope full of rubles to give Jack afterward.

A week later Kondrashev came back. This time focused more directly on Jack's Embassy work. It was Jack who first mentioned the code room and his functions there. This time Kondrashev left behind an envelope containing five hundred US dollars, the equivalent of about five thousand in today's currency.

The next encounter, which was Kondrashev's first direct payment to Jack, stuck vividly in his memory. He had stuffed into his suit jacket's breast pocket an envelope holding a thousand dollars. As they sat sipping tea, he told Jack specifically what he wanted to know while casually taking out the envelope and laying it on the table beside him. Jack eyed it hungrily as their talk progressed. Then just before stepping out of the room on some pretext, Kondrashev pushed it closer toward the code clerk. As he walked out, he saw Jack slip it under his saucer.

When they parted that day, Kondrashev told Jack he would get another envelope each time they met and hinted that there might be more in each.

The meetings continued at Nadya's two or three times a month. She was always present but would shrewdly excuse herself to go off to the kitchen. Jack sometimes wanted a whisky before beginning to talk, but Kondrashev told him, "Forget it. You'll soon have plenty of time—and money—for that."

Jack answered all of Kondrashev's questions. He also agreed to bring broken or used parts of cipher machines that he was supposed to dispose of. On one occasion he brought a broken rotor which, though lacking its wiring, was a help to the KGB's cipher-breakers. Each little wheel, rotating in varying speeds side by side (their number varying according to the type of machine) was wired with letters and numbers and punctuation marks, in order changing according to a key schedule. When Jack spoke of that schedule Kondrashev told him to bring it next time. Jack did so, and again whenever the key settings changed.

At first Kondrashev was coached for these meetings by "Misha," a cipher specialist of the KGB's Eighth Chief Directorate, the codes and ciphers equivalent of America's National Security Agency. But it soon became evident that they could move faster if Misha himself joined the meetings. Thereafter he attended almost every meeting, asking detailed questions and giving Jack concrete assignments. Once Misha asked him to encipher an arbitrary text on the machine in the Embassy code room and to give Misha its clear text. Misha also asked Jack to print out the alphabet backwards and then forwards and encipher all punctuation marks, then bring him the result.

By now Kondrashev handed Jack his envelopes without the delicate moves of the early meetings. At times he would leave up to $5,000 inside, but whenever Jack failed to produce what he had promised, Kondrashev left the room to remove some money. It didn't take Jack long to recognize the direct relationship and, greedy as he was, he tried to do better.

He did well. By the time Jack was transferred from Moscow in late 1949, he had received $50,000, and just before Jack left, at Abakumov's suggestion, Kondrashev gave him a send-off bonus of an additional $50,000 in cash. When one calculates dollar values of those days, this $100,000 amounted to more than a whole career's pay for Jack.

But for the KGB, the value of his services was incalculable. After the cipher-breakers had worked for a time on Jack's materials, Misha told Kondrashev in an excited, hushed voice, "It's working—we're getting clear text!" When later decorating Kondrashev for the operation, Abakumov said the cipher-breakers' chief General Shevelyov had told him Jack's information had enabled them to assemble a copy of the machine. The Soviet government could now read American secret communications not only between Moscow and

Washington, but also between Washington and other posts abroad, all of which continued throughout the months that the keys Jack had given remained valid.

Kondrashev looked back on this case not just with professional pride, but also with dismay, for with Jack he had inadvertently helped launch the Korean War.

• • •

Now came a critical moment: Jack's impending departure on routine reassignment.

Kondrashev got Minister Abakumov's authority to promise Nadya a passport and exit visa to leave the country before Jack's departure. Kondrashev told her he would help them arrange a "chance" meeting somewhere in Western Europe, after which the two could move on and make their lives together wherever they wanted. And he meant it, feeling that his service owed this gift to them for their enormous help, and he truly thought the service would carry out its promises.

Nadya and Jack started planning how they'd meet in the West, marry, and then go to the United States together. But it was not to be.

When Kondrashev and Abakumov discussed the subject in the presence of Counterintelligence Chief Pitovranov, it took Pitovranov only seconds to spot the flaw in the plan. The other two had sensed it, too, but had brushed it aside in their enthusiasm.

"Look," Pitovranov said. "Here's the picture you're painting. This American code clerk is traveling in Europe—West Germany, say— and what do you know? He happens to bump into this Russian girl he had known just a month or two ago when both of them were working in the American Embassy in Moscow. Now they suddenly fall in love and marry. Tell me, do you seriously think the Americans would accept that fairy tale? And how does she explain how she managed to leave the USSR?"

It was clear. To let Nadya out risked exposing the Soviet break of American ciphers, a risk that could not be taken because by now this cipher break was one of the country's most potent military assets. For months to come, at least until the expiration of the advance key settings Jack had given, the KGB would still be reading secret American communications. Those months might be critical—and as Abakumov later told Kondrashev, they actually were. Nothing was more important than hiding this success.

Of course Kondrashev agreed—how could any professional not? But he felt sick about the dilemma, feeling strongly that an intelligence officer's relationship with his sources must be based on absolute honesty.

There wasn't much honesty in what happened next. To strengthen Jack's confidence that they would get Nadya out of the country, Kondrashev and Abakumov threw an intimate little send-off party for them two weeks before Jack himself was to leave, both Markov and Kondrashev bringing special food and drink to the apartment.

So that Jack could see her leave, Nadya actually got on the westbound train, accompanied by Markov, who was going along ostensibly to make sure she would have no problem crossing the Polish border. To her dismay, he bundled her off the train at the first stop some hundred kilometers west of Moscow. Given a polite thanks and some money for her service, Nadya was then left to resume her life in Moscow. (Sergey remembered no more of her fate.)

Off went Jack at the end of his posting, thinking he would meet Nadya. But he never did.

• • •

THIS SUCCESSFUL RECRUITMENT AND cipher-breaking brought congratulations and prizes to Kondrashev. Minister Abakumov called him into his office to say he was presenting his name to the government to be awarded the Order of the Great Patriotic War. Nevermind that the war had been over for more than four years, he said, Kondrashev had achieved results of extraordinary military significance through this code-breaking source.

Abakumov must have kept thinking about it after Kondrashev left his office, for he called him in later that same day to ask whether there might be some more practical way he could help. There was indeed: Kondrashev and his wife Rosa were living in one room with their year-old son Igor[7] and would welcome an apartment of their own, even a small one.

"Done!" said Abakumov. "Sit down right here at my desk and write out the application." Then and there he added to it a hand-written command to the head of administration. A few weeks later the family moved into a small apartment in a recently constructed building of KGB apartments, the "house with the tower" on Malaya Kolkhoznaya (now Sukharevskaya) Square.

• • •

NOT LONG AFTER, STALIN's murderous scythe swept through State Security in a last purge that struck down Kondrashev's bosses Abakumov and Pitovranov and scores of others, and threw the whole service into turmoil.[8]

Because of this calamitous purge, years passed before the KGB could pull itself together enough to even think of reactivating Jack. Of the handful who even knew the existence of this case, Abakumov, Pitovranov, and Kondrashev's immediate boss were all in jail. The service finally got around to sending an officer to the United States after Pitovranov's release from jail and "no later than 1953," but Kondrashev foresaw and warned that it would be a waste of time.

The traveler did indeed, as Sergey had foreseen, return to Moscow empty-handed. But Sergey did not know or did not remember—or was unwilling to tell—why. Perhaps it had happened as he had foreseen: the KGB not having lived up to its side of the bargain, Jack refused any further help and neither wanted nor needed to run further risk. (The KGB could not pressure him because any exposure would harm the Soviets more than it would harm Jack.) Or perhaps it was because Jack had left the Army and gotten into some insignificant and uninteresting job. Sergey mentioned both possibilities, but did not specify. He wanted to make this important event a part of his life story, but without betraying the identity of his code clerk recruit.[9]

So the story remains incomplete, hanging there as yet another unsolved mystery of the Cold War.

Two:
Two Views of Culture

SERGEY KONDRASHEV'S LIFE in the most secret parts of the Soviet system would never have been possible if he had not concealed his own most dangerous secret. He could never have even begun his career under Stalin, nor recruited the code clerk "Jack," nor later supported Soviet policies around the world with "active measures." No matter how high he rose in the KGB ranks, Kondrashev remained haunted by the possibility that the secret might tumble out.

In another culture, it would have been no secret at all, but a source of pride. It was his true—and extraordinary—family history.

At each step in his life, Kondrashev had to fill out the infamous *anketa*, the autobiographical questionnaire that the regime compelled everyone to submit on entering schools, applying for a job, joining the Party, or even travelling abroad. Sergey never lied on one, but he did omit certain details.

He really was the child of two modest Moscow clerks, just as he wrote in the *anketa*. However, he omitted to mention forebears who had founded industries under the Tsarist regime and had become rich and titled landowners.

Thanks partly to the fallibility of KGB bureaucrats, who were at times less rigorous in checking backgrounds than their image in the West might suggest, Sergey succeeded in hiding that secret. But far greater thanks were due to his parents' foresight and self-sacrifice. When their son was just of an age to begin school, they tore up their deep roots and moved away forever from their town.

Sergey would eventually sense the irony of feeling grateful that he had been wrested from that picturesque home while enjoying the childhood pleasures of its nearby woods and fields. But had he then entered the first grade in that town Sergiyev-Posad (still widely recognized by its Soviet-era name of Zagorsk), it would have become part of his record. The security services would later have been more likely to check his background there, only seventy kilometers to the northeast of Moscow. Old townsfolk chatting innocently about his true family background would have inadvertently brought him down.

As Kondrashev described filling out the *anketa,* I could sense the hesitation and nagging fear he felt while pondering those questions running down the left margin of the blank sheet, and later while waiting during tense days or weeks for the reaction.

But as it happened, through all the years and all his *anketas,* no one went far behind the bare truth he had given: that he had lived in Moscow since early childhood and that his parents were obscure Muscovite office employees.[1]

. . .

JUST A STEP OR SO back on his life path that found him suborning American Embassy code clerks, Sergey Kondrashev had been busily helping visiting foreign writers. And just a step or so ahead on that same path, he would be managing spies abroad.

The Western reader might wonder what path might lead from guiding cultural figures to conducting subversive activities abroad, but Sergey obviously saw it all as one unbroken continuum. That made sense in the Soviet Union, where almost any creative mind, any foreign visitor, and anyone corresponding or socializing with someone outside the country, naturally came under the eye—and often the hand—of one and the same organization that spied and subverted and murdered abroad.

Kondrashev had been brought onto that path, and propelled along it, by his early and abiding affinity to foreign languages. It began already at the age of six, after he had been moved to Moscow with parents and grandmother to live in one room of a Moscow apartment. While his parents worked in their offices, he spent time with a German-speaking architect who occupied another of the apartment's three bedrooms[2] and often worked at home. Sergey didn't know whether Viktor Viktorovich Britzke was a descendant of Volga Germans or an immigrant from Germany, but this flat-mate made it a hobby to teach the little boy German words and phrases and eventually had him write page-long letters. His kindness and that of his wife instilled in Sergey a lifelong affection for the language and sympathy for the German people that even survived the terrible war that was soon to come.

Sergey's family encouraged his enthusiasm for languages. They arranged outside tutoring to supplement his school studies in German and French, and an uncle worked on Sergey's accent in French. The young man taught himself English and got a further push in that direction while studying aircraft-engine construction at MAI, the Moscow Aviation Institute (whose students were exempted from military service). An English teacher there helped him fight starvation during the war by paying in food for Sergey's translations of the technical manuals that the United States and Great Britain sent the Russians along with combat aircraft and engines.

• • •

IN 1944 THESE LANGUAGE efforts opened his career path. One day a family friend asked Sergey's mother, "Why not put his language talent to work? I know just the man who could use him."

The friend's friend turned out to be none other than Vladimir Kemenov, the chairman of VOKS, the Soviet regime's organization for cultural relations abroad.[3] At that moment VOKS was expanding. With victory now certain as the Soviet armies, already in Poland, moved inexorably westward toward Berlin, the Soviet regime was taking up more contacts with foreign writers and artists to promote the regime's image abroad.

Kemenov interviewed Sergey, confirmed that his command of English, French, and German was adequate, and offered him a job as the first member of a new "protocol department" to assist visiting foreign cultural figures.

That assignment pushed him straight into the arms of the KGB. Sergey had barely started work before he received an invitation to visit a room of the Hotel Moskva, where a man introduced himself as coming from the People's Commissariat for State Security, or NKGB as it was then called. "You must realize," the man told Sergey, "that not all foreigners who come here have friendly intentions toward us. We want you to get a feeling for the attitudes of those you meet, and tell us what they plan to do and whom they're seeing. We'll then judge whether they pose any threat to our security." For this, he said, the KGB would expect to meet him regularly. "My superior will be meeting you shortly to take care of certain formalities."

That superior, Fyodor Grigoryevich Shubnyakov, impressed Kondrashev with his striking appearance (he was of Gypsy origin), his vividly colored violet eyes, his darting movements, and his rapid speech. And later Sergey was to have ample reason to admire the quick mind behind it, for they were to share a long association.

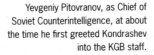

Fyodor Shubnyakov, pictured a few years before he recruited Kondrashev as a KGB informant.

Yevgeniy Pitovranov, as Chief of Soviet Counterintelligence, at about the time he first greeted Kondrashev into the KGB staff.

At that moment in 1944, Shubnyakov was chief of the "culture" department ("z") of counterintelligence, the Second Chief Directorate hence "2z." Three years later he would bring Sergey into the staff of his department, and ten years after that Sergey would become his deputy at the KGB residency in Vienna.

Shubnyakov registered Sergey as an informant and had him sign a secrecy oath. A few weeks later the overall chief of Soviet counterintelligence (SCD) went to that hotel room to look over the new recruit. Yevgeniy Petrovich Pitovranov, one of the outstanding figures in Soviet intelligence history, was also to become a lifelong friend.

• • •

KONDRASHEV WOULD BE ASSIGNED to one visitor for the duration of his stay in the USSR, usually two or three weeks. Sergey would suggest appropriate Soviet contacts and list others whom the visitor himself may have asked to see. After Kemenov approved his list, Kondrashev asked the people to meet or receive the visitor, and then he established a final agenda for the visit.

Stars from a dozen disciplines—famous writers, composers, film directors, artists, and scientists[4]—gladly participated in receiving foreign guests and taking part in conferences. Kondrashev thought they did so almost as much for the pleasure of working with

Vladimir Kemenov, with his erudition and pleasant manner, as for the foreign contacts that VOKS offered them.

Kondrashev reveled in this exposure to culture. He thought of VOKS as a private university and greedily soaked up views and insights. Hardly a week passed without stimulating lectures by writers, musicians, actors, and others from inside and outside the country. VOKS also promoted Sergey's language abilities, tutoring him in French and English.

VOKS also took him on his first trip abroad. In September 1945, he accompanied the first Soviet cultural delegation sent to Finland since before the war. Led by VOKS Chairman Kemenov, it included such prominent figures as the writer Leonid Leonov, the composer Dmitry Kabalevsky, film director Vsevelod Pudovkin, and the three artists-caricaturists who used the combined artistic name of Kukriniksy.

Soviet cultural delegation to Finland, September 1945. Seated, from left: Mikhail Kuprianov (of the "Kukriniksy"); Dmitry Kabalevsky; Malinovsky; VOKS chief Vladimir Kemenov. Standing from left: Kondrashev; Istomin; Leonid Leonov; Nikolay Sokolov and Porfiry Krylov of the "Kukriniksy"; Vsevolod Pudovkin.

To arrange the delegation's housing, supply, and transport in Helsinki, Sergey dealt with three members of the staff of the Soviet Control Commission under Andrey Zhdanov that was there to oversee the armistice that had ended the Finnish-Soviet war. All three were to become famous figures in Soviet intelligence history and were to figure in episodes later described in this book: Yelisei Sinitsyn, Mikhail Kotov, and Zhdanov's deputy Vasily Roshchin (KGB chief in Helsinki, using the name Razin), who was destined to become Kondrashev's father-in-law.

• • •

KONDRASHEV WAS SO IMPRESSED by the cultural figures he encountered in VOKS that he began to think, in his youthful optimism, that they might remove the dark, suffocating fear still lingering throughout Soviet society since the 1930s. He was soon to see these naïve hopes crushed. In Stalin's eyes, and hence the eyes of his KGB, these geniuses were potential menaces to be forced into line, arrested, or like the actor-humorist Solomon Mikhoels, murdered.

In fact, Kondrashev thought, there was hardly a better place than VOKS to see the contrasts in Soviet life. On one side were the bright horizons opened by artists and creators, on the other the mean and vicious darkness of the system in which they worked, a system run by people who had reached high position not by education or talent or wisdom but by cronyism and treachery and brutality.

In that environment, even a small slip could be dangerous. Minutes after Kemenov had left to make a statement to the Politburo on the work of VOKS for the period just elapsed, Sergey found two pages of the statement he had helped Kemenov prepare. Appalled that Kemenov might slip up in such company, Kondrashev grabbed the pages, rushed over to the Central Committee, and dashed up to the Politburo secretariat. But Kemenov had already been called in. Kondrashev begged the guards to let him carry the pages in to him, but in that holy-of-holies no such informality was even thinkable. (Kemenov survived anyway: When he came to the missing portion he improvised so well that no one noticed.)

Kondrashev spent more than a month escorting the British writer J. B. Priestley and his wife. Priestley's novels and plays were popular at that time in Russia for their "progressive" flavor. He was now visiting to develop the scenario for a play soon to be staged in Russia, based on his recent book about the situation in England, *Black-out at Gretley. A Story of—and for—Wartime.* When Priestley learned that Sergey was going to marry an English teacher, he inscribed a copy for her, which Kondrashev treasured.

There were politicians, too. Sergey's first American client was Harold Stassen, the youngest-ever governor of the state of Minnesota. Stassen had served in the wartime navy on the staff of Admiral Halsey in the Pacific, was a member of the US delegation to the founding meeting of the United Nations, and was a perennial candidate for the American presidency. The Soviet government treated Stassen as a potential president, so Sergey, escorting and interpreting for him, was given an early access to top Soviet leaders like Nikita Khrushchev and Dmitry Manuilsky in Kiev and Andrey Zhdanov (by then back in Moscow).

Stassen had brought along a rich political friend who had financed this trip and whose dirty jokes kept the party laughing. Kondrashev, in his role as an alert KGB informant, sensed that underneath his good humor, Stassen's friend thoroughly despised the Soviet political system. As they neared Kiev, he asked Sergey, with mock concern, whether the city had hotels or if they would have to sleep out in a field.

The most outspokenly anti-Soviet of all Kondrashev's foreign guests was the South Dakota Senator Karl Mundt, who called Stalin "all kinds of dirty names." That put Sergey in danger: just to report such shocking words would get him in trouble if they got back to Stalin unless he had vigorously contradicted them, yet it was not part of his role to argue with his guests. The American State Department official accompanying Mundt's delegation, George Frederick Reinhardt, comforted him. Patting him on the back, he said, "Don't worry, Sergey, that's just the way right-wing Republicans express their views."

British politicians came, too. In July 1946, Kondrashev worked with a delegation of members of Parliament from all three major parties, of whom the most colorful was the Laborite MP Konni Zilliacus, who while highly critical of the Soviet system "showed great respect for Russians as a people." The clergyman Stanley Evans was interested in many aspects of Soviet life, but his appreciation of Soviet science suffered from his visit to the toilet of the Armenian Academy of Sciences in Yerevan. He came back in a state of shock.

The shadow of Soviet reality hung over all this cultural activity. Kondrashev sensed it when organizing a VOKS reception for J. B. Priestley. He prepared a list of writers to be invited and submitted it to Kemenov, who struck out a couple of famous names without explanation. Only later would Sergey learn why.

All the while, Kondrashev reported to the KGB on his foreign visitors. The usual meeting place was in hotel rooms. His handler from Department 2z asked the same questions each time: which foreigners were criticizing the Soviet political system and which were showing sympathy for it. He didn't ask about the Soviet intellectuals whom these foreigners were meeting, but Kondrashev was under standing orders to report any blatantly negative views they expressed to foreigners. Happily for him, his reports were invariably positive.

As a secret informant for the KGB Kondrashev was also given a few operational tasks. As he was later often to do, he passed money to foreign communist parties, for example, to a delegate of the Italian CP leader Palmiro Togliatti, whose alias was "Ercoli."

• • •

HERE IS HOW KONDRASHEV met Stalin for the first time. The British parliamentary delegation had been disappointed at having failed to meet Stalin, but two days before they were to leave Foreign Minister Molotov received them in the Kremlin and said, "Comrade Stalin is on vacation in Sochi, but if you gentlemen are willing to stay on for a few extra days, I can arrange for you to fly south to meet him." Molotov told them that Kondrashev would work out the details, along with Molotov's assistant, Boris Podzerob.

At this point the visit became a political event. That very evening, Minister of State Security Viktor Abakumov sent a car to fetch Kondrashev to his office, where he impressed Sergey with the significance of Stalin's unusual decision. In contrast to his many meetings before the war, "The Boss" had met only a few foreigners since its end. If Stalin chose to receive these visitors now, Abakumov pointed out, he had in mind some high-priority objective connected with Soviet-British relations.

In Sochi everything was in the hands of Nikolay Vlasik, the chief of Stalin's personal security. Kondrashev was instructed to follow Vlasik's instructions and keep him informed about the visitors' attitudes and expectations.

At the airport Vlasik divided the arrivals into two groups, four in a car with the Foreign Ministry official who would be interpreting for Stalin, the others with Kondrashev. They drove to the area known as Bocharov's Brook and the spacious villa reserved for Stalin's guests, which was a considerable distance away from his own smaller villa. Vlasik went off to report to Stalin, and after about an hour messaged Kondrashev that Stalin could not meet the visitors until the following day.

That night, as they tucked into a largesse of wines and whisky and caviar, which must have seemed glorious after the privations of wartime Britain, the guests raised to Kondrashev the questions they wanted to put to Stalin. Although they would deal with such sensitive topics as political persecution, show trials, and the horrors that had accompanied the collectivization of agriculture, Sergey nodded with approval, thinking that he might get some answers for himself.

The next day they drove, again in two cars, to Stalin's villa. They passed through the two more security gates where Vlasik in one car and Kondrashev in the other were asked each time whether any unauthorized people were aboard.

Stalin came out to greet his visitors, dressed in a gray jacket buttoned to the neck and wearing high boots. Vlasik introduced Kondrashev who, like everyone meeting Stalin for the first time, was struck by how short he was (at 5'5"). To Stalin's questions Kondrashev replied that the visitors were having a good visit to the USSR and had passed a pleasant evening in the guest villa.

The interview lasted for more than three hours. Kondrashev was disappointed, however, since none of the questions got a satisfying answer. Stalin made it sound as if his decisions—which had caused famines, destroyed millions of lives, and shattered society—were the only decisions possible, using (as Sergey put it) "perverse argumentation and his own peculiar logic."

The visitors emerged subdued, even despondent. One laconically commented, "Now we understand what kind of leader you have." Others said nothing, and Kondrashev sensed that they didn't want to embarrass him by what they really thought. Later that year one of the visitors sent Kondrashev copies of two of his speeches describing their trip to Russia, but without a word about their interview with Stalin.

Kondrashev met Stalin again a few months later. When informed that Elliott Roosevelt, son of the late president, wanted to visit the Soviet Union with his wife, the actress Faye Emerson, Stalin wrote on the request, "He is *my* guest." Kemenov assigned Kondrashev to be guide and interpreter for the couple's entire month's stay.

To be the personal guest of Stalin made for an extraordinary trip. All doors were open. The Roosevelts were received by the Minister of Aviation Industry and visited a Moscow factory that produced fighter planes and medium-range bombers. They visited factories and farms in Leningrad, the Ukraine, and the Urals. Party and government leaders and prominent cultural figures received them, those in Georgia with particular lavishness. The Roosevelts wanted to meet the writers Konstantin Simonov and Ilya Ehrenburg, and Kondrashev arranged that each of them receive the Roosevelts at home.

On December 21, 1946, Sergey was breakfasting with Elliott and Faye in the Hotel National in Moscow when he was called to the phone. At the other end of the line was Fyodor Molochkov, the Foreign Ministry's Chief of Protocol. "You must bring Elliott with his wife tonight to visit Stalin in the Kremlin. A car will pick you up at the hotel at 6:30."

"How is this possible, Fyodor Fyodorovich? Today is Stalin's birthday!"

"Sergey Aleksandrovich, it's not for us to question an order from The Boss. We will obey!"

It would be unthinkable, Elliott said, to go without a birthday present. Luckily, he had brought with him two copies of his just-published book[5] in which he had described his father's impressions of Stalin and Churchill. He inscribed a copy for Stalin with a birthday salutation and wrote in the other copy, "To Sergey Kondrashov—our very good friend and confidant—We know that our friendship will continue for many years and our meetings will be many. Faye Emerson Roosevelt and Elliott Roosevelt." He also gave Kondrashev a portrait of FDR by a French artist.

Stalin was all joviality. The Roosevelts thanked him for his invitation to the country and told him some things they had liked.

Stalin was full of praise for FDR and underlined the importance to the final victory of their wartime contacts.

• • •

NONE OF KONDRASHEV'S MEMORABLE experiences at VOKS could compare with that of April 22, 1946 when he met the love of his life.

Kondrashev was at the reservations desk in Leningrad's Hotel Astoria arranging a railway car for the return to Moscow of a Yugoslav delegation when he noticed a lovely girl requesting a seat. On the spur of the moment, he went up to her and offered to help, subtly arranging that she would be seated in his compartment. As the train rolled southward hour after hour, they talked easily, and he became struck by her intelligence. Her name, she said, was Rosa, but he did not yet realize that she was the daughter of the Helsinki KGB Chief Roshchin (alias Razin) whom he had met the previous year while with Kemenov's VOKS delegation.

Her mother waited to meet her at Moscow's North Station. Rosa led him up and introduced Sergey with these words: "Mother, I'd like you to meet—my fate."

Rosa and Sergey were married a year later, on November 2, 1947, and remained devoted until her death on April 29, 1999. [Rosa accompanied Sergey to Berlin in 1995, where I had long talks with her in English and German, both of which she spoke fluently.[6]]

Vasiliy Roshchin

During the year of their courtship, Kondrashev came to admire and feel real fondness for both her parents. Roshchin was one of the top intelligence officers of the KGB and a key figure in operations in the German area since the 1930s.[7]

Kondrashev became deeply impressed by some of the Roshchins' friends. Among others, he met Vasily Ivanovich Pudin, who, after being detected and arrested in Bulgaria during the war, had killed a guard, escaped, and made his way toward the battlefront hundreds of kilometers to the northeast. Joining the partisans fighting behind German lines, he was wounded in the leg. Threatened with gangrene, he had his companions amputate it, and using a stick as a crutch—while fighting all the way—he made his way back through the lines.

Sergey also met a tall, grave, and imposing figure making one of his rare visits to his family in Moscow. His true name was Akhmedov, but at that time was serving in a Near Eastern country where, though an Illegal under a false foreign identity, he had risen high in the government. Kondrashev's admiration of these family friends was to influence his reply to a fateful offer that was about to be made to him.

• • •

In March 1947, Kondrashev got a different view of Soviet culture. He was called in to visit the Counterintelligence Chief Yevgeny Pitovranov in the company of Department Chief Fyodor Shubnyakov and his deputy Dmitry Tarasov. Now Sergey entered for the first time the big building on Dzerzhinsky Square, commonly known as "the Lubyanka" and to its workers as "House No. 2" (*Dom Dva*) for the first of its street entrance numbers.

Pitovranov told Kondrashev they were impressed by the work he had done in VOKS and wanted him to join the staff of State Security. He would be given the rank of Senior Lieutenant in recognition of his "unofficial" experience and would join Shubnyakov's department.

Kondrashev thus moved into Department 2z, the point from which the KGB looked over Soviet "culture" and did so quite differently from the way VOKS did. In the three months Sergey stayed in that department, he learned things about Soviet culture that few outside the KGB could fully grasp—not even its victims.

· · ·

To ENTER THE KGB staff filled Sergey with pride at becoming part of the nation's shield against foreign subversion. But he quickly learned how fuzzy in Soviet practice was the line between "security" and brutal repression.

The KGB's "sword and shield" emblem illustrated its double role as both of the state and of the Party—which meant, at this point in history, acting as the sword and shield of Stalin. As Kondrashev put it, the shield protected The Boss not so much from foreign threats as from his own rivals and those he in his paranoia imagined likely to oppose him, and the sword was quick to be unsheathed against them. On paper, Department 2z's function was "counter-intelligence": to defend the state against the supposed efforts of foreign spy services to subvert Soviet writers, artists, and musicians. In practice it was there to keep a stern eye and hand on their conformity.

It was here that Kondrashev came to see the true, hidden links among the security service, the Party, the state, and the "creative unions" of writers and musicians. All were meshed in one single machinery devoted to maintaining Stalin's grip on power. The "creative unions" acted as the Party's arms, keeping its leaders abreast of what artists were up to ("Fadeyev is starting to write a book on this or that subject, with this or that angle"; "Marshak's new volume on Robert Burns has an over-enthusiastic introduction") so the Party could cope with any perceived menace. The Party would decide whether a newspaper article would be published, a play staged, a concert or exhibition hall made available, or who would (or would not) receive financial support and vacations in the union's resorts.

For this machinery the KGB provided the biting power, investigating and stopping or punishing anything that excited the Party's—Stalin's—unease.

Stalin himself looked at any significant manuscript that was to be published. He could and did wipe out theater projects with a stroke of his pen. He also saw every new Soviet film and ordered changes to parts he didn't like (he appointed his personal projectionist as Minister of Cinematography). Through his KGB, Stalin got up-to-the-minute appraisals of the attitudes of all these artists, inevitably slanted to accord with his own prejudices.

Now inside this machinery, Kondrashev came to recognize that a counterintelligence officer like himself in 2z, knowing little of music or art or literature but pandering to Stalin's whims (for fear of his own career and even survival), was in a position to stifle the output of creative minds and talents.

He saw now why his admired VOKS boss Kemenov had publicly criticized Picasso: It wasn't Kemenov's own appreciation, but the imposed Party line. He saw now why Kabalevsky and other composers had applauded Stalin's deadening Party decree on musical "correctness" in 1948: They all feared for their own and their families' lives.

· · ·

WHILE OTHER 2Z OFFICERS dealt with musicians, playwrights, and filmmakers, Kondrashev was given the field of writers. Here he watched over and managed the files of people he had admired, even idealized, and saw them shrink to mere objects of suspicion and surveillance. He had long been grateful to Ilya Ehrenburg for inspiring the embattled nation to stand against the German invaders, but here he found a different Ehrenburg in thick volumes of KGB reports of his private remarks to friends, his meetings with foreign visitors, even his restaurant conversations captured by microphones hidden in vases or ashtrays. Kondrashev saw questioned in all seriousness what sinister reality might lie behind Ehrenburg's love of France and the French language. Why, *really*, had the French government awarded him its *Legion d'Honneur*?

Now Kondrashev saw why his VOKS boss Kemenov had struck the name of the Tadzhik translator and writer Lahuty from Sergey's invitee list for the reception for J. B. Priestley. The Writer's Union had reported Lahuty's complaints of excessive control over creative work, so the Party was unhappy with him and the KGB had come to suspect him of secret contact with the Iranian police. (After all, he had lived his early life in Iran, hadn't he?)

Department 2z's informants were keeping a close eye on Samuel Marshak, widely admired not only for his own poems, but also for making Robert Burns's language sing even in Russian. During evenings of poetry reading in a close circle of fellow creators, he had expressed admiration for Britain and for poets like Burns. That was too much in the xenophobic Stalinist environment. Moreover, Marshak was Jewish. (He narrowly escaped arrest and death.)

Though Sergey thought his department chief Shubnyakov was handling these "suspicions" with as much restraint as possible, and mitigating the damage Stalin was doing, it was not for this sort of life that Sergey had signed into State Security. He had expected to defend the country against real foreign threats.

• • •

ONE INCIDENT FROM THIS time in 2z remained engraved in Kondrashev's memory: His brush with one of the most infamous tragedies of the immediate postwar time.

One day in April or May 1947, he was directed to act as interpreter in a certain room that Kondrashev knew to be part of the Department for Investigation of Specially Important Cases (described in Chapter 4). He walked in past a soldier stationed in the corridor. A man was seated at a small table on the right. On the left, perhaps two or three meters away, sat an interrogator on whose desk lay some files. Sergey took his place alongside the interrogator, and the questioning began.

It lasted more than an hour. During the questioning and answers, the interrogator checked the files for information that he had earlier received.

Kondrashev was not told the identity or anything else about the man being interrogated and was clearly expected not to ask any questions. At the end of the session, the interrogator called in the soldier to take the prisoner back to his cell and told Kondrashev not to write any report on this talk.

Sergey remembered vividly the man being interrogated, for he conducted himself unlike anyone he had seen or would ever see in such circumstances. Under hostile interrogation the man was calm, thoughtful in his answers, fearless and self-confident without being in any way defiant, although, as Kondrashev later learned, he had

Raoul Wallenberg

been imprisoned for two years without even knowing why.

Kondrashev later saw the man's photograph in the foreign press—it was Raoul Wallenberg.

In 1944, that brave Swede had been sent from his neutral nation to Nazi-occupied Hungary where he saved tens of thousands of

Jews from deportation and murder. He had disappeared in January 1945 in Budapest just after the Soviet forces had captured the city. As a genuine hero, as the emissary of the American President Roosevelt, and as a member of one of the most prominent and powerful banking families of Sweden, Wallenberg had become the subject of long and intense international efforts to find him or find out what had happened to him. It was evident that he must have been abducted by Soviet forces, but for decades the Soviet government steadfastly denied any knowledge.

Kondrashev had assumed, noting the prisoner's calm and confident manner, that nothing very sinister awaited him. That was why in July or August of that year, when he happened to meet in the corridor a friend who was working in that investigative department, he felt no compunction about asking, "Whatever happened to that man I helped interrogate?"

The answer was shocking. "It's finished with him," his friend said, using a Russian expression that left no doubt that the prisoner had been killed.

"What?" Sergey exclaimed, surprised.

"Sergey, don't ask. Don't get involved. Just forget it."

It was clear to Kondrashev that he was getting very serious advice. And it was not until a half-century later, when a Swedish investigating team visited Moscow, that he ever spoke publicly of the matter. To them, he described his brief participation in this sad and sinister episode.[8]

• • •

KONDRASHEV HAD ONE MISSION abroad during his short stay in 2z. In July of 1947, he was made part of the Soviet delegation to the First World Youth Festival in Prague. Komsomol chief

Aleksandr Shelepin and his deputy Vladimir Semichastniy, both "youth leaders" destined to become KGB chairmen, led the delegation. Kondrashev's job was to prepare and publish the Russian edition of the festival's newspaper.

The Soviet leaders had initiated this festival through their front organization, the World Federation of Youth and Students, to boost Soviet prestige in the postwar struggle for power in the East European occupied countries as well as to galvanize left-wing forces throughout the world. It was no coincidence that Prague had been selected as its locale. That country was reaching a turning point; the Communists were losing the popularity they had won by the Soviet Army's liberation of the country from the Nazis.

To prepare for the Festival, the Party staged meetings and cultural events throughout the USSR. It called on each Union Republic to select participants from among its most loyal and fervent young Communists, a good percentage of whom were KGB informants sent to watch the others and detect and thwart Western efforts to counteract the Festival's pro-Communist impact.

Aside from such undercurrents, Kondrashev felt a lot of good cheer and friendly contact between young people of different nationalities. These memories were still fresh thirty years later when he was negotiating the Helsinki Final Act on Human Rights. He was happy to support measures that would help reunite families and permit young people to marry those of different countries.[9]

· · ·

To KONDRASHEV'S JOY, THAT mission to Prague marked the end of his time in the repressive Department 2z. Although he had not complained or knowingly revealed his unease, he told Shubnyakov and Pitovranov that his interests and language abilities pushed him toward foreign affairs. But it was probably mere coincidence that shortly after his return from Prague toward the end of August, Pitovranov called him in.

"We need someone with good English in the American Department," Sergey was told. "It's a job that takes diplomatic tact and experience in dealing with foreigners. It will give you broader responsibilities, too."

Thus did Kondrashev become deputy chief of the section working against the American Embassy in Moscow.

Three: Target: The American Embassy

FROM THE MOMENT in 1933 when the United States first established an embassy in Moscow, the building and its occupants became the object of unremittingly hostile attention from a dedicated, aggressive element of Soviet State Security. Into that element, called at the time 2b-1,[1] Sergéy Kondrashev moved in the late summer of 1947.

The arrival of the embassy appeared to the eyes of the Communist leaders not as a welcome symbol of friendship with an America that had belatedly recognized the legitimacy of their rule, but as a new center for anti-Soviet subversion. That view never changed (nor has it to this day), so it is not surprising that Kondrashev saw his new position as a welcome opportunity to thwart the "main adversary" to his country's aims. He entered as one of the section's two deputy chiefs.

Western embassy officials and newspapermen mixed quite freely with Muscovite officials, writers, researchers, and scientists during and after the war, and trusting relationships had developed. By 1947, seventy-two Soviet women, some related to government officials, had married Western citizens, mainly Americans and British. Kondrashev's unit was warned from on high that government secrets were leaking through these connections.

Because there were so many connections and because only a fuzzy line separated friendly conversation from the passing of information that Soviet leaders deemed "secret," the KGB had trouble finding the leaky channels. Kondrashev and his colleagues were kept busy recruiting informants from among the many Russians consorting with Americans of any sort, important or not.

Each section officer was assigned to watch a specific Embassy official and family to detect any spying and also to spot vulnerabilities that might permit the KGB to recruit them as spies. To these ends, many but not all Americans' offices and apartments were bugged and phones tapped. Surveillance squads shadowed them on foot and by automobile to identify their Russian contacts. Russians who worked as Embassy clerks, cleaners, language teachers, drivers, or babysitters informed officers of the KGB's American-Embassy Section about the personalities, habits, contacts, and movements of their employers.[2]

Although their American targets may have felt themselves under permanent surveillance, KGB realities made that impossible. Kondrashev and his colleagues never felt that the KGB's 7th (Surveillance) Directorate gave them enough street-surveillance teams, which forced them to review priorities constantly and shift their focus from one American individual to another. Though they had microphones and phone taps in some offices and residences, Kondrashev complained to me that the section never had enough English speakers available for the time-consuming task of transcribing the take.

And, he added, it wasn't even easy to deal with those Russian sources whom they themselves had planted inside the Embassy and its apartments. Those servants, clerks, drivers, and others found themselves getting salaries and privileges unthinkable in Soviet workplaces, and they became reluctant to take risks that might get them fired if caught, risks such as copying apartment keys or inserting detection devices into their employers' clothing.

The servant of one news correspondent and his Russian wife was, however, "persuaded" to perform a very compromising act indeed: poisoning the family cat. The couple had such an unusually well informed circle of acquaintances that Kondrashev and his men saw them as security threats requiring a microphone in their apartment. Either the newsman or his wife seemed always to be home, but then Kondrashev's people spotted a vulnerability: the couple had a cherished cat.

Kondrashev asked the chief of the KGB's special laboratory[3] whether there was a drug that might make the cat appear sick so that, while her husband was away, its loving mistress would have to take it to a vet. The lab chief came up with a solution, literally and figuratively: eye drops that would make the cat's eye bug out frighteningly, but not permanently.

The servant woman, armed with the KGB's eyedropper, succeeded in surreptitiously dropping some into one eye. Horrified at the sight, the wife dashed out with the cat in her arms, whereupon the KGB men sneaked in and planted the bug.

Not even the Russian wives offered easy access to their American husbands, Kondrashev said. "We failed as often as not" to use them as informants. Most of them bent over backwards to avoid compromising their marriages. Even after agreeing to meet with a KGB officer, they seldom gave the hoped-for details. "Worse, even if we had a bug in their apartments, we would be likely to hear the wife telling her husband what an ass her KGB contact was." The handler, hearing himself thus made to look foolish to his colleagues, lost interest in pursuing the target. In fact, husbands were learning more about Soviet conditions than the KGB was learning about the husbands. When the wife had relatives in important positions, this deficit became a matter of concern.[4]

Nevertheless the Section enjoyed successes. In Kondrashev's time, as described in Chapter 1, they brought about the defection of one American military code clerk (McMillin) and recruited another in place ("Jack"). And just before Kondrashev joined the section, they had arranged the defection of an Embassy attaché.

As Kondrashev described her, Annabelle Bucar was a "big blonde" of Croatian origin from a miner's family in Pennsylvania who felt an emotional bond with Slavs. KGB surveillance had spotted her beginning an affair with Moscow actor and well-known ladies' man Konstantin Lapshin. Norman Borodin, deputy chief of the American Department, approached "Kostya," who was ready to help the KGB (mainly to boost his own theater career) by leading Bucar on. Under Borodin's skillful guiding hand, the relationship developed to the point that Annabelle defected to stay with Kostya.

After her defection, the KGB used her for propaganda purposes. She willingly cooperated with Borodin in producing an anti-American book under her name. Titled *The Truth About American Diplomats*,[5] it portrayed the Embassy as a "vast espionage net" and called its officials, some by name, immoral and incompetent. Afterwards (without Lapshin), she worked as an announcer at Radio Moscow until shortly before her death in 1998.

• • •

Annabelle Bucar and the cover of her KGB-written book *The Truth About American Diplomats*.

KONDRASHEV'S SECTION STRUCK ANOTHER both propaganda blow and counterintelligence coup by surreptitiously photographing the American Military Attaché's personal diary. They published several pages along with outraged comments that twisted routine military attaché observations to look like war preparations.

This episode of General Grow's diary has been told and retold as a piece of Cold War history.[6] However, Sergey Kondrashev's inside account, though its details were sketchy and reluctantly told, reveals that underneath the commonly accepted version lay a still-hidden KGB success. The KGB, he revealed, had not acquired the diary the way history recorded it, but instead through a still-undiscovered spy inside the American military attaché's office.

Major General Robert W. Grow, the distinguished commander of the 6th Armored Division in George Patton's 3rd Army, became the US Military Attaché in Moscow in July 1950. His performance there was so energetic that it impressed not only the Pentagon, but also the KGB men who followed him. Grow and his officers systematically travelled first throughout Moscow and then in and around other cities, to collect data on such potential wartime bombing targets as industrial plants, airports, military installations, and bridges. They did so much and so well that the KGB's concerns were brought to Stalin's personal attention. He told them to have it stopped—and Stalin's word was law.

It was therefore welcome news when a spy reported to Roman Markov that General Grow was keeping detailed notes on his obser-

vations and contacts in a personal diary, and that it was accessible, in a locked desk drawer in his apartment. (Kondrashev would not identify the source beyond the fact that he or she worked "inside the Military Attaché's office.")

General Robert W. Grow, clandestinely photographed by the KGB.

The KGB checked with an agent in the Moscow military-attaché milieu, Swedish attaché Colonel Stig Wennerstrom, who confirmed that he had seen Grow taking notes in a booklet.[7]

Now the diary became a priority target of Kondrashev's section.

Markov's source provided the key to the drawer. A KGB operative managed to enter the apartment undetected, unlocked the drawer, photographed the diary, and replaced it seemingly undisturbed.

It proved to be a boon for the KGB. Grow's diary gave details of his observations, exposed the workings of the Embassy's joint intelligence committee, explained the nature of some Russian and diplomatic contacts that the KGB surveillants had observed, and convinced the KGB, rightly or wrongly, that the military attachés were running spies. Moreover, names Grow had jotted in the diary helped Kondrashev's section to select, from among his many contacts, the ones on whom their surveillance would most profitably focus.

Kondrashev quickly perceived that the diary would make a propaganda coup if publicized. Some of Grow's notes, taken out of context and edited to look aggressive, would contribute to the current Soviet efforts to brand the United States, then battling Communist invasion in Korea, as an irresponsible and aggressive warmonger.[8]

A ready-made outlet was at hand. The KGB happened at that moment to be composing a book for that very purpose. Ostensibly written by British Army Major Richard Squires, who lived in East Germany after defecting to the Soviet side in 1947, the book was to be published there under the title *Auf dem Kriegspfad (On the Warpath)*.[9]

The manuscript was not yet complete, so the KGB now inserted a chapter about Grow's diary. As soon as the book was published in January 1952, they followed up with articles in two East German newspapers that screamed "America prepares to bomb the Soviet Union!" Two months later, even the American press pitched in, adding to the KGB's desired effect. The *Washington Post* splashed the story on its front page under banner headlines: "Red Agents Reveal US General's Diary," subtitled "Secret Writings of Moscow Attaché Tell of Search for Bomb Targets."[10]

To explain how he got hold of the diary pages, the defector Squires was told to say that a British journalist friend had given them to him in East Berlin in August 1951, having himself obtained them from an American Army officer in Frankfurt.

Kondrashev considered this cover story too thin. He was concerned that the revelation might draw attention to their real source inside the American Military Attaché's office. But happily for the KGB, a much better cover story fell into their lap. Just before the KGB actually photographed the diary in Moscow, Grow had travelled to the West in the summer of 1951 for a conference in West Germany followed by a vacation with his wife in Majorca. Grow had stayed twice at a US military guest house in Frankfurt where an East German agent was later discovered to have worked. Damaging his own situation, Grow himself admitted that the German hotel staff would have had ample occasion to see the diary exposed in his room.[11] He became convinced that it had been photographed there while he was on his way back to Moscow.

Today, more than a half century later, that story still stands as history, and the true spy has never been suspected.[12]

This KGB-sponsored campaign soon blew over, but its victim, a distinguished and capable officer, was recalled to Washington and court-martialled. Kondrashev said he regretted this unplanned coda to the affair.

· · ·

ALL THIS TIME, WHILE Kondrashev and his section were enjoying these successes, a storm was breaking over the USSR, over the KGB, over its American Department—and over Kondrashev himself. Stalin had launched purges.

Four:
Inside a Deadly Purge

"LIKE THE FIRST** winds of a gathering storm," Sergey Kondrashev felt the onset of Stalin's postwar campaign against foreign influences.

Stalin was setting out to eradicate what he perceived as threats to his absolute power brought on by the recently ended war. So long and hard did the fighting and suffering drag on that he came to doubt that the people would go on defending "communism," so he instead called on their love of their raped homeland; "Mother Russia" had been given precedence over "Father Stalin."

Russians were told they had fought the "Great Patriotic War," likened to the "Patriotic War" of 1812 against Napoleon's invasion. Valor was rewarded with new orders named for Russian military leaders of much earlier times, like the Order of Kutuzov for the commander who beat back Napoleon at the battle of Borodino, the Order of Suvorov for the man reputed never to have lost even one of his ninety-three battles in the eighteenth-century, and the Order of Ushakov for the admiral who never lost any of his ships in all of his forty-three sea battles.

To keep the people's loyalty in those embattled years, Stalin eased his persecution of the church, and to go on fighting he accepted vast amounts of war aid from his declared enemies Britain and

America, revealing them as friendly allies rather than the ferocious enemies he had taught the people to hate and fear.

Just as threatening to Stalin's regime, Red Army soldiers advancing into Europe had a first look at the West, where even workers' tenements looked like bourgeois luxuries compared to Soviet conditions. Stalin saw a threat, too, from Muscovites who had been socializing with Westerners, adopting their habits and enjoying their popular music. Kondrashev remembered as just one example the painter Aleksandrov's open-house receptions in his atelier. There, Soviet citizens mixed with British and American diplomats and correspondents and heard—and even expressed—political opinions far outside the Party line.

To rid the country of such "contamination" when the war ended, Stalin launched a violent "struggle against cosmopolite tendencies" that would revive the people's deep-rooted mistrust of foreigners. Russians who had been in contact with the West or Westerners, including returning soldiers and even liberated prisoners of war, were arrested and tried on spurious charges and shipped off to the Gulag.[1]

Literature and art were culled of foreign influences. The Party-controlled "creative unions" denied to "cosmopolite" writers and artists the chance to publish, exhibit, or perform.

From its outset, the campaign took on a frenzied, anti-Semitic tone. It attacked Jews as "rootless cosmopolites" and their organizations and leaders as treasonous. High among its targets was the Jewish Anti-Fascist Committee, no matter that Stalin's regime had set it up during the war for propaganda purposes. In early 1948, Stalin ordered Security Minister Viktor Abakumov to liquidate its leader, the prominent and popular humorist Solomon Mikhoels.

The campaign melded step by step into a series of interlocking purges against anyone and anything that, in his growing paranoia, Stalin imagined as a potential threat to his power inside and outside the Party. Following the Jewish Anti-Fascist Committee purge, he imagined "plots" like the "Leningrad affair" for which he decimated the party leadership of that city and the "Aviators case."[2] He struck down his own nearest protector Nikolay Vlasik, and in the "Abakumov affair," the closest of all, his own head of State Security, along with scores of his lieutenants. Tens of thousands were arrested, many were murdered or died in prison camps. And finally with the "Doctors' Case," Stalin moved toward his top Party "rivals," Beria and Malenkov, until in early March 1953, they (or a happy coincidence) brought Stalin's life and these purges to an end.

• • •

THROUGH THIS ENTIRE STORM, thunderbolts kept striking near Kondrashev. That he emerged unscathed and even vaulted up in rank appears almost miraculous, and it would surely have been impossible had he entered the KGB staff only a couple of years earlier.

Kondrashev's troubles began in December 1947 when Stalin turned on the family of his second wife, Nadezhda Alliluyeva. She apparently committed suicide in 1932 with the pistol of her brother Pavel, who died during Stalin's purges of 1938. Pavel's sister Anna and his widow Evgeniya ("Zhenya") had good reason to believe that Stalin had poisoned Pavel, resented his having had Anna's husband shot in 1938, and harbored doubts about the circumstances of Nadezhda's suicide. Like many others, they suspected Stalin of having killed her. Now in late 1947, Stalin had both Zhenya and Anna arrested and sentenced to long imprisonments. As he said to his daughter (their niece) Svetlana, "They knew too much and they talked too much."[3]

These events hit perilously close to Sergey Kondrashev. In or next to Zhenya's big apartment in the well-known "House on the Embankment" lived Kondrashev's mother's sister, Aunt Zoya, with her husband "Uncle Georgy." Air Force Lieutenant General Georgy Uger was chief of the department for radar surveillance of the Ministry of Defense. Kondrashev had often visited them with his parents (this affectionate uncle had helped the young Sergey learn French) and had come to know Zhenya well, along with her children and nephews and niece. Stalin must have thought the Ugers, living so closely by Zhenya, would also have come to "know too much," so he had them arrested at the same time. (Like Zhenya and Anna, the Ugers were not released from jail until after Stalin's death more than five years later.)

Their arrest set a trap for Kondrashev, who by this time in 1947 had just attained full staff status. Strict rules compelled members of State Security to report the arrest of any relatives to the Personnel Department. But if he did that, it would alert his bosses to his connection to Stalin's family. Sergey himself might be arrested, along with his mother, who by then had attained an important trade-union post in the Ministry of Aviation Industry. Therefore, Kondrashev made the potentially fatal decision not to report the arrests, and for weeks thereafter he anxiously watched for changes in his superiors' attitude toward him.

The connection was never discovered, but Sergey looked back on his fears as typical of those that gripped almost everyone in Stalin's security services at the time. No one was secure, and mere rumors and casual connections could change—or end—lives.

While living under that cloud, Kondrashev was moved from the "cultural" into the "American" Department, which acted as one of Stalin's instruments to reduce foreign influences. There, he was to find that not even Stalin's executioners were immune from his flailing ax.

● ● ●

ONE DAY IN FEBRUARY 1949, Kondrashev's internal-counterintelligence directorate (SCD) was notified that the Party leadership had ordered the establishment of an "officers court of honor," a sort of court martial to deal with violations of the honor code. One had already been convened a few months earlier for the foreign-intelligence directorate, and Kondrashev and his colleagues felt a foreboding.

Two weeks later, all SCD officers were called to assemble for the first of their "courts of honor," which would deal with accusations against two officers of its American Department.

Kondrashev felt a chill. The accused were two of the very best and, even more frightening, they were the two closest to Kondrashev himself. Norman Borodin was the American Department's deputy chief and leading operative. Along with Kondrashev, Mikhail Nadyozhkin was one of the two deputy chiefs of its section working against the American Embassy. Sergey knew they were no more guilty of any crime than he was.

The "trial" was held in the KGB Club's large auditorium. On one side of the stage, the panel of "judges" sat side-by-side at a long table. Alongside the chairman sat the KGB Party Secretary as "prosecutor." Also, three others were present from the Second Chief Directorate: its chief Yevgeniy Pitovranov, his deputy Leonid Raikhman, and its Party Secretary. Facing them at another table sat the two accused.

The KGB Party Secretary read out the two charges. The first one, Kondrashev recognized immediately, was spurious: "reaping personal profit" from Western goods acquired from official contacts in the American Embassy. This could not conceivably be, as the accusation put it, "conduct contrary to the officer's code and the spirit of patriotism." Everyone in the department knew that Borodin and Nadyozhkin (as well as others) had long been getting from their Western embassy contacts rare goods like whisky, Western cigarettes, and another item that might not sound very exotic today: ball-point pens, then newly developed. They had been passing them on to their superiors. If this procedure was suddenly a punishable offense, why wasn't it being handled, as such things always were, by the Ministry's Party organization and personnel department?

The second charge accused Borodin and Nadyozhkin of "cosmopolite tendencies." Now Kondrashev and the others got the point: Stalin was purging his own defenders in State Security.

After several of hours of ritualistic accusations and questioning came a recess ostensibly for "deliberation." But from the moment Pitovranov and Raikhman had joined in accusing the defendants, Kondrashev knew there was nothing to deliberate. Both were friends of Borodin and Nadyozhkin and their intervention could only have been ordered from above. The whole thing was being staged as a sacrificial rite—and as a warning.

When the court delivered its judgment and sentence, no doubt decided long in advance, Kondrashev shuddered. These excellent officers were reprimanded, relieved of their posts, and lowered one step in military rank. Thus did this "court of honor" transmit its message to everyone in the SCD: Watch out! When dealing with Westerners in the course of your jobs, don't overstep the line of "cosmopolitanism," however invisible that line might be.

Worse followed. Two days later, Norman Borodin was arrested, and then his father Mikhail, too. With that, the atmosphere within the service changed abruptly, increasing animosity toward Westerners, sharpening its scrutiny of informants among Westerners, and cutting back their numbers. The painter Aleksandrov, for instance, was warned that he and his guests would suffer if he were unwise enough to continue his "open houses."

In Kondrashev's words, he and his colleagues "cracked our brains" trying to figure why Stalin—and he knew it had to be Stalin personally—had selected the Borodins, two of the very best, to set the example. It must have been partly because they were the best, both professionally and personally, highly respected and popular in Moscow society.[4] How better to intimidate lesser men than to cut down such stars?

Norman's father, Mikhail Markovich Borodin, well-known to history, had lived abroad for many years between the revolution of 1905 and the beginning of the Bolshevik era. In the United States, he had been an early member of the American Socialist Party and played an active role in developing the workers' movement in Chicago, where Norman and his brother Fred had been born and brought up. After Lenin came to power, he invited Mikhail to return to Russia, and in 1923 sent him off to China to serve as principal counselor to the revolutionary leader Sun Yat-Sen. Borodin helped to shape Sun's Kuomintang Party in the pattern of the Soviet Communist Party, but two years later, Sun's successor Chiang Kai-Shek dropped Communists from the Kuomintang and expelled Borodin and other prominent Soviets. Back in Moscow, Mikhail became the first editor-in-chief of the English-language daily newspaper *Moscow News* and was still active there when he was arrested in March 1949.

One reason Mikhail Borodin was arrested was surely that his English-language newspaper was a natural target for Stalin's campaign against "cosmopolitanism." It maintained all sorts of foreign contacts in Moscow, as indeed it had to. In addition, Mikhail was friendly with the American journalist and China specialist Anna Louise Strong, whom he had known in China. The KGB had now come to suspect her of working for the "American secret service," and an officer of Kondrashev's department was looking into what might lie hidden behind her work with and for Borodin.

Mikhail's son Norman had been enjoying striking success in his work against the Americans in Moscow. He controlled sources in and around the American Embassy and had brought about the defection of the attaché Annabelle Bucar. Kondrashev credited some of this success to Borodin's fluent command of English, but there was also his sense of humor, his self-confidence, and his ease in establishing contact with people, perhaps a result of his American upbringing. Norman Borodin was a close friend of Minister Abakumov, who every Thursday evening would invite twenty or thirty top officers to a small projection room on the fourth floor of the Lubyanka to see American or British films. It was an invitation that all considered a privilege, and Borodin was there to supply simultaneous interpretation.

Kondrashev was certain that the Borodins's contacts with foreigners played a major role in their downfall. It would be hard to find anyone more "cosmopolitan" than the polyglot Norman and his father Mikhail. Their Jewish origin made them vulnerable (the family name had been Grusenberg). But other Jewish officers remained unharmed, so this could not entirely explain why these two were singled out.

Mikhail Borodin was never released. Though no charges were ever brought against him, he died in prison in May 1951, still in his sixties.

Norman Borodin was kept in jail for a year, without a shred of evidence of any wrongdoing. He emerged in bad health, banned from the service or Party membership, and was exiled to Kazakhstan. After working as a journalist there, he was "rehabilitated" after Stalin's death. He returned to Moscow and not long thereafter to KGB service. In 1962, Kondrashev with Ivan Agayants at the top of the "active measures" service, made Borodin chief of its department that worked inside the news agency Novosti.[5] But his health never fully recovered, and he died in 1974 at the age of sixty-three.

• • •

THE PURGE HAD A huge impact on Kondrashev's life. With Deputy Department Chief Borodin in jail and Kondrashev's fellow Deputy Section Chief Nadyozhkin demoted and discredited, Minister Abakumov called in Sergey and said, in these words, "The post of Deputy Department Chief is vacant. It requires good English. You take it." With those words, Kondrashev jumped two steps in the hierarchy to join State Security's leadership ranks. Just twenty-six years old and only a senior lieutenant, he found himself deputy to a general—and about to take the general's place for a while, too.

• • •

THE PALL THROWN OVER State Security by the "courts of honor"[6] soon grew thicker, and the darkness spread toward Kondrashev. One day in 1951, MGB officers received an information copy of what Kondrashev called the shortest and strangest order he had ever seen. It said simply: "Lieutenant Colonel Vasily S. Ryumin is hereby appointed chief of the Investigative Department for Especially Important Cases of the MGB USSR. Stalin."

This was shocking. The terse message was signed by Stalin personally, not by the Chairman of the Council of Ministers, as it would have been normal. Strangely, it named a middle-level official to head an extraordinarily powerful department, and it had inexplicably promoted him. As Kondrashev later learned, Stalin personally invited Major Ryumin to come see him in the Kremlin, talked briefly with him, and an hour later had sent Lieutenant Colonel Ryumin back to succeed a full colonel and perform many sinister tasks.

To understand the impact on KGB officers, one must know about that department. "Investigative" departments per se were an integral part of every regional KGB and of various headquarters components in Moscow. They prepared and brought to court cases that KGB operations had developed. But what now became Ryumin's department stood apart.

"Especially important affairs" were crimes too important or too sensitive to be judged by ordinary courts, including those given the dreaded label of "terrorism" or "counterrevolution." This department usually referred its cases to the so-called Special Board, the quasi-judicial body that Stalin set up in 1934 after the assassination of Kirov and empowered it to sentence people to death, among whom, by no coincidence, were some of Stalin's rivals. The Special Board had become the prime instrument of Stalin's terror until it was abolished three years after Stalin's death when Khrushchev's "secret speech" revealed some of the thousands it had falsely convicted and condemned.

The troubles anticipated by Ryumin's strange appointment were not long in arriving. On the heels of the "Leningrad Affair,"[7]

Stalin accused a number of doctors of having killed by purposeful medical mistreatment his close associate Andrey Zhdanov[8] in 1951. This "Doctors Plot" launched a new purge that would rid Stalin of any others he saw as potential rivals.[9] For this, Stalin elevated his tool Ryumin yet again, to be Deputy Minister of State Security.

Thunderbolts began to slam down upon State Security.

Every State Security veteran of the time remembered that shocking summer night of July 1951 when the news came of the arrest of Minister Viktor Abakumov himself. Into prison, never to emerge alive, went the man closest to Stalin's secrets and, by some reckoning, the second most powerful man in the Soviet Union. And close to Kondrashev: Abakumov had personally overseen some of Kondrashev's work and had helped and promoted him.

Now anything might happen to anyone on almost any excuse. Soon it would be the turn of Abakumov's deputy, Kondrashev's overall boss in the SCD, Yevgeniy Pitovranov.

One summer day, one of Kondrashev's agents, an actress with American Embassy contacts, dropped a hot and unwanted piece of information in his lap. She casually mentioned that she had been forced to spend a night of sex with Lavrenty Beria (in this respect she was one of scores, if not hundreds of women who had struck Beria's fancy).[10] Sensing the danger, Kondrashev went directly to Pitovranov and got an instantaneous response: "Drop her!" he exclaimed. "We don't need her any more. Retire her file to Archives immediately. And don't write a word about it, and don't mention it to anyone!"

But not even such caution would save Pitovranov, who stood too close to one of the most vicious rivalries in Stalin's entourage. The two rivals whom Stalin saw as contenders for his power were Beria and Georgiy Malenkov. And Pitovranov's and Malenkov's wives were sisters.

In October, the thunderbolt struck him. As Pitovranov told Kondrashev long afterwards, he was summoned to the Politburo where, in the presence of others, Beria accused him—his own right-hand man—of negligence in connection with the Leningrad affair and Zhdanov's death. "Comrade Pitovranov," Beria said, "we have overestimated your abilities and your understanding of the situation. You have disregarded your responsibility for the safety of the leaders of our country."

"No," Pitovranov replied, "that is not so. A couple of strange accusations by crazy doctors do not mean that Counterintelligence has 'overlooked' anything."

Beria replied coldly, "You failed to notice the presence of enemies of the state in the Leningrad party organization. You can go."

Pitovranov was arrested within hours. At one moment, he was Chief of Counterintelligence; at the next, he was downstairs in prison. And within days he was joined in the cells by his deputy Leonid Raikhman, with whom Kondrashev had handled the McMillin defection, and some twenty other senior State Security officers. One was Fyodor Shubnyakov, the man who had recruited Kondrashev into the KGB ranks.

Then Kondrashev's immediate boss was arrested practically before his eyes.[11] It was about 11 o'clock at night, still office hours for them, when the chief of the American Department, Major General Georgy Valentinovich Utekhin, summoned his deputy Kondrashev. It was supposedly to discuss a telegram from an outlying office, but Kondrashev remembered that when it had arrived earlier that day, Utekhin had waved it off as trivial. The real reason he called Kondrashev now became clear: Acting Minister Ogoltsov had suddenly called Utekhin to come talk about it.

Utekhin took the telegram in his hand and started out the door. "Wait for me here while I go to Ogoltsov," he said. There was a wry smile on his face, for at this time everyone in the service knew that any unusual call to see a higher-up could be the harbinger of terrible things.

Ten minutes later the door flew open, and a major from the Administrative Security Department whom everyone knew was the head of its arrest squad, burst into the office. Kondrashev instantly knew that Utekhin had been detained. A jumble of thoughts crossed his mind. "Why? What could he have done?" (Sergey later marveled at his own naiveté at the time even to have asked himself such a question.)

"Is this Utekhin's office?" the major asked. Told that it was, he ordered brusquely, "Let's close and seal the safe." Kondrashev helped seal it and collect the documents on Utekhin's desk. The major took them all away, along with Utekhin's coat and rubber boots. As he left he said, "Don't leave. You may be needed."

Hearing those ominous words, Kondrashev knew this might be his last moment of freedom, but he nevertheless decided to go home. He phoned his wife, "Rosulya, the situation is grim, anything might happen. But I'm coming to see you." He wouldn't be away for long because she was then practically next door in her parents' apartment.

When he arrived, he told Rosa and her mother (her father was away in Berlin) what was happening and tried to comfort them. He had nothing to fear, he said, because he had done nothing illegal or against the Party or government, but they all knew he was whistling in the dark. Neither innocence nor loyalty mattered.

The very next morning Ryumin's deputy called him in. Kondrashev never forgot his first words. In a matter-of-fact tone and without any small talk, he said, "You are now Acting Department

Chief. You will produce evidence of the criminal activity of your leaders!"

Kondrashev knew that his fate hung on his response. Somehow he managed to say, "It would be hard for me to satisfy such a request. If there has been any irregularity in my own cases, I stand ready to answer any questions you have about my work and the cases I'm working on."

The investigator launched into a crude tirade that ended with a warning, "I'll give you twenty-four hours to come to your senses. Remember, you are playing with your life and the lives of your family."

That night when he recounted this threat to his mother-in-law, she recalled that in the 1930s her husband's life had hung in the balance, too. She reminded Sergey that Roshchin had survived because he stuck to the truth, and after a jobless period, he had even been restored to his place in State Security. She also mentioned that many of those who denounced others had themselves been executed.

This advice helped. The next morning when Ryumin's deputy replayed the scene, and again the day after, Kondrashev kept repeating the same response, after which he was left in peace.

Utekhin was replaced as American Department Chief by Gleb A. Strokov who, like Utekhin, had had long wartime experience under Abakumov in Military Counterintelligence. But Strokov, too, was doomed. Ryumin's deputy called him in and demanded, as he had from Kondrashev, a report on criminal activity, serious errors and blunders committed by leaders of counterintelligence and of the MGB as a whole.

In those days, Kondrashev pointed out to me, no one had any trouble finding fault with his colleagues. Amid the all-consuming fear, no one dared take a step or make a decision; it would have been harder to find anyone whose work was not insufficient.

Strokov approached Kondrashev about collaborating on a statement of the sort that had been demanded. "No," Kondrashev answered, "but do what you think best. Whatever either of us does is on his own conscience and his estimate of his own best interest." Strokov went off and wrote a denunciation. After vainly asking Kondrashev to countersign it, he turned in his accusatory document, which indeed caused arrests and interrogations.

That did not help Strokov. Ryumin accused him, along with others close to Kondrashev—like Pitovranov, Raikhman, and Shubnyakov—of failing to spot criminal acts committed by security authorities. Strokov was jailed, and even though released after Stalin's death, was dropped from State Security.

Kondrashev did not judge Strokov or any other officers who took the path of denunciation. All too many of them trod a thin line between life and death, and in fact many were executed or driven to suicide.

You could feel the tension everywhere in the service, Kondrashev recalled. In the gloomy atmosphere of the executive dining room reserved for them, deputy department chiefs and higher gathered and looked around to see who was missing that day. In nervous whispers to those they trusted with their lives, they exchanged the latest news or rumors.

• • •

IN THE ARRESTED MINISTER Abakumov's place sat temporarily his deputy Sergey Ogoltsov, until Semyon D. Ignatyev was appointed in September 1951 to replace him. To replace the competent

Pitovranov at the head of Counterintelligence, the new Minister brought in a crony of Beria, the Byelorussian State Security Chief Lavrenty Tsanava.

Maybe, Kondrashev commented, one could look back on the time that followed as a fleeting moment of farce, had it not involved such deadly actors.

The first act of the new leadership turned almost to comedy. They assembled the party activists—including Kondrashev—to select a new Party Committee for the Ministry. One candidate, sure to be elected, was Tsanava and because few in Moscow knew much about him, they invited him to tell about himself.

Up to the rostrum he strode and began to list every council he had ever been elected to, from the top—the Supreme Soviet of Byelorussia—down to some remote district soviet in Georgia without omitting any.

Up to this point, the delegates listened with at least a semblance of seriousness, but they became restive when he began citing every one of his numerous decorations. He then enumerated every wound he had received at the hands of the regime's enemies, six bullets and sixteen stab wounds, each described in detail. The audience took care to stifle its collective laughter; while they had not known all this about Tsanava's past, they had heard plenty about his vindictive character.[12]

Kondrashev remembered Tsanava constantly doing petty things to humiliate or impress his subordinates. He made them wait patiently in his office while he finished a long phone conversation in the Georgian language with Beria so everyone would know that he was close to this powerful Politburo member. He was, but it was also widely known that Beria had put him atop the directorate to wield its enormous investigative powers through this abject toady.

Tsanava called in the now-acting American Department chief Kondrashev for a "professional" chat, pretending interest in how Kondrashev's people recruited foreigners. Sergey launched into a description of how one would first explore the target's interests and weaknesses to find a basis for development, then touch, gently at first, on his work in his office, and then . . .

Tsanava cut him off with an abrupt gesture. "Rubbish! All of this! You want to know how to recruit? I'll tell you how I recruited Dashnaks [nationalist "bandits"]. I'd put a knife to their throat or a pistol to their chest—and that was all it took: they cooperated!"

He habitually dismissed the opinions of experienced officers until finally Kondrashev and the others gave up and obeyed his stupidest orders without question. When someone told him that an American oil engineer was traveling to Dagestan, Tsanava curtly ordered Kondrashev, "Get on a plane and go recruit him." Sergey looked through the file, which included reports from the man's time in Poland, and found not the slightest prospect of success. He tried to point this out, but Tsanava wouldn't listen. With a shrug, Kondrashev flew off on this waste of time. He boarded the train the American was riding and managed to strike up a conversation. A probe of his political attitudes confirmed what Kondrashev had read in the file.

After arriving at the destination, Kondrashev went to the local State Security Office and phoned Tsanava on a secure line. Tsanava cut him off: "You have my orders," he snapped before hanging up.

Now Kondrashev was in a potentially fatal bind. His only recourse was to explain to Tsanava's deputy, one of the few reasonable people still remaining in the leadership.[13] "Forget it, Sergey Aleksandrovich," Ogoltsov told him comfortingly. "Just come on back to Moscow. I'll explain to Tsanava."

Kondrashev's spirits lifted, but only briefly, for now he knew that a frustrated Tsanava would be as dangerous as an angry bear. Indeed, from then on, Kondrashev could feel his hostility but, happily, Tsanava never said another word about this matter. Once again, in the random world of who survived and who didn't in Stalin's secret services, Kondrashev was spared.

Kondrashev saw an example of Tsanava's indifference to others when the well-known Soviet diplomat Maxim Litvinov died. Litvinov had been shabbily treated during the last years of his life, reduced to an insignificant position as counselor with a little office where he would show up punctually every day, though usually only to read TASS bulletins.

As Kondrashev arrived at work on the first working day of 1952, he was told that this historic figure had just died. Within minutes Tsanava called him in, along with the deputy chief of the British Department, Colonel Smirnov. Tsanava had obviously gotten a rocket from Beria or maybe from Stalin himself: He ordered Smirnov to go immediately to Litvinov's apartment and remove a certain photograph of Litvinov with Stalin.

Two hours later, Smirnov reported back to Tsanava, again with Kondrashev. He had gone in and before the distraught widow's eyes had scooped up every photo he could find that showed Litvinov and Stalin together. Looking through the pile, Tsanava said one was still missing; Smirnov must go back and get it.

"But the widow is there, surrounded by her close family. The body is lying in the room. Perhaps this isn't the ideal moment," Smirnov timidly suggested.

Tsanava rudely cut him off with one sharp word: "Execute!"

Thankfully, Tsanava's leadership did not last long. After a few months he was transferred. And after Stalin's death and Beria's downfall, he was arrested and shot before the end of 1953.

Any hope that conditions might improve were quickly squelched when Tsanava's replacement as head of Counterintelligence was named: a little known functionary, Vasily Stepanovich Ryasnoy. Whispering behind his back to friends they trusted, officers called him "Vasily the Dark," a nickname richly merited by his ignorance, pettiness, stubbornness, and disregard of others' opinions. One incompetent leader had simply been replaced by another, and the atmosphere remained oppressive.

. . .

IN OUR TALKS, KONDRASHEV would frequently return to those purge years, recalling them as a recurring nightmare and the source of much that was still amiss in Russian society today.

He recalled a man whose fate, among others, he considered symbolic: Leonid Fyodorovich Raikhman. Sergey had worked closely with him from 1947 until Raikhman's arrest in 1951. After his release, they remained on friendly terms until Raikhman's death forty years later.

Soon after Raikhman's release, Kondrashev met him by chance in the corridors of the Lubyanka and asked about his health. His answer stayed engraved on Kondrashev's memory: "Thanks, Sergey Aleksandrovich, everything is more or less okay. Except my teeth are gone. The bastards knocked them out."

Raikhman had been getting medical treatment and some financial remuneration, but he had then been fired without pension. No consideration was given to his rank, war experience, or lifetime of loyal service. He was simply sent off without even a certification of his service. With deep disgust, he told Kondrashev that he was getting by only through the support of relatives and friends who had helped him get his last job as legal consultant to a society of the blind.

Kondrashev saw him as an example of a reality of Stalin's rule: obey or die. Raikhman had entered State Security at the beginning of the 1930s, a time when able and decisive State Security officers found themselves being used as puppets in Stalin's play, which had little to do with "state security" and everything to do with tightening Stalin's grip on power.

In 1939, Raikhman found himself in a leading position in Poland after the Soviet Army occupied the eastern half of that country following German invasion of the western part, as prearranged by the infamous Molotov-Ribbentrop Treaty that triggered the Second World War. The Polish Army surrendered more willingly to the "friends" coming in from the East. Raikhman was in the chain of command when Stalin ordered the NKVD to kill all the Polish officers and non-coms. Raikhman signed off on the order and has been pilloried by history for playing a key role in what became known as the Katyn Massacre. The KGB—then NKVD—slaughtered tens of thousands[14] of Polish officers, non-coms, and prominent civil and religious leaders from at least three camps. Some bodies have been found, more than four thousand of them in the Katyn Forest, which gave its name as a symbol of the larger massacre. After a half century of denials, blaming it on the Nazi Germans, the Soviet regime under the reformer Mikhail Gorbachev finally confessed to this massacre and released Stalin's fatal orders.

It was clear to Raikhman in his time that the true story was neither fully known nor likely to come out. He knew quite precisely what had really happened and how. In late 1989, he tried to get it on the record, even if only for the KGB's chairman.

He phoned Kondrashev, then Chief Senior Consultant to the KGB Chairman. "Look, Sergey Aleksandrovich, you know I have things to say about Katyn. I'm the only one alive who knows the full truth. Please go tell [then Chairman Vladimir] Kryuchkov that I want to tell him the whole story before I die." Kondrashev had no idea what Raikhman intended to say, but was sure he was not seeking to exculpate himself, so he passed the message.

Kryuchkov brushed Kondrashev off, telling him to go see his deputy, who flatly refused any meeting. He told Sergey to tell Raikhman to write up whatever he had to say and drop it in the post box designated for citizens to pass information to the KGB.

When Sergey passed this on, Raikhman threw up his hands and dropped the whole subject. He understood: The KGB leadership was unwilling even to touch this hot potato, and he did not want to put his friend Sergey into an embarrassing position by unloading the story on him. Raikhman died a few months later, in March 1990, the year Gorbachev released Stalin's fatal order.

That the Soviet rulers were still so anxious to hide the full, terrible truth of their history illustrated for Kondrashev how their regime had drained the nation of humanity and kindness and instilled cruelty and suspicion and fear. Even as he and I spoke a decade after the collapse of Communism, Kondrashev could still feel the impact on society of the purge periods like that of 1951–53. He thought Russia would suffer for decades more from the bitterness and mutual suspicions left behind.

Kondrashev still felt unable to fairly weigh the good and the bad of Raikhman's life's work. He took pains not to justify cruelty, either Raikhman's or his torturers', and on Raikhman's bad side was his involvement in the deportation of nationalities (especially Volga Germans) in 1944, the bloody liquidation of Ukrainian and Polish resistance, the persecution of the Jewish Anti-Fascist

Committee, and the arrests of Wiktor Alter and Henrykh Erlich of the Polish Jewish Bund. But, Kondrashev stressed, this was reality under Stalin. Had anyone in the KGB failed to carry out any order or even questioned any suggestion that emanated from the Party leadership—meaning Stalin himself—he would find himself and his family, by a simple stroke of Stalin's pen or a casual word from his mouth, in the same position as the victims. Once engaged in Stalin's State Security, the only real alternatives were obedience or suicide.

• • •

THOUGH KONDRASHEV SURVIVED STALIN's final year, he had learned all too well how intimately and inextricably "counterintelligence" was linked in the Soviet system to repression. He disliked the work and realized after his narrow escape that he might fall into another hazard at any moment. He began thinking of how to get away from it, out of Counterintelligence and out of State Security altogether.

At that time, no one could leave the service of his own volition, as all KGB officers knew. Those who did were looked upon as lepers if not traitors, and might never find any employer willing to entrust them with responsible work.

So desperate was Kondrashev that he went ahead anyway. In March of 1952, he wrote a request for release, saying he wanted to pursue formal studies in the field of philology. It went to Counterintelligence Chief Ryasnoy—but bounced back with a curt notation: "I don't need students at work. Ryasnoy."

Kondrashev turned to the Personnel Department, where his situation put the deputy chief into a quandary. The file clearly reflected Kondrashev's achievements. "Look," said Pyotr Vasiliev, "your only real way out is to be fired—and with your record and your languages, we can't just fire you. And," he added after a moment, "neither can we just reject your request out of hand."

He scratched his head, and came up with an idea. "I'll pass this to the chief of the FCD." Foreign Intelligence had recently returned to State Security after years under the Committee of Information, so he sent Kondrashev's file to FCD Chief Sergey Romanovich Savchenko.

Savchenko was willing to interview him, so off Kondrashev went to FCD headquarters. After his recent experiences in Counterintelligence, Kondrashev was struck by the pleasant and unassuming way he was received. Savchenko welcomed Kondrashev's qualifications and, in view of his hierarchical status as a deputy department chief, proposed that he enter the FCD as a deputy chief of its American Department, part of what was then a two-pronged American-British Directorate headed by Anatoliy Gorskiy.

Thus in March 1952, Sergey Kondrashev left the Counterintelligence Directorate forever, and without regret. It had boosted him into the supervisory ranks of the KGB, but had involved him all too deeply in the dark repression that had gripped the country.

Five: Into Foreign Intelligence—and London

THE CHEERY WELCOME by his new boss Anatoliy Veniaminovich Gorskiy (nicknamed "Vitaminovich" for his bustling energy) coming on top of the pleasant reception by Savchenko made Sergey Kondrashev happy that "Vasily the Dark" had rejected his application to quit the service. As he told me fifty years later, he had remained glad throughout his long career in foreign operations.

But here in Foreign Intelligence, Kondrashev found the same turbulence he had left behind in Counterintelligence. Throughout the continuing purge and then Stalin's death and the rise and fall of Beria, senior officers were being swept in and out of key positions to the day in September 1953, a year and a half later, when Sergey himself was moved abroad.

Hardly had Kondrashev come in as a deputy to American Department Chief Pavel Mazur than Mazur departed. His deputy and replacement was busily instructing Sergey in the ways of operating against the United States when within weeks he, too, was gone. Then Kondrashev was shifted to the British department headed by Aleksandr Feklisov.

Then in came as FCD chief none other than Ryasnoy, the "Vasily the dark" whose ineptitude as SCD chief had contributed to Kondrashev's earlier decision to quit State Security altogether.

He had barely arrived before he managed a spectacular gaffe: To assert his new authority and views, he called in the chiefs of residencies abroad for a general meeting in Moscow—all at the same time. This, of course, as Kondrashev observed with disgust, would enable Western counterintelligence, analyzing travels of Soviet officials, to identify all the KGB's top men abroad (although, as I think now, the CIA missed this golden opportunity). But Kondrashev took comfort from his observation that Soviet Foreign Intelligence, while never immune to ineptitude, usually rid itself rather quickly of incompetent leaders. Ryasnoy was removed after little more than two months.

And then Anatoly Gorskiy himself fell. He had managed a surprisingly large number of the KGB's historically most important agents: in England, the famous "Five of Cambridge" (Kim Philby, John Cairncross, Donald Maclean, Anthony Blunt, and Guy Burgess) and in America, Elizabeth Bentley and her network of spies inside the United States government. But Gorskiy's luck had already begun to decline. In 1945, Bentley defected and exposed the American spies, and in 1951, Burgess and Maclean fled to Russia and Philby and others had fallen under suspicion. Now in Moscow's current atmosphere of purge and intrigue, some ill-wisher discovered a long-buried secret. On the autobiographical questionnaire that Gorskiy answered when he entered State Security many years earlier, he hid a fact that would have kept him out of the service altogether: His father had been a gendarme in Tsarist times. The omission itself was bad enough, but Gorskiy had also entered the personal data of a different person. He was fired.[1]

• • •

THE KGB HAD TWO reasons to transfer Kondrashev into British operations and then to London.

The first was the massive British counterintelligence investigation that followed the flight of Burgess and Maclean. To protect surviving spies, like the "Cambridge Five," the KGB suspended contacts and recalled their handlers, both the *rezident* Boris Nikolayevich Rodin (working under the alias Nikolay Borisovich Korovin) and his deputy Yuri Modin. English-speaking replacements were needed.

And there was a new mole—a traitor within British intelligence—who would need a handler in London. That handler needed to be unknown abroad as a KGB officer and needed to speak English, and it would be a great plus if he had counterintelligence experience. Such a combination was rare enough throughout the FCD, but among officers qualified for the top level of a residency abroad, it was practically nonexistent.

Kondrashev now prepared not only for his secret operational work in London, but also for the overt position he would hold in the Soviet Embassy. That would be no mere "cover job": Sergey was to be the real Cultural Attaché. That, at least, would be easy enough: Sergey had genuinely worked for years in VOKS, the organization he would represent there. Finally ready by late August 1953, off he went to London with the overt title of Cultural Attaché and the covert position of deputy rezident and acting rezident pending the arrival of a new one.

• • •

THE KGB RESIDENCY IN London had enjoyed extraordinary success since the mid-1930s. The depression had caused wide despair with capitalism and a corresponding sympathy for the Russian "socialist" experience. British students and intellectuals moved through infatuation with Marxist teachings toward the Communist Party, where they were nudged toward secret collaboration with what some thought was the Communist International (Comintern). During and after World War II, these spies leaked to Moscow such close-held Allied secrets as the development of the atom bomb and the breaking of Soviet ciphers (now best known by one of its code names, Venona).

So precious to Moscow—and thus held so tightly secret—were some of these sources, like "the Cambridge Five," that despite the ongoing public speculation about Philby and the other suspects, even Kondrashev was not told their identities. He was told only that because of British investigations, contact had been suspended with "some important sources." He would be given further details "when and if the situation might require action." In the meantime, he was warned simply to take special care in his operations.

Even Kondrashev was not to know the identity or details of "a valuable source in the Admiralty" "Shah," who was being handled by a *rezidentura* officer named Nikita Deryabkin. "Give Deryabkin every support possible," he was instructed—and nothing more. [As Sergey later learned, "Shah" was Harry Houghton, in whose uncovering six years later I myself was to play a part.[2]]

And no one beside Kondrashev himself, not even the new rezident, would know the identity and position of the British intelligence mole whom Kondrashev was to handle.

Kondrashev's overt assignment as Cultural Attaché gave him access to a broad range of British officials and cultural figures. Despite the prevailing atmosphere of distrust between governments, he and his wife Rosa moved easily in diplomatic social circles, contributing simultaneously to both his overt and covert missions. As cultural attaché, he organized visits by and receptions for Soviet academics, scientists, ballet troupes, and renowned musicians like violinist David Oistrakh. He became a member of the Musicians Club, where he met prominent figures like Master of the Queen's Music Sir Arthur Bliss and the conductor Andrew Bolt. When the editor of the Moscow magazine *Ogonyok*, Andrey Safronov, came, Kondrashev accompanied him to visit the playwright Sean O'Casey.

His acquaintances among young Conservatives taught Sergey how rising politicians were thinking and arranged his access to prestigious clubs. These overt contacts, the normal stuff of diplomacy and cultural relations, produced insights that were useful for the KGB and were numerous enough to confuse any British surveillance checking him for possible covert contacts.

· · ·

HARDLY SIX WEEKS INTO the job, an incident disturbed his relations with the recent rezident Boris Rodin, now head of the British Department in Moscow. Rodin was not inclined to listen to the views of his subordinates or to clarify or explain his orders, and he was abrupt, even discourteous, to their wives. In this incident, the wife in question was Sergey's Rosa.

Coming to join Sergey in London in October 1953, she decided to bring along their boxer, but hadn't bothered to tell Sergey about the dog until she phoned from Strasbourg en route. He was taken aback. "Why didn't you look into British quarantine rules?" he asked. "But I did," she answered, "I asked Rodin." Although Rodin, who had recently been serving in London, knew its conditions well, he simply told her offhandedly that it might be better not to. Asked whether this was opinion or recommendation, Rodin said it was just his opinion, and told Rosa nothing of the complications that would ensue. She stuck to her plan and on her arrival, of course, the dog was led off to a kennel for many months costing money and visiting time that the Kondrashevs could ill afford. Rodin could easily have averted this nuisance, but such was not in his character.

• • •

ONE OF KONDRASHEV'S OCCASIONAL KGB functions was to act as bag man. The British Communist Party depended largely, and its newspaper almost entirely, on subsidies from Moscow. The Central Committee of the Soviet Communist Party (the CC CPSU) provided funds about twice a year, Party to Party, but to ensure that this subsidy remained secret, it called upon the KGB to deliver the funds in clandestine fashion. It was not a huge amount, Kondrashev remembered, perhaps ten or twenty thousand dollars at a time, always cash and usually in dollars.

Each time the CC CPSU sent money, Kondrashev rendezvoused with the British Communist Party chief Harry Pollitt. On the occasion of diplomatic receptions at the Soviet Embassy, they retired to a secure room in the embassy. At other times, they met on a certain narrow road that passed through a wood outside London, but within the forty-mile radius within which Soviet diplomats were allowed to move without notifying British authorities in advance. Kondrashev drove at dusk into the woods from one side, Pollitt from the other, and at the point their cars crossed, Kondrashev tossed a shopping bag filled with money into Pollitt's open car window while Pollitt reached out and handed over a receipt.

The British Communist Party always needed more. When Pollitt asked Kondrashev, "Have you had any mail recently?" Kondrashev understood the shorthand. He then cabled Moscow recommending that the next payment be sent soon.

• • •

AN INCIDENT IN THE summer of 1954 that seemed, on its surface, to be farcical threw Kondrashev into real trouble: the case of the wrong box.

Technicians who came from Moscow to inspect the Embassy's internal phone system recommended that the obsolete switchboard be replaced by one offering better security against penetration by British counterintelligence. As acting rezident, Kondrashev was responsible for Embassy security, so he asked the Center in Moscow to send a suitable replacement.

Several months later, it arrived via sea freight in two large boxes. Moscow had sent it as ordinary cargo and not by diplomatic mail where it would have avoided British customs inspection and possible tampering. Kondrashev warned Moscow of this danger, and was told to send the boxes back as possibly having been "contaminated." In return they would send another switchboard by diplomatic pouch.

The boxes had arrived on the same ship as two similarly large crates that contained framed portraits of Politburo members and other government leaders. After they reached the Embassy, Ambassador Malik asked Kondrashev to help him decide how to distribute the new portraits in various offices. They told an Embassy administrator to open the boxes—and that happened to be Nikita Deryabkin, a KGB officer under this cover who was handling a valuable source.[3] Deryabkin rushed into Kondrashev's office, pale and practically speechless.

"What's wrong, Nikita?"

"Big trouble, Sergey Aleksandrovich. Big trouble! I've really screwed up!"

When told to send the switchboard back to Moscow, Deryabkin had pasted on the boxes a label, "Returned, not needed here," and sent them away. Now in opening what he thought to be a crate of pictures, he had found the switchboard. It was the boxes holding the Politburo portraits that he had sent to Moscow. The Embassy had been put in the position of telling Moscow that it didn't want pictures of the Politburo!

Today, one can only laugh. Those grim, touched-up pictures of a lot of old men would have added neither dignity nor cheer to Embassy offices. But at that moment in Soviet history, the incident could have been construed as the deadly crime of political subversion.

Kondrashev knew how violently Ambassador Malik would react. Always touchy, it never took much to set this man into a rage and moreover he resented KGB people because they were largely outside his control. Kondrashev told Deryabkin to rush to the port and, if the ship had not gotten too far out to sea, to send out a fast cutter to catch it and return these unfortunate boxes. Off Deryabkin dashed—too late to catch the ship—while Kondrashev went to report the situation to the ambassador.

Even when telling me about it decades later, Kondrashev could hardly describe Malik's fury. He couldn't calm the ambassador down. "Deryabkin must go!" Malik exclaimed, and sat down then and there to write a cable telling the Foreign Ministry to recall the hapless Deryabkin immediately.

Kondrashev, who had been instructed to give special support to Deryabkin, told Malik firmly that the KGB residency could not do without him at this moment. But no matter how forcefully Sergey repeated himself, Malik refused to listen.

This called for fast action. Kondrashev saw only one way out. He ordered the Embassy communicator to keep the line open after sending the ambassador's cable, and immediately afterward sent his own, with higher priority, to KGB Chairman Ivan Serov.

Serov went straight to Party Chief Khrushchev and by the next morning, long before the Foreign Ministry could have reacted to Malik's angry message, in to London flashed a KGB cable signed by Serov himself. Without referring to any incoming message, the KGB Chairman congratulated Deryabkin for his important operational work, informed him that he had been awarded the Order of the Red Star, and expressed confidence that his good work in London would continue.[4] Serov's cable added that Kondrashev should show this to the ambassador and tell him flatly that Deryabkin would stay.

The Soviet system had transformed a trivial farce into a potentially explosive incident—and then the same system had defused it.

• • •

MALIK'S SHORTCOMINGS LATER COMPLICATED a critical moment in Soviet-British relations, one that impressed Kondrashev once again with the contrast between British good manners and the cruder behavior of his own society.[5]

In the spring of 1955, the Ministry of Foreign Affairs cabled Malik the text of the Soviet government's position on the Suez Canal crisis. (The Egyptians were nationalizing the canal and the Soviets were promising them the intervention of military "volunteers" if the British were to oppose the measure by force.) The ambassador was told "immediately" on receipt of a follow-up signal to hand the message to the British Foreign Secretary. Malik asked Kondrashev to accompany him and to memorize the text to support Malik's presentation.

When the go-ahead signal arrived, Kondrashev phoned the British Foreign Office's duty officer asking for an immediate meeting with Foreign Secretary Sir Anthony Eden. He was given Eden's home address and told that Eden would be expecting the ambassador there.

Malik and Kondrashev were cordially received by Sir Anthony and Lady Eden in a warmly lit living room filled with comfortable chintz-covered sofas and armchairs. Lady Eden personally served tea from a sparkling silver set and then gracefully excused herself with a pleasant "I'll leave you to your men's talk."

Malik knew English pretty well, but when excited he could not enunciate clearly even in Russian. After Malik read the message aloud, Kondrashev saw from Sir Anthony's expression that he had no idea what it was all about. Malik repeated it, but with no more success. After an embarrassed silence Malik turned to Kondrashev: "Now you repeat it." Kondrashev did so with careful emphasis to make the essence of the message clear. Sir Anthony nodded, thanked the ambassador, and said that the cabinet would consider the text urgently and give a reply through the British Embassy in Moscow.

Then came the moment that impressed Kondrashev. As Eden was escorting them out, he took Kondrashev's hand and said in a low voice inaudible to Malik, "I am much obliged to you, Mr. Secretary." In the West this may seem a natural courtesy, but to Kondrashev it was profoundly touching. In his country no government leader would pay attention to a mere interpreter, much less thank him, and even less when tensions were high between their two countries.

• • •

ALTHOUGH KONDRASHEV'S POSTING TO London ended in the fall of 1955, he was soon to return, if only temporarily.

In April 1956, KGB Chairman Ivan Serov phoned. After only the briefest greeting Serov said, "Look, Sergey Aleksandrovich, I have to go to England tomorrow to make security arrangements for the visit of Chairman Khrushchev and Prime Minister Bulganin. You're just back and you know our problems there better than anyone else. I don't have time to prepare someone else for this job, so you'll be flying with me." When Kondrashev started to say he needed time to get a British visa, Serov cut him off. "Forget it. My assistant will take care of everything." Serov did not even bother to ask whether this trip might interfere with any of Kondrashev's business.

The next day Sergey found himself aboard a plane to London. The only other passenger besides Serov was a man from the KGB's 9th Directorate that supplied and protected Politburo members. He would be heading the close-in physical protection of Khrushchev and Bulganin and running a regular shuttle on this aircraft between Moscow and London, bringing the visiting delegation its correspondence, briefing materials, and even food.

The plane was a TU-104 on its first flight abroad in its civilian adaptation from a medium-range bomber. At an RAF airfield they were met by an honor guard and RAF senior officers led by Air Chief Marshal Lord Tedder himself. Expressing interest in the plane, the RAF officers were invited aboard. In the cockpit, Tedder wryly pointed out that the plane was so fresh from its military functions that parts of the bomb sight had not yet been removed.

Kondrashev accompanied Serov on visits to British officials responsible for organizing and protecting the Soviet visitors. It must have severely tested the tact of these British counterintelligence people to receive the infamous chairman of the KGB, whose presence was being attacked in the British press. But they handled the situation admirably, Kondrashev said, dealing respectfully with Serov as a fellow security professional and avoiding any allusions to politics or to the press campaign. All quickly agreed on the measures needed to protect not only Khrushchev and Bulganin, but also other prominent figures who would accompany them.

Among the obvious precautions was an electronic sweep of the Claridge's Hotel rooms that the Soviet leaders would be occupying. No microphones were found, although it was later reported in the West (Kondrashev did not know how accurately) that some had been planted.

Khrushchev and Bulganin arrived at Portsmouth several days later aboard the new Soviet cruiser *Ordzhonikidze*. Their visit was not to be without incident.[6]

Breakfasting in the dining room of Claridge's on the morning of April 19, Sergey got an urgent call to Khrushchev's suite. He found him sitting at breakfast with Serov and Bulganin. All three looked tense and concentrated. "We've just received a worrisome message from the captain of the *Ordzhonikidze* in Portsmouth," said Serov. "We don't know the details but he is concerned about some sign of action against his ship. Get down there right away and find out."

Serov and Kondrashev exchanged glances. Each knew what the other was thinking. They had been told (either in Moscow or now by the KGB resident in London) that British Intelligence planned a surreptitious inspection around or under the ship's hull and especially its screws,[7] and that the job would be done by an experienced British naval diver named Commander Lionel Crabb. In recounting this to me a half-century later, Kondrashev did not identify the source—if indeed he knew—or speculate on how that source might have got such detailed advance knowledge of this highly secret and irregular operation.

With Serov's approval, Kondrashev asked the head of the British security group to help him get to Portsmouth as fast as possible. A few minutes later, he was in a police car driving through the streets at a hair-raising speed and then along the sometimes narrow highway, often with lights flashing and siren wailing.

At the dockside, Kondrashev crossed the gangway to the *Ordzhonikidze*. Its executive officer told him they had heard suspicious noises under the hull and had spotted a frogman in the water close to the ship. Sergey did not tell me what, if anything, the crew had done about it—but there it was: confirmation of their advance warning. [8]

Soon thereafter, as if by chance, the British announced publicly that Commander Crabb had gone missing while testing underwater apparatus miles away from Portsmouth. Twelve months later, the headless body of a frogman washed ashore miles from the harbor and was identified as Crabb's.

Clearly, the British Intelligence plan, known only to a handful of people in the world, had been betrayed to the Soviets by someone in that narrow group. Of all the East-bloc spies officially exposed during or since the Cold War, not one could have known. An undiscovered mole thus takes his place among the unresolved mysteries of the Cold War. [9]

Six:
A Mole and a Tunnel

ONE SUMMER DAY in 1995, I was riding in the back seat of Markus Wolf's little car, followed by a TV camera crew, as he drove to the spot in Berlin where back in the 1950s Soviet soldiers had "accidentally discovered" a mile-long underground passageway that had been dug by American and British Intelligence to tap into Soviet military phone lines—the now-famous "Berlin Tunnel."

"Mischa" knew the way more or less (he had headed East German Intelligence back then), but he was getting some guidance—"a left turn here, now right"—from his front-seat companion, who was using a city plan and a copy of a little sketch of the tunnel's route.

It was not just any sketch. That scrap of paper had in its time been the hottest secret of the Cold War in both West and East. A little group of American CIA and British MI6 planners had drawn it in great secrecy in London, but one of them was a traitor and gave it to his KGB handler before even the first spadeful of dirt was dug.

This wasn't the first time the front-seat passenger had handled that sketch: He had been that KGB handler in London. It was Sergey Kondrashev, and the traitor who had handed him that sketch nearly forty years earlier was MI6 officer George Blake. My presence in the back seat added a touch of irony to that scene, because I had handled for CIA the operation that uncovered Blake!

In telling me how he came by that sketch, Sergey offered a look at how the KGB handled moles in Western intelligence services and revealed how many—how amazingly many—of their own secrets the Soviets would sacrifice to shield such moles from Western discovery.

. . .

IN THE EARLY SUMMER of 1953, Sergey's boss called him into his Moscow office. "You're being given a very important and responsible task in London," said Anatoliy Gorskiy. "You've been working in counterintelligence, you've dealt with foreigners, and you've produced some of our most important sources. Now you'll need every bit of that experience. You'll be handling an officer of British Intelligence."

These were the words that introduced Sergey Kondrashev to the case of George Blake, one of the most dangerous moles of the Cold War.

Though he was not to depart for London for months, Kondrashev started immediate preparation, delving into the file on this agent codenamed "Diomid," to grasp the back history, acquaint himself with any problems that had developed, and to get a firm idea of Blake's personality and motivation.

Luckily for our talks after the Cold War, Kondrashev's memory had been recently freshened. The old "Diomid" case file had been made available to him for his contribution to the book *Battleground Berlin*. What's more, he and Blake were still friends in Moscow, so while telling me about these events, Sergey was able to go back and ask Blake to clarify minor points.

. . .

GEORGE BLAKE HAD SERVED the British Secret Intelligence Service undercover as the British Embassy's vice-consul in Seoul. When the North Koreans invaded South Korea in June 1950 and captured Seoul, they interned Blake along with the rest of foreign embassies staffs. After months of internment, during which internees had been allowed to send complaints or requests to the Soviet Embassy in Pyongyang, Blake wrote a note asking for contact with a Soviet intelligence officer. As Sergey recounted, the first to interview Blake was Nikolay A. Loyenko of the KGB's Vladivostok regional office, after whose positive evaluation Moscow sent Colonel Vasily A. Dozhdalev. Blake convinced Dozhdalev of his sincere desire to cooperate with the Soviets after the internees were repatriated and together they planned for re-contact in Holland where Blake would go spend time with his mother's family.

Why did this British Intelligence officer go over to the enemy? Kondrashev seemed to have taken at face value Blake's own vacuous rationalization of his deadly treason. Blake's story was that he had felt such horror at the killings of civilians by American bombs during this Korean War, on top of his memory of Allied bombings in wartime Holland, that "he had come to realize," as Kondrashev recounted to me with a straight face, "that peoples of opposing nations and viewpoints must somehow bridge their differences." Accordingly, Blake had decided that he might reduce the chances of future such killings by connecting to the adversarial side.

Kondrashev may have believed (or wanted to believe) this version, but it would surely require deeper, more personal drives and influences to impel an intelligence officer of a democratic government to betray not only his country, but also the very people he worked with day after day and called friends, and to expose and send to the executioner's bullet brave men who were secretly opposing their country's repressive rule.

Whatever Blake's personal drives—whether spite, resentments, frustration, a need to feel secret power, or greed—his treason must have been eased by his lack of any real sense that Great Britain *was* his country to betray. Born in Holland of a Dutch mother and a naturalized British citizen of Spanish and Turkish-Jewish origin, Blake had never spent much time in Britain. Only thirteen when his father died, he was sent from Holland to live with relatives in Egypt where, as he later told Kondrashev, his views were shaped by an older cousin, Henri Curiel, an Egyptian Communist Party member. (Curiel was later to assist KGB operations in France, as I had learned during my time in CIA.) Young Behar then spent the wartime years with his mother in Holland and had never set foot in England before he went there late in the war as an escapee from German internment. At that point, he changed his family name from Behar to Blake and served for a time in the British Navy. After the war, thanks to his foreign experience and languages, he was taken on by British Intelligence (MI6).

. . .

To HANDLE BLAKE WOULD be a challenge for Kondrashev. To get maximum cooperation of an experienced intelligence officer in the enemy camp, Sergey would have to win and hold his respect by demonstrating exceptional professional care and competence.

Blake would know more than he, for example, about the British surveillance techniques under which they would have to meet, so Kondrashev would have to arrange their contacts skillfully. To do so, he carefully studied the KGB's files on the MI5 security force's impressive surveillance methods. He took note of their use of London cabdrivers and traffic policemen, for example, and their permanent observation posts at various points in the city, not only around the Soviet Embassy. Kondrashev made notes on the cars the British surveillants used and learned about their radio communications.

Kondrashev knew that if he found himself under routine MI5 surveillance, evading them and going ahead with a planned contact with a spy would be foolish. While he might shake the tail, his maneuvers would expose him as a professional engaged in secret work. Forever thereafter he could be sure that MI5 would marshal so many surveillants against him, using such sophisticated procedures that he might never be able to shake them and might inadvertently lead them to his clandestine contact and himself into a trap.

Kondrashev comforted himself with the thought that one reason he had been given this delicate assignment was his counterintelligence experience. He had dealt closely with Moscow's surveillance squads and, knowing their ways, had even suggested improvements that they adopted.

Having played the hound, he would know how to play the hare.

• • •

THE WAY KONDRASHEV WOULD first meet "Diomid" had been pre-planned in June 1953 by Blake and the KGB London rezident Boris Rodin in Holland where Rodin had gone, according to arrangements made by Blake and Dozhdalev in Korea.

That Rodin-Blake meeting in Holland worried Kondrashev. Having served in England for five years, Rodin was exposed to the British as a senior KGB officer. The KGB was aware that Dutch Counterintelligence routinely informed MI6 of known British-based KGB men coming to Holland and sometimes surveilled them. Moreover, the British themselves might be keeping a special watch on Blake the way the KGB would on any Soviet official returning from Western imprisonment. Sergey feared the Dutch might have spotted Rodin's visit to Blake.

When he expressed this concern to Rodin in Moscow, Rodin simply brushed it off. Kondrashev could only shrug; there was nothing to do about Rodin's arrogance, overconfidence, and indifference to others' views and problems. Though Rodin had faced many of the dangers and obstacles that Kondrashev would confront in London, he made no effort to help him prepare. In fact, he seemed hostile to the appointment, perhaps (or so Kondrashev thought) because he resented any colleague with greater counter-intelligence experience. Sergey would just have to work out on his own the safest way to contact Blake.

Kondrashev arrived in London in September 1953 and, before meeting Blake, he spent weeks establishing a normal pattern of diplomatic life. As described in the previous chapter, he moved into British cultural circles and played an active part in promoting Soviet culture in Britain. Still, when it came to meeting time, he couldn't shake his unease. Might he be stepping into a trap?

Kondrashev took a long and circuitous walk on his way to the meeting place, passing two checkpoints where watching rezidentura members could spot a tail. Only after getting "all clear" signals at both points did he proceed to the bus stop where, at a precise moment, he stepped onto a double-decker bus. Spotting Blake on the upper level, he sat alongside him and exchanged prearranged passwords.

As the bus rolled along, the two swapped ideas about how to meet safely and pass documents. "I can give you a very small and sophisticated camera our technicians have developed," Kondrashev told Blake, "but you wouldn't want it to be found in your possession. It would be safer to use something you could have bought in any store." Blake agreed, and they settled on the Minox, the popular commercially-sold tiny "spy camera" that any intelligence officer might own. But even then, Kondrashev took special precautions. Not wanting to be seen buying a Minox in London, he arranged that one be bought in another country. From then on, most of the secret documents Blake provided came in the form of undeveloped Minox film.

Blake described to Sergey the things he was in a position to reveal, emphasizing British taps on Soviet Bloc phones and communications lines in the West and microphones in Soviet installations, the product of which he was personally handling.

They talked about indirect contact but agreed that dead drops were too liable to accidental discovery. Quick brush passes without staying together for a meeting would be safer, and they agreed on sites that Kondrashev proposed. In the contacts that followed, after Blake brush-passed undeveloped film, they met again after Kondrashev had time to pass this compromising material to a colleague. Their actual meetings, about once a month and always in different places, lasted no more than a half-hour and were usually held outdoors, on narrow streets, although twice on upper level of buses. On two occasions, they met in movie theaters where Kondrashev could see Blake come in and anyone who might be following him.

The KGB took great precautions to hide and protect this agent. Even Kondrashev's boss in London, Rodin's replacement as rezident Sergey Tikhvinsky, did not know of Blake and was told little more than that Kondrashev was handling a source of special value and deserved any and all support. Kondrashev wrote all his reports, enciphering parts of them, photographed them, and sent them in undeveloped film to Moscow Center where no more than three people, he said, knew the "Diomid" source's identity.

• • •

George Blake about the time of Kondrashev's early contacts with him (left), and in Moscow when Kondrashev was consulting him for details for this book.

KONDRASHEV REMEMBERED WITH SPECIAL clarity his third meeting with Blake, on January 18, 1954. Forewarned that Blake would then be passing important documents, Kondrashev planned his entire day so that his actions would fit into a normal pattern. He left the Embassy in the morning in his overt function as Cultural Attaché to accompany a departing group of Soviet chess players to Heathrow Airport. After that he strolled and shopped in town, went to the movies, and then did the customary long walk past anti-surveillance checkpoints to a certain bus stop that served two separate lines. Blake approached from a different direction, signaling that he was not under observation. They mounted separately to the bus's upper deck where Kondrashev took the material from Blake. A few stops later, Kondrashev got off alone. In a nearby alley, a car with a rezidentura driver waited to drive him back to the Embassy.

The most stunning item received that day was a carbon copy, not a film, of the minutes of a secret conference Blake had attended in London a month earlier. The MI6 and CIA had worked out plans for an operation "Gold," a mile-long tunnel from the Berlin's American Sector to tap into Soviet military phone cables just over the Sector border. An extract from that protocol illustrated the dangers that "Gold" posed for Soviet security: "The last available information . . . shows that there are three cables . . . Cables 151 and 152 are believed to contain 81 Russian speech circuits, of which 19 are voice frequency telegraph circuits."

The KGB was startled by the huge "take" MI6 and CIA expected and the vast resources they were willing to invest in sophisticated listening apparatus and the hundreds of people needed to transcribe and handle it.

At the next meeting, Blake again thrilled the KGB with an undeveloped Minox film of a ninety-page MI6 report titled "Banner 54/1" exposing a similar British tunnel-tap in Vienna, codenamed "Silver," listening to Soviet Army personnel talking between Austria and Hungary. Blake confirmed something the KGB had heard from other sources: more secrets were leaking through taps on Soviet phone lines near borders with Norway and Finland. Blake also exposed British bugs in official installations abroad of Poland and other Eastern European satellite states.[1]

The KGB leaders were impressed. Blake made them realize how badly they had underestimated the danger of technical penetration of their official installations abroad, and the secrets such bugs and taps might reveal. This inspired the Soviets, Kondrashev said, to develop their own capabilities—to dig their own tunnels. As he said to me, "Certain KGB operations in later years had their roots in our knowledge of the Tunnel."

• • •

THE WESTERN BUGS AND taps that the KGB discovered on their premises offered enticing channels through which they could drop misleading information into enemy ears.[2] But to use the Berlin Tunnel this way would involve too great a risk to Blake. In Berlin better than elsewhere, the West might detect deception, for they would presumably be getting similar information from other secret sources amid the large, nearby Soviet military presence. If by comparing results they came to recognize that the

Soviet side was passing deceptive material through the Tunnel, they would wonder how the Soviets had discovered it and an investigation would inevitably point toward Blake.

So—as Kondrashev was uniquely qualified to know—the KGB never used the Tunnel lines for deception. He personally primed the KGB deputy chief Arseny, Tishkov to reject any proposals that bore any chance of alerting the adversary to the KGB's knowledge of the Tunnel.

• • •

Although Soviet military personnel who used these phone lines in their daily work were never told that they were being eavesdropped, KGB Chairman Serov did feel compelled to warn high commanders of the danger, at least in general terms. In September, he sent to Defense Minister Bulganin the "Banner 54/1" report revealing the British tap on Soviet military phone lines between Austria and Hungary, whereupon Bulganin issued a general order to his officers to be wary in phone conversations.

The warnings evidently didn't do much good, as Kondrashev learned after the Cold War. During the year and a half that the Soviets left the Tunnel untouched to protect Blake, it had exposed a wealth of secret data. The CIA produced about 1,750 intelligence reports based on almost 400,000 telephone conversations between officers of the largest Soviet military force outside the USSR during a period when the outbreak of war was constantly threatening.[3]

All that was sacrificed simply to protect a mole. It sounds hardly believable to Western civilians, but as Kondrashev pointed out, it was not unique. The KGB made similar sacrifices to protect the still-undiscovered mole in Western intelligence who uncovered for the KGB the treason of GRU Colonel Oleg Penkovskiy.[4]

• • •

BLAKE AND KONDRASHEV WENT on meeting once or twice a month, always in different places, and Blake continued to produce information of great value to Moscow. At his subsequent trial, he confessed that there was not one official document of any importance to which he had access that he did not pass to his Soviet contact in London and, later, in Berlin.

Although the Western and Soviet press later reported that Blake had exposed large numbers of Western spies,[5] Kondrashev brushed this assertion aside, insisting that Blake had told little of real interest to the KGB in that respect. Whatever spies Blake did expose, Kondrashev said, were mostly among the Russian émigré community and already known through the KGB's "very adequate" penetration of that milieu. In fact Kondrashev could not remember the man's ever having revealed any significant source previously unknown to the KGB, and he doubted that there were any. (Kondrashev flatly denied published allegations that Blake had uncovered CIA's spy in the GRU, Pyotr Popov.)

• • •

WORRIES AROSE FROM TIME to time. When Blake failed to show at one scheduled meeting and then missed the alternate date as well, Kondrashev was sick with apprehension in a way, as he put it, "that only a case officer or a parent could understand." What could have happened? When Blake did not appear at a second alternate meeting the following month, Kondrashev even proposed to Moscow that he try to spot Blake on his way to his workplace, but even that seemed to Moscow too great a risk. It was decided to wait another month.

The final alternative meeting had been scheduled for a London cinema where Blake and Kondrashev were to sit in specified seats. If Blake spotted Kondrashev, he would get up after a while and go outside. If Kondrashev saw nothing suspicious, he would follow after an appropriate delay and meet him out on the street.

Kondrashev entered the cinema—and saw Blake. His heart leapt with relief. They met as arranged, and Blake explained his absences. Just when they had been scheduled to meet, he was sent to Geneva to oversee the installation of listening devices in the premises of the Soviet delegation to hear a conference on Vietnam. The first alternate meeting date happened to coincide with Easter weekend, and he couldn't get free. Then in early April he heard that the KGB rezident in Australia, Vladimir Petrov, had just defected to the West. Fearing that Petrov might have known something that could throw suspicion in his direction, Blake thought it prudent to stay away while he kept an eye out for any change in his boss's attitude toward him. Having noticed nothing amiss, he had come to this third, final alternate meeting.

When Kondrashev reported this sequence, Moscow ordered him to do all he could to get transcripts of the Australians' interrogation of Petrov. One of Kondrashev's "trusted contacts," a high-level lawyer (QC—Queen's Counsel barrister) managed to get him a copy. Happily for the KGB, there was not a word there about penetrations of MI6 or Blake.

• • •

WHEN IN EARLY 1955 Blake was informed he would shortly be leaving London on permanent assignment to Berlin, he and

Kondrashev worked out a series of possible meeting places there with alternate dates and times. Using this information, Moscow Center worked out with Berlin a sequence of meeting arrangements that might be used at any future date "just in case some eventual important source should come along." Though Kondrashev then had no idea who might make first contact in Berlin, he learned afterwards that it was Boris Rodin, British Department Chief in Moscow, who, as we have seen, had met Blake in Holland.

Blake continued to produce for the KGB in Berlin, but he had nothing whatsoever to do with the tunnel operation, which was strictly separated from the rest of the MI6 station. As Blake later told Kondrashev, no one outside a special tunnel unit except for the station chief was allowed to know anything at all about it.

In April 1959, Blake was transferred back to London headquarters and five months later to Beirut. He was in Lebanon when Western counterintelligence uncovered his treason. Recalled to London on a pretext shortly before Easter 1961, Blake had a passing flash of worry—a British woman in Beirut asked innocently, "Why are you being recalled? Are you accused of something?"—but he shook it off. Once back in London, he visited his mother, reported for duty the following day—and was arrested on the spot.

The KGB did not know at first how Blake had been uncovered, but later learned (Kondrashev did not specify how or when) that a KGB advisor to Polish State Security in Warsaw, apparently with a misplaced desire to help, had ignored standing orders to clear through FCD Deputy Chief Tishkov any use of information from "Diomid." He had given the Poles a list of MI6 recruitment targets in Poland.

They were right. The Polish Intelligence officer Michal Goleniewski had told the CIA in an anonymous letter (that I had handled for CIA) that his service received this British target list from the

KGB. The CIA passed this news to MI6, which identified the document and traced it back to Blake. Thus, by extraordinary coincidence, I had been personally involved in the undoing of this most important agent of my future friend Kondrashev.

Blake confessed. At his trial in May 1961, he pleaded guilty to violating the Official Secrets Act. The maximum sentence for betraying official secrets in peacetime was limited to fourteen years but the court, appalled by Blake's betrayal, chose to count separately each of the three places where he had betrayed: London, Berlin, and Beirut. Thus he was sentenced to forty-two years in prison.

• • •

BY AN ASTOUNDING COINCIDENCE, Kondrashev was the first KGB officer to see Blake after his daring escape from Wormwood Scrubs Prison in October 1966. (Though the KGB had heard echoes of Blake's earlier plans to escape, some of which became known to prison authorities, Kondrashev insisted that the KGB had nothing to do with the escape.)

Kondrashev and Blake became lifelong friends in Moscow[6] and to assist Kondrashev's writing his autobiography, Blake gave him a long written account of his escape.[7] Blake made his own way across the Channel and into Germany smuggled in a hiding place in the van of a vacationing British couple. Knowing well from his Berlin days the various crossing points into the Soviet sector of the city, he directed them to a remote one in the south manned only by East German border personnel. There, he asked the border point commander to notify the KGB's Berlin headquarters that he wanted to talk with them.

The coincidence was that Kondrashev, then chief of the KGB's German Department in Moscow, happened to be in Berlin-

Karlshorst with KGB Deputy Chairman Nikolay Zakharov for the annual review of the work of the KGB Apparat. Following drinks and dinner after one of their sessions, everyone went off to bed. Kondrashev had hardly fallen asleep when Zakharov entered his bedroom and said excitedly, "The duty officer reports that some Englishman at the border is asking to meet a Soviet official. Maybe it's him!"

"Him" of course meant Blake, for like the rest of the world, the KGB had read newspaper accounts of Blake's escape a couple of weeks earlier. "Maybe you should go yourself and check," Zakharov suggested.

Kondrashev dressed and went off in the night to that remote border crossing. There, to his astonishment, was Blake sitting in a waiting room.

Blake couldn't believe his eyes. "*You? Here?*" he exclaimed.

Blake never could be brought to believe that it was truly by chance, Kondrashev told me; he continued to believe that the KGB must somehow have known where he was and when he would appear.

Blake stayed in East Berlin for a few days in a KGB villa while he bought clothes and other personal items. In the meantime, an apartment was prepared for him in Moscow. He was flown there in a KGB plane and has lived there ever since.

• • •

Since Kondrashev had been selected and assigned to England primarily to handle Blake, it came as no surprise that after Blake left for his Berlin post, a cable from KGB headquarters informed Kondrashev that he would be reassigned to Moscow. Because his normal two-year tour of duty was coming to an end anyway, his departure so soon after Blake's did not attract any Western suspicions.

Kondrashev did not know which job awaited. An assignment to the British Department would have been logical, but Rodin, who was chief there, had shown that he was no supporter of Kondrashev, and KGB assignments depended more on relations with leaders than on performance. Sergey's worries grew when he was told on arrival that his next assignment would be discussed only after his vacation.

But in the end things worked out well: He got the job he most wanted, Deputy Chief of the Austro-German Department.

Seven: "Why Do You Need All Those People Here?"

"WHY DO YOU need all those people here? We're giving you all the information you need!" complained Erich Mielke, the head of East German "Stasi," to the visiting chief of the KGB's German Department.[1]

Erich Mielke had a point, that visitor wryly admitted to me long afterward. "Those people"—the KGB staff in Germany that Sergey Kondrashev oversaw—numbered more than a thousand.

• • •

KONDRASHEV ARRIVED IN THE German Department when he returned from England in 1955, remained as its deputy chief for nearly two years before being assigned abroad again to its residency in Vienna, and in 1964 became the Department's chief.

Sergey had focused on that country since childhood, learning its language as a child practically as a game. World War II indelibly demonstrated that Germany would always be a menace or at least a problem to the Soviet Union and raised Germany permanently into top place among his interests in foreign places. And as we have seen, he practically married into KGB German operations, with his wife so fluent in the language and his father-in-law having served with distinction in the area since the 1930s.

Kondrashev's KGB superiors noted his penchant in this direction from the outset of his career. Even while working against Americans in Moscow, he was sent to Berlin on a mission only distantly related to his functions.[2] When he later entered Foreign Intelligence to work against England and America, its chief presciently remarked, "You'll surely have a lot do with German operations here." Toward that end, Sergey was put together with three top veterans of German operations to brush up their German in private tutoring. Within months he was sent to Berlin to review files of German officer prisoners of war with an eye toward spotting individuals the KGB might enlist for use after their liberation.[3] Only weeks afterward, he was the junior member of a high-powered delegation to inspect the KGB's Vienna representation (described in Chapter 9).

And even after heading the German Department for three years, he continued to oversee KGB activity in the German-speaking area for the rest of his career, as head of worldwide "active measures," as Deputy Chief of Foreign Intelligence, and as Chief Senior Advisor to the KGB Chairman.

• • •

GERMANY AND AUSTRIA OFFERED Soviet Intelligence golden opportunities. Tight control of the East German population and its connections with the West presented innumerable channels toward top-priority American and NATO targets in West Germany and beyond. And all from a secure base: Tightly policed East Germany prevented the Western side from enjoying similar access to the East. Nowhere outside the Soviet Union did the KGB put more officers into action.

KGB presence in Germany had undergone repeated reorganizations,[4] but when Kondrashev served in the department's leadership in the mid-1950s and again in the mid-1960s, it consisted essentially of three arms: 1) the so-called "Apparat" based in Karlshorst, East Berlin with subordinate units throughout East Germany; 2) the rezidentura in West Germany; and 3) the security services of the Soviet Group of Forces in Germany.

The largest element, the Apparat, represented not just foreign intelligence, but the KGB as a whole. Accordingly, its chief was the senior KGB representative in Germany and enjoyed a position roughly equivalent to that of the FCD chief himself. It included hundreds of officers and technical personnel, who supervised outside offices of ten to fifteen officers in each of the five East German provinces. They advised the Stasi as well as running their own operations against West German targets.

The largest Apparat department collected political and economic intelligence and spotted, recruited, and handled spies in the West. A counterintelligence department mounted operations to thwart and penetrate the numerous Western intelligence services in West Germany and saw to the security and loyalty of Soviet civilian personnel. Yet another department collected scientific and technological secrets from German institutions and firms, while an information group edited and evaluated intelligence reports coming from the Apparat's secret sources and from the Stasi and passed them along to Moscow.

The West German rezidentura was based in the Soviet Embassy in Bonn and the trade mission in Cologne. It communicated directly with Kondrashev's German Department in Moscow, but also coordinated some of its work with that of the East Berlin-based Apparat through visits and secure telephone communications.

Some KGB units in Germany, even some responsible to the FCD itself, bypassed Kondrashev's department, although he was kept aware of and coordinated their work with that of the others. An independent directorate took in scientific and technological intelligence from West Germany, while the FCD's Illegals Directorate selected and trained and documented officers who would work entirely outside of any Soviet installation, and sent them abroad, some to East Germany, on "staging" missions to acclimatize to the West and develop their fictitious life stories or "legends." Only when finally dispatched to work in the area of their assignment, as in West Germany, did they come under the control of the responsible geographic department.[5]

No Illegal could be sent to work in Germany without Sergey's approval. And if one of them should defect there, it could cost him dearly. In mid-1967, Yevgeniy Runge, a Soviet citizen and ethnic German, was about to be reassigned to West Germany where he had already operated for years. Kondrashev spotted a problem: Runge and his wife had a school-age son who spoke little German. That lack would raise suspicions among the couple's German neighbors and the boy's schoolmates and impose an impossible strain on the child's discretion. Kondrashev proposed that the lad remain in a boarding school in Russia. Runge insisted on taking him, and this raised Kondrashev's suspicions; he recommended against the assignment—luckily, in writing.

While Kondrashev was away on vacation, his deputy, unaware of the recommendation, approved Runge's reassignment, and later that year Runge and his family defected to the CIA in West Germany. Kondrashev escaped blame by pointing to his written negative recommendation and to his absence at the time. Those who had approved the mission received letters of reprimand.[6]

• • •

"WHY DO YOU NEED ALL THOSE PEOPLE HERE?"

BEFORE WE SAT DOWN to write his autobiography, Kondrashev had already published a lot about the KGB's Germany structure and operations using Moscow files that had been opened to help him write his 1997 book *Battleground Berlin*. And since German unification, scores of books and articles have been written describing the vast operations of the KGB's East German satellite, the Stasi. But now, reminiscing with me, Kondrashev made other points that deserve a place in the history of this time and place.

When Erich Mielke complained, "Why do you need all those people here?" Kondrashev admitted he had a point. The KGB might not need so many officers in Germany, and definitely not certain individuals. Entering the leadership of the German department, Kondrashev recognized that German operations were overstaffed with ill-qualified officers who busied themselves with sources who, during the turbulent postwar years, had been taken aboard with little regard to their long-range value. Their numbers increased with the release of former prisoners of war who had agreed to collaborate.

Sergey saw that he would have to cut the numbers of officers and sources and improve their quality. Up to this point the officers had done all right within the sprawling framework of military occupation, but they lacked the finesse, language ability, or geographical knowledge needed to deal with the kinds of sources that could meet the KGB's new priorities.

Kondrashev made his needs known to the KGB Party organization, which sent out a request to Party organizations throughout the Soviet Union to identify Party members who spoke German or knew the area and would be willing to spend two to three years there on contract. At the end of that period, they could return to their previous jobs with the gratitude of the KGB or could stay on for a career. This effort bore results, and Kondrashev noted a gradual rise in the quality of recruiters and agent handlers.

· · ·

THIS NEED FOR NEW people with new qualities had become urgent because history was reaching a turning point just as Kondrashev arrived on the job.

The Soviet Union could no longer hope to unify Germany into a neutral and disarmed state. Only a year earlier in 1954, Moscow had still retained enough hope to carry out a massive overt and clandestine program in France to abort a European Defense Community that would have incorporated West German forces.[7] But then the treaties of Paris gave full sovereignty to the Federal Republic and placed it firmly within the Western alliance. By May of 1955, sovereign West Germany joined NATO and began to build its own armed forces. In Austria that same summer, the State Treaty finally came into effect, ending Soviet domination of much of that country.

In recognition of this new situation, the Kremlin leadership invited to Moscow West German Chancellor Konrad Adenauer, the very man who had most staunchly opposed Soviet efforts to create a neutral Germany, now to establish the basis for formal diplomatic relations. Aside from trade and cultural matters, he would discuss the release of the hundreds of thousands of German prisoners of war still held in the USSR ten years after the war's end.

Adenauer's five-day visit in September of 1955 became a major concern and an opportunity for Kondrashev and his department. Along with three other KGB officers, he was personally attached to the visiting German delegation to ensure its security and to ease its work—and to go behind the scene to assess individual delegates as targets for cultivation as potential agent recruits.

Adenauer had not simplified their task. In the process of accepting, he announced that his staff would travel on its own train with their equipment and his official Mercedes automobile. The train enjoyed diplomatic status from the moment it entered Soviet territory, under permanent guard by West German security personnel and off limits to Soviet workers. Even at the border the Germans did not let the Soviets close. To shift the train's cars onto the wider-gauge wheels required for Soviet rail lines, another train went first, equipped with a powerful crane, and did the job itself.

Adenauer and his closest associates flew in on two airplanes on September 9th at about the same time the train arrived with the rest of his delegation and his car. The delegation members, who were perfectly aware that the KGB would take special interest in them, took precautions. The KGB moved agents and bugging equipment into their hotel. But all hope of listening in on private discussions were dashed—the West Germans retired to the train to talk privately.[8]

• • •

THE KGB WAS, FOR all practical purposes, fully informed on West Germany, and not only from its vast presence in the country,[9] but also from elsewhere. KGB spies in the French and British governments, for example, gave details of relations with West Germany and their own evaluations of that country's policies, plans, developments, and personalities. From cables and dispatches sent by Western embassies to their foreign ministries that the KGB intercepted or stole, came insights into troublesome issues between those countries and West Germany. (Kondrashev's Active Measures department would then exacerbate these troubles, as we shall see in Chapter 13.)

Erich Mielke's Stasi was, as he told Kondrashev, "giving all the information you need." His HVA foreign-intelligence component was doing a splendid job at its assigned task, "to elucidate the internal political and economic situation of West Germany, by establishing agent networks inside the Bonn government and its institutions [. . . and to elucidate] the policies and tasks of the occupying powers."[10]

Just how splendidly the HVA was doing was, of course, a secret at the time, but was more fully recognized when files were opened after the dissolution of the East German state in 1989. In the single year before that[11] the HVA got some 180,000 reports from its sources throughout both Germanys and abroad, to a total of some 15,000 per month or 500 a day. While many of these reports were trivial, the HVA labeled no fewer than 2,500 of them—say, 75 a day—as "valuable."

The HVA's coverage of just one West German political party, the "Greens," during that same year 1988, exemplifies its coverage of the whole political scene. In addition to what it was learning about party leaders through phone taps and mail coverage, no fewer than 368 informants inside and close to the party were reporting, some copiously (43 of them providing more than 10 reports each, 25 of them more than 20 reports each, while one gave more than 150).[12]

Of all this intake, the HVA sent to the KGB's Berlin Apparat perhaps half of the most important reports, more than a thousand of them, which amounted to about five every working day. Here were inside accounts of West German policy discussions and planning at the highest levels, intimate looks at leading personalities, details of new scientific and technological developments, and the West's spy operations against the East.

While the KGB generally trusted the HVA's judgment and good faith, Kondrashev said they occasionally had reason to question whether they were getting everything, or whether certain of the HVA's unidentified sources really had direct access to the information they reported or to the high personalities they cited. To get clear on such questions, KGB officers nosed about with their "trusted contacts" inside the HVA staff.

The information exchange was a two-way street, for the KGB's own spies were learning things that affected East German interests. For example, the KGB mole Heinz Felfe, who headed the West German Intelligence service's counterintelligence work against the East, revealed successes of his own service in recruiting East German officials or controlling as double agents HVA spies in the West.

Similarly, the KGB benefited from the East Germans' most sensitive—undeclared—sources, like Willy Brandt's close aide Günter Guillaume and other spies inside West German intelligence and counterintelligence agencies.

When, as in Felfe's or Guillaume's cases, the existence of such KGB or HVA sources was too sensitive to be revealed to the other side through routine liaison, both sides fell back to their top-level informal relationships. Kondrashev and a few other top KGB German specialists had long-standing trust and friendship with Security Minister Mielke and HVA chief Markus Wolf. They simply confided in one another and developed ways to pass information so that only they personally would know of the real source.

The KGB never officially informed the MfS of its penetration agents like Felfe, but in these informal exchanges at the top, Mielke, Wolf and perhaps a handful of their top people became well aware of their existence and in some cases of their identities.

In short, Moscow was fully informed on West German internal affairs and its relationship with NATO and other Western governments.

． ． ．

FROM HIS VANTAGE POINTS in the Center, Kondrashev watched the rising influence of West Germany's Social Democratic Party during the 1960s. It had been Soviet policy to discredit Social Democrat leaders, but now with the growing possibility—once hardly conceivable—that it might even come to power and work toward rapprochement with the East, the Soviet view changed. The KGB began to look for clandestine ways to boost and even shape SPD policies.

Kondrashev and his deputy Vasily Sitnikov separately discussed with KGB chairman Andropov, who took it up with Soviet leader Brezhnev, the idea of establishing direct links with SPD leaders. The Politburo gave the KGB the green light to set up an unofficial "back channel" through which Brezhnev could communicate with the Social Democrat leader Willy Brandt outside formal diplomatic channels.

The KGB already had a route in that direction. Vyacheslav Kevorkov, a longtime veteran of KGB operations in Germany now heading the SCD department that covered Germans inside the USSR, maintained close relations with Valery Lednev, editor of the magazine *Sovetskaya Kultura*, who had interviewed Brandt's close Party associate Egon Bahr. Kondrashev and Sitnikov recognized that Bahr, who had long shown himself to be sympathetic to Soviet initiatives, would be the ideal conduit to Brandt, and Kevorkov the ideal intermediary. Following their conscious decision to keep the channel independent of formal diplomacy, they gave Kevorkov cover as a news correspondent.

Introduced by Lednev, Kevorkov told Bahr about his connections to Brezhnev. Bahr proved not only willing, but eager to pass Brezhnev's messages to Brandt and Brandt's to Brezhnev. The channel worked for years.[13]

Kevorkov consulted with Kondrashev on several occasions about what to tell Bahr. Kondrashev regularly discussed the matter with Andropov and in critical situations with Foreign Minister Gromyko. (Kevorkov also reported directly to Andropov and, when Andropov recommended it, to Gromyko.) The messages that Kevorkov passed to Bahr promoted Soviet objectives of the moment, while for his part, Brandt passed his own ideas and questions through Kevorkov to Brezhnev.

Thus, with the Socialists in power, West Germany's policy came under clandestine and direct Soviet influence.

• • •

ALREADY BY 1952, KONDRASHEV had participated in the KGB's search for potential spy recruits among German prisoners of war. More than two million German soldiers had fallen into Soviet hands and many remained confined. The search became urgent in 1955, soon after Kondrashev went to the German Department, with the arrival of West German sovereignty and the Soviet agreement with Adenauer to release all those remaining.

It would be the final phase of a process that had been going on for more than a decade. During the war and immediate postwar years, the KGB and GRU had been interrogating captured senior German commanders and intelligence and counterintelligence officers. The Soviets wanted to find out how the Nazis had uncovered Soviet Intelligence networks in Germany and whether the Germans had uncovered agents whom the Soviets had dropped

behind their lines or infiltrated into German Intelligence operations. KGB interrogators sought the full inside story of intelligence
operations like "Zeppelin," in which the Germans had dropped
hundreds of parachutists behind Soviet lines. They hoped to identify still-undiscovered German spies and Russians who had collaborated with the Germans.

As time went on, Soviet interest shifted from these counterintelligence questions toward recruiting Germans for secret cooperation
after their release. KGB officers, including Kondrashev, reviewed
files to find those whose attitudes in the camps had seemed least
hostile and whose past (and hence future) civilian occupations
might offer the best intelligence. They signed up many POWs who
had little or no prospect of ever being useful for the Soviets (or, for
that matter, of ever cooperating later in Germany). But as Kondrashev put it, the KGB considered that out of this mass of thousands,
a few might both rise in the world and cooperate. And some, he
said, did.

One who did not was a former German diplomat from a
noble family, a man whose name Kondrashev would not divulge.
He had told a KGB informant in his POW camp that he was
convinced that the future belonged to the Soviet Union and
that he would be willing to help. The KGB signed him up and
let him go home, where he took a high position in an industrial
enterprise.

Kondrashev went to Berlin where he had the ex-diplomat invited
to a Soviet Embassy reception. There, he sidled up and addressed
him with the prearranged "parole." The German started, his eyes
darting about, but then composed himself. "Yes," he replied, "I
thought your people would find me, and I'm really quite glad
you did. I still sympathize with your country." After a pause, he
added, "But you know, the situation is different today. The relative

power of the two sides is by no means as clear to me as it was in those days. And frankly, until it becomes clearer, I don't want to commit myself." And try as Kondrashev might to persuade him, the German remained politely adamant.

Recognizing that to threaten a man of this stature and self-confidence would have been foolhardy, Kondrashev dropped the case, and as far as he knew his service never had any further contact with him.

• • •

KONDRASHEV BECAME AWARE OF something almost no one in the world knew: the location of Hitler's remains. And it was he who instigated their final disposal.

They had been found in May 1945 just after Soviet troops had secured the Reich Chancellery area. In a shallow grave near a large bomb crater outside Hitler's bunker, a military search party found a group of half-burned bodies that they tentatively identified as those of Joseph Goebbels, his wife, and their six daughters. Nearby were two others that the search party thought must be Hitler himself and his wife Eva Braun.

Stalin ordered that the bodies be tested to determine beyond doubt that Hitler's was among them. The charred remains were taken to a secret location in Berlin and submitted to months of research and tests. Parts of Hitler's skull, including his jawbone, were sent to Moscow along with bloody fragments cut from the bunker's leather couch on which survivors reported he shot himself. The blood matched Hitler's blood type, and the skull, carefully reconstructed from the pieces available, conformed to Hitler's dimensions. But the final, conclusive evidence came by comparing the intact jawbone with Hitler's dental records.

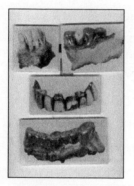

KGB photos of Hitler's teeth.

The parts of Hitler's body that had been sent to Moscow are still retained there today. Kondrashev was given pictures of the jawbone and teeth.

After the identification had become certain in early 1946, the KGB took the remains to Magdeburg, seventy miles west of Berlin, and buried them under concrete on the grounds of a Soviet military installation, a location known only to a handful of Soviet leaders. When Kondrashev arrived in a leading position in the German Department, he was told this by Aleksandr Korotkov and Vadim Kuchin, both of whom had been in Berlin when the remains were found and tested.

When Kondrashev learned in 1970 that the Soviet Army was to turn over the Magdeburg military installation to East Germany, he warned KGB Chairman Andropov that the bones might be discovered and the tomb become a neo-Nazi shrine. Andropov reported to Brezhnev, who ordered the KGB to dispose of the remains once and for all.

The operation, codenamed "Archive," was carried out in great secrecy on the night of April 4th. KGB troops sealed off the area around the military camp and erected a tent over the site. Thus hidden from curious eyes, five KGB officers with pickaxes and shovels dug through the night and found five boxes holding ten bodies. After counting the bones to ensure that none were missing, they loaded them onto a military truck and drove to a remote corner of a nearby Soviet military training area. In the dark of night, they incinerated the remains and immediately threw the ashes down a manhole into the Magdeburg city sewer system. From there, the currents took them down the River Elbe and into the North Sea.

Eight: A Unique Look at the Hungarian Revolution

"**O**UR TROOPS CONTROLLED the airport in Debrecen, but as we came in to land, small arms fire rose up at our helicopter. Aleksandr Korotkov leaned down toward me from the co-pilot's seat, pointing to the machine gun alongside me in the lower compartment, and shouted, 'Do you know how to use it? We're going to have to shoot our way in!' I didn't, really, but finally managed to spray fire at surrounding bushes and trenches to cover our approach."

As Sergey Kondrashev recounted his personal participation in the historic events in Hungary in October and November 1956, I realized that I was hearing something no one in the West had ever heard. Here was a high KGB participant on the scene telling from the inside how this core element of the Soviet regime had viewed and coped with those events.

Kondrashev, too, recognized that his is the only such testimony. One of his senior KGB colleagues in that episode had indeed published his memoirs—but without a word about his very active part, close to Kondrashev, in the bloody suppression of the Hungarian Revolution.[1]

So I have left the story as I helped Sergey compose it in English for his autobiography, the manuscript that the KGB deemed too sensitive to publish. Here is Kondrashev's account, in his own words:

• • •

I WAS PULLED ABRUPTLY—VERY abruptly—into the Hungarian Revolution by a call from KGB Chairman Ivan Serov.[2] On Saturday afternoon, October 25th, 1956, I was sitting quietly at home with Rosa. Our chat about what we'd do the next day was interrupted by a phone call. A KGB duty officer informed me that Serov had called from Budapest and ordered me to join him there immediately. And that meant *immediately*. I barely had time to pull together a few essentials for the trip before the car pulled up at our address. I jumped in and we sped off. After a short stop at the storage center to select whichever weapon I wanted to take along, it took me straight to the central military airport.

At the airport I was handed a suitcase-sized package of food with the warning, "We really don't know when or whether you'll be able to get food there." These packages were being supplied to each of our officers going into the Budapest maelstrom. Only a few moments later, with two colleagues who had similarly been called, I boarded the aircraft, it taxied out, and we lifted off—barely two hours after that phone call.

This call had been a surprise, but the situation I was stepping into was not. While supervising intelligence work in Germany and Austria, I had been keeping our government abreast of the fast-developing and deeply worrying unrest in East Germany and Poland. Now it had impacted in deadly fashion on Hungary: Shooting had begun in Budapest, and it seemed that a full-scale revolution was in the making.

I was to play a role in dark deeds that, while in the short run helped preserve Socialist rule in central Europe, were to bring no credit to our government or to any of us who participated. In retrospect, they look like steps toward the collapse of Communist Party rule in that area and eventually in Russia.

That is why no member of our little group has wanted to speak or write candidly about our work there. And that is why my mine will be the first inside account.

•   •   •

MINE WERE NOT THE only warnings that had reached the leaders of our government and Party about this growing threat since—and because of—Stalin's death in early March 1953. The East Berlin riots in June of that year already showed how intense and dangerous the popular discontent was. If that weren't enough, we in Foreign Intelligence had been getting reports from our Eastern European security services and from inside Western foreign ministries and intelligence services, that a crisis was brewing throughout the area. But seemingly indifferent to all this, the Politburo continued to support the rigid old-timers who were the focus of that discontent: Ulbricht in Germany, Novotny in Czechoslovakia, Rakosi in Hungary, and Bierut and Ochab in Poland.

An explosive element had been added to the mix in April of 1956. In Khrushchev's London talks with leading British politicians about the Near East and Suez Canal issues, he had been shocked by their determination to defend national interests, including their readiness to use force. And he had exploded with anger when he found that the British Left's Labour Party leaders, whose views he had imagined to run parallel to those of the Socialist Bloc, were in fact staunchly supporting their government's line. Talking afterward to Soviet party leaders, he said bitterly, "They've taught us how to defend our own interests everywhere." I believe that this realization influenced Khrushchev's decisions about Hungary that he was soon to make.

Heated by disorders in Poland, the situation in Hungary had evolved into a crisis by mid-October. Up to this point, we had observed and managed the Hungarian situation and exercised influence on the Party leaders through our ambassador, Yuri Andropov, while the local KGB residency had depended on the Hungarian State Security service. But Andropov, though a prominent member of the Central Committee of the Soviet Communist Party, was not authorized to make decisions on his own. Now as things began to fall apart and sensing that they might quickly get out of hand, Andropov made recommendations that, to me, demonstrated his political astuteness.

Citing the gravity of the moment and the impossibility of keeping abreast of such fast-evolving events from distant Moscow, Andropov recommended the establishment of a political command center in Budapest, including a standing representation of the Politburo itself along with top level security services. I don't believe for a minute that Andropov's concern was just command and communications: I knew him as an astute politician who recognized the value—to his own survival—of spreading the eventual responsibility.

Moscow concurred. Politburo members Mikhail Suslov and Anastas Mikoyan travelled to Budapest where they stayed sometimes together, sometimes one at a time. Andropov again demonstrated his instinct for self-preservation by separating himself geographically from the eventual fallout from their decisions. Although there was plenty of room in his Embassy building, he set up their offices not there but in an Embassy-owned building down the street.

In flew the security service top level: KGB Chairman Serov himself accompanied by two close colleagues, Aleksandr Korotkov and Yelisei Sinitsyn.

To assess the situation, Serov first heard the Hungarian State Security service's reading, then took a hard look at its ability to handle the crisis and to cope with possible Western intervention. He was not comforted by what he saw nor by the ability of the standing KGB representation in Hungary to cope with a crisis of this magnitude.

The presence of Soviet troops in Hungary made it inevitable from the very beginning of the unrest that if things got out of hand, Moscow would use whatever means were required to restore order. Soviet troops in neighboring areas were put in alert status.

On the 23rd, hundreds of students demonstrated in Budapest in support of the Polish workers and students. Their numbers swelled into thousands as they called for improvements in Hungary, too. They issued a set of demands for relaxation of political and economic restrictions, for changes in the government leadership, and for Soviet troops to leave the country. That night they tore down the huge statue of Stalin and exultantly dragged part of it through the streets.

As people assembled in front of the radio station the next morning, shots were fired from the building. Violence spread not only in Budapest, but also to other Hungarian towns. Soviet tanks in the country took up positions to defend certain buildings, the shooting spread and soon became open warfare. Rebels took over town administrations and supported the students' demands. Now we were dealing with a full-scale revolution.

With the very survival of the Hungarian regime at stake and the security of Soviet troops in Hungary coming into question, the KGB's role took center stage. Serov quickly saw that Hungarian agencies would not be able to find out enough about what the Western powers were doing or planning, so he focused his whole foreign intelligence service on that aspect of the crisis. He called on Moscow center and KGB residencies everywhere to send to Budapest officers who spoke Hungarian or had friends or sources in Hungary or inside Western institutions connected with Hungarian affairs. The officers handling such agents were to come with arrangements to meet their sources on the spot.

In rushed Soviet intelligence officers, including my father-in-law Vasily Roshchin who, though retired, called in several of his journalist, government, and business sources from his decades of operating in Germany, Austria, and Scandinavia. Korotkov brought in at least one source from Austria. From my own German Department came Oleg Ivanov and from the Vienna rezidentura Sergey Votrin, both of whom spoke some Hungarian. Aleksey A. Krokhin, a specialist in operations in France and at this time a deputy chief of foreign intelligence, brought in sources with good contacts in the French diplomatic and intelligence services. (While in town making contact with one of them, he was shot in the buttocks and was flown back to Moscow.) With me in the plane from Moscow came Nikolay A. Kosov, presumably to exploit contacts from his earlier service under journalist cover in the United States, and Vladimir P. Burdin, with wide contacts from his long service in Canada. Something like a dozen KGB officers in all came from other areas during this time, plus a number of Illegals (KGB officers operating under false Western identities).

Their Western contacts spread out, seeking to elicit information and evaluations of the situation from co-nationals in Western embassies and Budapest business offices and from whichever Hungarians they knew.

Top priority for all sources was to find out whether and exactly how the American, British, and French governments, and specifically their secret services, supported or planned to support the rebellion. Our mission was to anticipate and foil any direct Western intervention and clandestine help to the rebels.

We had no doubt that Western governments were in fact supporting the insurrection. Our service had assembled so much information on the Hungarian reformers' Western contacts that even now I am still persuaded that Westerners were influencing and encouraging developments. And I say so while recognizing that our views at the time were exaggerated by preconceptions inherited from the paranoid Stalin times.

· · ·

IT WAS TO HELP Korotkov develop these efforts and ensure real-time reporting that Serov had summoned me. Our plane landed at a military airport near Budapest on the morning of the 26th. To my surprise, Serov was there to meet us. He led us to a nearby armored troop carrier that would carry us into the city.

"Why are we going in *that*?" I asked.

"Just wait," Serov replied. "You'll see soon enough." And in fact as we drove into town we heard shooting, saw houses with bullet and shell holes, even felt a shot ping off our vehicle.

We were dropped off in front of the Soviet Embassy, where a tank stood at the corner and troops were positioned to defend it. Serov led us down a little side street to a two- or three-story house. "This is where Korotkov and Sinitsyn are staying," he told us. "You'll stay here, under Korotkov's direction. Keep us up to the minute on what's going on, what the rebels are planning, what the Westerners are doing, and how things are developing. Work out among yourselves how to do it."

Some officers who came in answer to Serov's call stayed with us in that house, while others made their own arrangements to lodge with friends from the local KGB residency or in vacant flats of absent Embassy personnel. Essentially, we were an ad hoc KGB center with its own, imported sources keeping the local Politburo representation apprised of the situation hour by hour.

We worked out how our imported officers would pick up information from their sources. As that information flowed in, they helped us prepare reports in our house and walked them over to Serov in the Embassy at any time of the day or night. He then informed Andropov, who saw to their transmission to the Politburo representation here and in Moscow. Our operation was entirely independent of the Embassy as such and solely under the command of Serov, whom I saw much more often than I saw Andropov.

Living there in that little house, we prepared our own meals from the food packages given us in Moscow, later replenished by regular deliveries of more of the same. After a few days we were given a car and managed to augment this menu by driving to a market that somehow continued to function where, talking only English or German to each other in front of the Hungarians, we loaded up with apples and vegetables.

A few days after our arrival, we acquired what we considered direct evidence of Western support for the rebels. Korotkov, who wanted to assess the situation in the east of the country, arranged that he and I be driven by car to Debrecen. En route we encountered a column of Red Cross trucks and Korotkov—in the full uniform of a Soviet general[3]—stopped them and asked me to check their cargo. As I walked along the line of trucks, I saw something thrown out to the side of the road. It was a pack of hand grenades. After waiting a few seconds in case a pin had been pulled, I picked it up and went back to question the driver. He "couldn't imagine" where it came from or for whom it had been intended. After confiscating the grenades and drawing up an official document to certify it (the driver refused to sign), we allowed the convoy to proceed. We were left with the strong impression that Red Cross aid was intended primarily to help anti-Soviet rebel groups.

Because of this delay, we decided to return to Budapest for the night. The next day Korotkov arranged a faster way to Debrecen: a military helicopter—our descent under fire there is described in the opening paragraph of this chapter. The town of Debrecen was now in the hands of rebels, so we spent the night with the Soviet Army unit holding the airfield, and then in an armored personnel carrier we accompanied an armed convoy back to Budapest.

On the way back, Korotkov proposed to visit a Hungarian Army unit based an hour or two from Budapest to get an idea of their mood and intentions. When we told the sentry we wanted to talk with the commander, a major came out and invited us into his office. He politely assured us that the army did not want to fight against Soviet forces, but reminded us forcefully that its sworn task was to defend the interests of the Hungarian nation. Its decisions would be based on the situation, not on Soviet preference.

On the basis of this visit and the information being supplied by our sources, Korotkov reported to Serov that the Hungarian Army was against us and might fight. I think this conclusion contributed to the eventual decision to use overwhelming Soviet force against the rebels.

A talk with a young Soviet tank commander who had faced oncoming crowds on a Budapest square showed me the pressure our troops were under. "I had no orders to shoot," he told me, his nerves about to crack, "but I had to do something when they came at me. They could have tossed a Molotov cocktail into us. I fired over their heads, but they kept coming. Then I fired down onto the pavement. I didn't intend to hit them!" However, bullets that hit the cobblestone surface ricocheted up, and several people had fallen. The young man was practically in tears, and there was little I could say to comfort him.

It was clear to us that getting rid of the hated Communist Party Chief Matyas Rakosi had been a good first step. (I believe it was Ambassador Andropov who persuaded him to retire to the Soviet Union; I cannot confirm written reports that Politburo members Suslov and Mikoyan did it.) But then, having got rid of Rakosi, Soviet authorities let his almost equally detested deputy Ernö Gerö succeed him. Although I do not know exactly who played the key role in persuading Gerö to bend to popular demand and bring back Imre Nagy as prime minister, I do know that at that time Soviet leadership considered Nagy a reliable friend of the USSR.

The change didn't help. Nor did things cool down with Gerö's exit and replacement with the less unpopular Janos Kadar. The rebellion continued.

Even before shooting began on 23–24 October, new Soviet divisions with hundreds of tanks had moved into Hungary from several sides. And when the two Soviet divisions regularly stationed in Hungary were ostensibly "withdrawn" on October 30, they only moved out of Budapest to nearby positions where they stood ready to move back in case of any Western intervention

The uprising gained strength. Revolutionary councils took power in cities and towns throughout the country. Rebels paraded the national flag with the communist hammer-and-sickle centre-piece cut out. On November 1st, Imre Nagy bent to popular demand and called publicly for "neutrality" and withdrawal from the Warsaw Pact, an impermissible move that shocked and fright-ened the Soviet leadership.

Two days later, the situation had gotten completely out of hand. Someone—I presume Suslov and/or Mikoyan, after phoning Khrushchev in Moscow—gave the order to unleash the Soviet Army. They struck the following day, and the poorly armed resist-ance soon collapsed. Imre Nagy and some others took refuge in the Yugoslav Embassy that day, but the Soviet Army captured and jailed members of his government, prominent reformers, and mili-tary leaders, some of whom were snared by false promises.

A few days later we celebrated in our little house the anniver-sary of our October Revolution—ironically after our forces had put down the Hungarians' October revolution. We had food and drinks, and a picture was taken of us all together with a live turkey on the table in front of us.

● ● ●

NOVEMBER 22 WAS A date that remains a dark blot on my memory even though I had nothing to do with the arrangements that led to it. I participated in moving Imre Nagy from the safety of the Yugoslav Embassy.

Our aim, in our Serov-directed unit, was solely to assure Nagy's safe transportation to a place that he had chosen. I have read (but cannot confirm as I never discussed it with Andropov) that Nagy had been induced to leave his refuge by an agreement between the Yugoslavs and the new Soviet-installed, Soviet-controlled Hungarian government. That agreement, which was said to include the assurance that Nagy would not be harmed, gave him the choice of going to his home in Budapest or safe passage to Romania or Yugoslavia. He chose the former.

Serov planned the actual move. A Volkswagen minibus and three escort cars, confiscated from Hungarians to assure its safety, would pick up Nagy when he left the Yugoslav Embassy. Each vehicle would be driven by one of the officers of our little KGB group. A Hungarian State Security officer in the front seat beside us knew the route to the place to which we were to escort Nagy.

We waited outside the Yugoslav Embassy. I saw Nagy emerge. When offered the chance to ride either in a car or in the minibus, he chose the latter and got in with one other person who I was later told was his assistant. No one else entered the minibus or any of the cars.

Serov stood off to the side watching as we drove off in a column, the minibus driven by Sinitsyn leading the way. My car was in the middle of the three behind it. I cannot remember seeing any escort or surveillance in front or on the sides. The street seemed strangely deserted that morning.

We drove for some fifteen minutes to our destination, a villa in Pest where someone came out and exchanged words with Nagy and his assistant. Nagy and his companion left the bus and entered the villa. He did not seem in any way reluctant to do so. Our mission of assuring his safe passage was thus accomplished.

"Where was that place we took Nagy?" I later asked one of my colleagues. He thought, as I had, that it was some Hungarian government house or office, but he did not know more. Neither then or later did any of us find out, nor had we any idea what was to happen to Nagy. We were all shocked to hear that about a year later, the Hungarians had transferred him to Romania where he was executed.

I have read various published reports that we drove Nagy to the Soviet military command headquarters, and that Yugoslav diplomats accompanied us, that we were escorted by armored cars, or even that our convoy was stopped by armored cars and Nagy taken out and driven off in one of them. None of this is true.

After dropping Nagy off, the four of us drove back to our lodgings, feeling relieved that Nagy was safely back among Hungarians and no longer a problem for us. In retrospect I recognized—as did all my colleagues—that our role was not unlike that of Pontius Pilate washing his hands. The incident certainly did not enhance the international image of my country.

In Budapest, I talked several times with my father-in-law. I remember Roshchin's warning: "Keep quiet, Sergey. Don't let yourself become prominent in or identified with these events. They're unpredictable, and they won't reflect credit on any of us."

Our group stayed on until early December, but I left earlier in a medical emergency. A sudden and acute stomach pain sent me to a Soviet Army field hospital, far safer for a Russian patient than a Hungarian hospital at this time. The ailment was diagnosed as an inflamed appendix, and Korotkov arranged a military flight to Moscow where my appendix was removed. Soon afterward, by the end of November, I returned directly to my job in the Austro-German Department.

The pain in my stomach symbolized my feelings about the Soviet intervention in Hungary. It blatantly exposed the failure of the system of government that I had so long served, and it portended ill for the future of my own country.

Nine:
Spy Center Vienna

NOWHERE IN THE West did the KGB have a more convenient base for its spy operations than Vienna, where Sergey Kondrashev arrived as its deputy chief in February 1957.

For the Soviets, the city richly deserved its oft-cited sobriquet, "turntable of espionage." This capital of a western country lay far to the east, half surrounded by Communist lands. Borders only minutes away facilitated the KGB's secret contacts and movements to and from the West—movements including kidnappings: Austria became notorious as the site of KGB abductions of anti-Soviet Western activists or spies lured there from farther west.

The KGB had made good use of the Soviet and Allied postwar occupation of Vienna. For one thing, they had planted friends and clandestine collaborators in key Austrian positions. They took on so many policemen as secret helpers that they finally couldn't handle them all and (after a 1953 reorganization described on the following page) culled the numbers from more than three hundred to a more manageable fifty or so.[1] They acquired villas and apartments that continued for many years to serve as venues for meetings with spies who could travel "innocently" from their own countries to this tourist mecca to consult at leisure with their KGB handlers without having to get telltale eastern travel stamped into their passports. The history of Cold War espionage is replete with

KGB meetings in Vienna with western traitors like CIA insiders Edward Lee Howard and Aldrich Ames and the American Navy cryptographer John Walker. Soviet Illegals preparing missions in the West could more safely live here (sometimes papered with authentic documents supplied by some of those Austrian secret helpers) while accustoming themselves to Western ways and firming up their legends.

Earlier history added to Vienna's espionage potential. Thousands of Czechs, Slovaks, Hungarians and others had settled in this former imperial capital and whenever possible the KGB's Eastern Europe satellite services exploited the family or business ties of their descendants. The KGB rezident and his deputy stayed in close touch with the local chiefs of the Czechoslovak, Hungarian, Polish, Bulgarian, and Romanian state security services and sometimes made use of their secret assets.

Moreover, the 1955 State Treaty ending the occupation had established the country as neutral. Austrian security services would thus keep a less close eye on Soviet intelligence officers' movements and contacts, and if they should do so, one of the KGB's inside sources might give warning.

• • •

THE STRUCTURE OF VIENNA'S KGB residency was the result of a reorganization of 1953 in which Sergey Kondrashev himself had participated to resolve a problem that had festered since the war's end. The KGB had set up a counterintelligence residency independent of military counterintelligence and independent of whatever unit its foreign-intelligence component might establish. Thus until 1953 the KGB had had two separate residencies (aside from military counterintelligence), both housed in the same building with overlapping missions. Inevitably, an unhealthy rivalry sprang up.

Heading the counterintelligence ("KR") residency was a Colonel Gorkov who had been plucked from some region of Russia. He thought this job required him to cast his eye onto the doings of all Soviet citizens in Austria—including those of the KGB's own intelligence residency. To his provincial eye, their contacts with foreigners looked suspicious and threatening.

Having someone poking into his secret work would have irritated any foreign intelligence officer—after all, his very purpose was to develop such contacts—but the one who commanded this particular foreign-intelligence residency would be the least likely to abide it. Colonel Vasily Romanovich Sitnikov, as Kondrashev described him to me, was a brilliant officer with an impressive command of German history and language but notably impatient with disagreement, even from higher-ups, and unable to conceal his intellectual superiority. Deteriorating relations between the two residencies were hampering the work of both.

In early 1953, a four-man inspection team went out from Moscow to straighten out the situation. If they were to delve into the secret work of both residencies, these inspectors would need unusually high authority, and they had it. To lead the team was none other than Pavel V. Fedotov, who had commanded successively both Counterintelligence (SCD) and Foreign Intelligence (FCD) and was soon to take over the SCD again. To second him went Andrey G. Graur, an FCD deputy chief well versed in bureaucratic tangles, having headed the KGB's huge and administratively complex East Berlin structure. The chief of the Austro-German Department, Yevgeniy I. Kravtsov, was the third member.

The fourth was Sergey Kondrashev. He had been brought into this exalted company because of his experience in Counterintelligence, his command of the German language, his hierarchical status as a deputy department chief, and no doubt because he was already marked for service in the German-language area.

In their weeks in Vienna, they saw that drastic repair was called for, and Fedotov's recommendations were immediately put into force. Although the solution was labelled a "merger," the counterintelligence residency was disbanded and Gorkov reassigned to a regional office inside the USSR. A unified residency was taken over by Kravtsov himself later in the year, with Sitnikov charged with its highest-priority work of targeting Americans in Vienna. One of its sections (SK, for "Soviet Colony") would take over Gorkov's former role of watching over Soviet civilians throughout Austria.[2]

That inspection mission to Vienna was marked by a bizarre moment. As the team sat together at breakfast in their hotel, General Graur suddenly mentioned quite casually that he had been recruited by British Intelligence.

"*What?*" exclaimed Fedotov.

Yes, Graur answered matter-of-factly. British operatives wearing white doctors' coats had broken into his hotel room the previous evening, injected him with drugs, and forced him to divulge secrets and agree to become their agent.

Fedotov, with admirable composure, replied in a mild, conversational tone. "You know, Andrey Grigoryevich, all this work has tired you out. You need a rest, my friend, as I'm sure you agree. So don't worry about those British doctors, just go on back home and take it easy for a while. I'll arrange the details." Kondrashev arranged a military flight with a doctor to take Graur to Moscow the next day. He entered a mental institution, and though he eventually recovered, he was retired from the service on medical grounds.

. . .

KONDRASHEV WELCOMED HIS POSTING as deputy rezident not only because Vienna was a prestigious posting, a fine operating base, and a pleasant place to live, but also because nowhere in the West did he and his wife feel more at home (she having gone to school there as a child). Sergey arrived in February 1957 under cover as First Secretary (later to become Counselor) of Embassy, to serve as deputy to Fyodor Shubnyakov. When Shubnyakov departed in 1958, Kondrashev served as acting resident for two or three months—as the fates would have it, replacing, if only temporarily, the very man who thirteen years earlier had recruited him as an informant on Soviet cultural figures.

• • •

THE KGB RESIDENCY UNDER Shubnyakov and Kondrashev enjoyed successes. In his time there, Shubnyakov was twice awarded the Order of the Red Banner and in 1956 received a gold watch and the KGB chairman's congratulations for his successes. When I asked Kondrashev, "Why did Shubnyakov get such rewards?" I was clearly striking a nerve. Sergey brushed off my question: "Oh, that was probably routine stuff, for length of service, birthday, or something." That sent the clear message that he was not going to tell—and was leaving yet another Cold War mystery still to be resolved. However, Kondrashev confirmed that two spies were labeled as "valuable" and hence worthy of such special security precautions that even Kondrashev, as acting and deputy chief, was not allowed to know more than their general location and positions. I knew from other sources that American intelligence, specifically CIA, was high among the KGB's top targets in Vienna, and wondered if these successes had been enjoyed at CIA's expense.

• • •

THE ONLY SPIES OF the residency about whom Kondrashev was willing to speak were an Austrian Foreign Ministry official whom Sergey himself had recruited and a member of a French intelligence office whom Sergey had handled. The latter had brought him a notable accomplishment.

It began when disturbing news and instructions came to Sergey from Moscow: "Soviet secrets are being betrayed in Vienna. Find out how!" Moscow had learned—presumably from a mole inside French Intelligence though Kondrashev did not specify—that Paris was getting important Soviet political and economic secrets and, according to the KGB's "analysis" (as Sergey put it), from French "military channels" in Vienna.

Kondrashev set out to find the source of the leak and succeeded. "This was one of our best achievements in Vienna," he told me proudly, "and it far surpassed the initial task set for us and for me personally."

Sergey was running an agent inside a French military intelligence office, most likely the very one through which Moscow knew the leak was passing. He decided to break into its files. With help of his agent, he studied the layout of that office, which was situated on the second floor of a big house not far from Vienna's city center. They copied the keys and, during "tedious hours over a period of weeks," worked out in minute detail how KGB technicians, brought in from Moscow, would enter and which safe or safes they would open and how they would copy and replace documents without leaving a trace.

In the first attempt to enter late one night, the newly-made key to the house stuck in the lock. During "nerve-wracking" moments, Sergey and a colleague managed to free it, but it was too late to carry through the entire operation. The second try was the charm: The technicians got in and photocopied French intelligence reports of contacts with Soviet diplomats and trade representatives in Austria. These reports persuaded Moscow that they had discovered the source of the leak, and Kondrashev was commended.

It was not clear from Kondrashev's guarded account whether the Soviet official who had leaked the information to the French had been intentionally treasonous or simply indiscreet, nor whether that official had been punished and, if so, how.

. . .

IN EARLY JUNE 1961 the new American President John F. Kennedy met with Nikita Khrushchev in Vienna. That was a time when the Cold War threatened to turn hot: East Germans were fleeing westward through Berlin in such numbers as to pose a threat to the survival of this vital Soviet satellite and even of the Soviet Bloc itself. Khrushchev, who threatened to sign a peace treaty with East Germany that would cut Berlin from the West, called it "the most dangerous place in the world."

The KGB made the local preparations for this historic encounter, and Sergey Kondrashev was able to add bits to its history.[3]

Nikolay S. Zakharov, the head of the Moscow directorate protecting and supporting the Soviet leadership, came to Vienna to plan the details. Together with Sergey, he met presidential assistant Pierre Salinger in an American Embassy secure room to agree on the schedule of events.

The first day's meeting would include lunch and take place on June 3rd at the American ambassador's residence. A state dinner would be hosted by Austrian President Adolf Shaerf that evening. The second and final day would be spent in the Soviet Embassy, where a room would be set up for the president's private use and communications.

Kondrashev was designated as liaison officer between the two delegations. He saw to the ordering of new furniture for that private office and had it checked for bugs by Soviet technicians. (He assured me with apparent sincerity that the room was in fact not bugged.) At Salinger's request, he personally checked the functioning of an American-installed direct line from the Soviet Embassy to the White House. Salinger assured Kondrashev and Zakharov that the Americans would hang a special phone line between the American and Soviet embassies, its entire length to be guarded by US Marines.

Kondrashev was one of the six Soviets accompanying Khrushchev to his meeting with Kennedy at the residence of the American ambassador.[4] As the last to enter, Sergey signaled to the American security chief, who immediately took a solid, determined stance athwart the entry, a formidable obstacle to any of the assembled officials or reporters who might try to follow them in.

At the Soviet Embassy after that meeting, Khrushchev told his team his impressions of the talks, including what was said during his post-lunch one-on-one stroll with Kennedy in the garden. Contrary to some published reports that Khrushchev had crowed about his dominance of the younger and less experienced Kennedy, Kondrashev remembered that Khrushchev expressed respect for the president's conduct in the talks.

Khrushchev then directed Kondrashev to deliver his presents to the Americans. Sergey drove to the American residence and lay the gifts for display on the entry hall floor. Jacqueline Kennedy shuffled through them all, examining even those destined for others. When Sergey raised an eyebrow, she smilingly asserted her right to inspect them all. The president then came down and after briefly looking over the presents, ordered whisky and invited Kondrashev for a drink, which was happily accepted.

Khrushchev had Sergey procure the presents he would take back to his colleagues in Moscow. Here was a glance into Kremlin practices: There were to be five hundred packages of the best Austrian wines, a hundred to contain six bottles each, two hundred of three bottles, and another two hundred of two bottles. Through a prominent Vienna wine merchant, Sergey made the selection and arranged the transport.

At the state dinner at Schönbrunn Palace, Kondrashev found himself interpreting for both Nikita and Nina Khrushchev with both John and Jaqueline Kennedy and—in three languages—for Khrushchev with Austrian President Adolf Schaerf and President Kennedy. Only ten minutes of this strenuous task had Kondrashev damp with perspiration, but here, once again as so often in his life, his linguistic talent had drawn him into an extraordinary position.

Kondrashev (second from right, standing), interpreting for John F. Kennedy, Nikita Khrushchev, and (seated between them) Austrian President Adolf Schaerf.

Kondrashev interpreting for President Kennedy and Nina Khrushchev at state dinner, Vienna.

Ten:
The KGB's Nazi Underground

SERGEY KONDRASHEV AND I had both enjoyed long tours of duty in Vienna and sometimes talked about its pleasures. One sunny day in a Brussels garden restaurant we were reminded of Vienna's Heurigen, those homey restaurants and gardens with their fresh white wine. When our reminiscences drifted back to our job at hand, bringing up his memories for his autobiography, Sergey said something that reminded me how tightly the KGB had held its secrets within the circle of those who really had a need to know. "I'm afraid your KGB did a lot better job of that than my CIA did," I remarked.

Sergey nodded absently, his mind still on our reminiscences of Vienna, and murmured, "Like that day in the Heuriger . . ."

He had been sitting at a table in the wine-growing suburb of Grinzing, he said, while not far away in the woods, some deep KGB intrigue was afoot—and even he—the local KGB chief—had not been permitted to know about it.

We didn't go further that day, but later when I asked, he told me more, although the explanation was far too dangerous to be part of his autobiography. It was, nevertheless, a tale that demanded to be told.

• • •

KONDRASHEV'S PART IN THAT story began in Moscow in February 1957 when the chief of KGB Illegals, General Aleksandr Korotkov, took him aside to talk privately. They were both about to leave Moscow, Sergey to become deputy and acting chief of the KGB's Vienna residency and Korotkov to take command of the huge East Berlin KGB Apparat.

"Look, Sergey," Korotkov said, "I've going to make a very important meeting in Vienna, and I'll need your help there. But only yours; I can't trust anyone else. And you can't tell anyone about it, not here, not in Vienna."

Two months later Korotkov slipped into Vienna without notifying the Soviet Embassy or the KGB residency. Sergey picked him up at a street corner and, at his direction, drove into the Vienna Woods near Traiskirchen. Korotkov pointed out a spot where he should be picked up exactly four hours later. He spelled out what to do should he fail to show up there, including how to sound the alarm in Moscow. After they had driven a bit further, Sasha asked Sergey to stop, and left the car. Kondrashev drove on to that Heuriger in Grinzing, had lunch and a long walk, then at the prescribed time drove to the pickup spot.

Korotkov popped back into the car and let Sergey know all had gone well, but said no more about it. And Sergey said no more either, until our lunch in the Brussels restaurant nearly fifty years later, about his brief role as chauffeur and warning bell for Korotkov.

That was, indeed, tight compartmentalization. Sergey was at the top level of the Austro-German Department when Korotkov asked him to play a supporting role in some Germany-related action, and he was acting chief in Austria at the time that action played out there, yet was not told details. No matter that Korotkov trusted him so deeply that only Sergey could do this job. Nevermind that these long-time colleagues had recently been under fire together in the Hungarian Revolution. If Korotkov, well-known for being close-mouthed, had wanted to say more, he would have.

Now I asked Kondrashev what he had not ventured to ask Korotkov: What activity in Vienna might be so secret?

"As I said," Sergey replied, "he never specified." After a brief pause he added, "But you know about Korotkov."

Evidently Sergey knew more than he was telling. I looked at him quizzically.

"He was meeting some German," Sergey said, "someone he had worked with long before." Evidently deliberating how far he could go, he added, "Some of those were former Nazis. They were contacts known and coordinated only at the highest level of our service."

I did not press further. We had come close to an answer, perhaps closer than Sergey had anticipated. Not only did I "know about Korotkov," but I also knew something about these Nazi contacts. By extraordinary coincidence I had personally heard from no fewer than three of the handful of people in the world who could have known anything about this matter. Now I understood why Korotkov hid his secret even from Sergey. You see, the KGB had hidden the bloodiest Nazi war criminal and used him and other high Nazi survivors as postwar tools against the Soviet Union's wartime allies.

• • •

SOMETHING OF A LEGEND in the KGB, Aleksandr Mikhailovich Korotkov had by 1957 operated for nearly a quarter-century in German affairs and was its leading operator in the area. Tall, blue-eyed, dark-haired, and handsome, he inspired awe but sometimes irritation at his temper and intolerance of disagreement. Some of the criticism stemmed from jealousy, Sergey thought. Indeed, few could boast such a record as Korotkov's. He had commanded a large part of KGB German operations before, during, and after the war. He oversaw the KGB's most secret operatives, the Illegals, for so long that a post-Cold War biographer labelled him "King of the Illegals." Already a deputy head of Foreign Intelligence, he was regarded as a potential KGB chairman.

Even more lustre of the KGB sort shone from earlier deeds dating from the mid-1930s. Korotkov was an Illegal in France, said to have played a role in the assassinations of KGB defector Georgy Agabekov and Leon Trotsky's aide Rudolf Klement. In wartime Berlin, as a Soviet trade official using the name Aleksandr Erdberg, he handled key members of the now famous network "Red Orchestra." Even after Germany invaded Russia in June 1941 and interned Korotkov with other Soviet officials, he was said to have duped his captors into giving him a moment free, during which he slipped contact arrangements to a "Red Orchestra" agent, Grete Kuckhoff. Repatriated to Russia in the German-Soviet exchange of internees, he then performed KGB missions in Afghanistan and India and became wartime chief of the German Department. He is said to have recruited, prepared, and dispatched several German prisoners of war to be dropped as spies behind German lines, at least one to Berlin itself.[1] He also screened other POWs for possible postwar KGB use.

Amid the ashes of the German capital, Korotkov helped prepare the German surrender ceremony. (In one photo of it, he can be spotted behind Field Marshal Keitel signing the act of capitulation.) He worked with Ivan Serov and alongside Viktor Abakumov's SMERSH, seizing Nazi Intelligence files and personnel—the stuff of future KGB operations.

• • •

Korotkov pictured shortly after the war, and again in early 1961 toasting the medal given him by East German Stasi Chief Erich Mielke for his long oversight of Mielke's work. On June 28, 1961, Korotkov died of a burst aorta while playing tennis with KGB Chairman Ivan Serov at the Dynamo sport club where, as a teenager, he had got his start in the KGB as an elevator repairman.

WHEN SERGEY KONDRASHEV REMARKED, "You know about Korotkov," he was reminding me that Korotkov's Illegals Directorate (partitioned as it was from the KGB's geographic departments) handled specially-delicate operations. Under its wing at times were such functions as assassination and kidnapping abroad.[2] And Sergey's remark also pointed me toward Korotkov's well-known work in Nazi Germany.

After the 1943 battles of Stalingrad and Kursk and after D-Day a year later, it had become clear to any rational member of the Nazi German leadership that defeat was inevitable. Each had to think about what he would do when the end came, and the most compromised of them could expect no forgiveness for their crimes. Some contemplated suicide and stored cyanide pills. Others prepared false identities, including documents, disguises, and even plastic surgery. Alone or in concert and using the contacts and money abroad of German Intelligence, some set up escape routes (which became known as "rat lines") and laid down gold and other valuables in hiding places in remote areas of the Austrian Alps, in Franco's Spain, and in South America. Others looked at possibilities of organizing military post-surrender groups to keep the Nazi flame burning and harass the incoming occupiers, like the much-touted "Werewolf" units that were expected to, but never did, strike from hiding-places in the Bavarian mountains. Still others made peace feelers through neutral countries, or sought secret contact with the enemy—East or West—to save their skins.

Hundreds of German war criminals escaped and survived. They were helped to escape and settle abroad by pro-Nazis in governments like Franco's Spain, Peron's Argentina, and Stroessner's Paraguay, from German emigrants, and even from Catholic institutions. Some, like Adolf Eichmann, were finally found and brought to justice. Others defied long worldwide searches and, like the Auschwitz "death doctor" Josef Mengele, died decades later accidentally or by natural causes.

In the process, loose organizations evolved not only to facilitate escape and survival, but also to preserve Nazi ideology and restore it to power in an eventual Fourth Reich. These associations have been fictionalized in novels like *The Odessa File* (the title is an acronym for *Organisation der Ehemaligen SS-Angehörigen* or Organization of Former SS Members). Some were said to take names such as The Spider. As late as the 1960s, some had congealed into far-right political parties or study organizations. One was the Nazi-rescue "Society in Argentina for the Reception of Europeans" (SARE), set up in 1948 to provide "visas and resources for immigration" for the hundreds of arriving war criminals and Nazi collaborators.[3]

· · ·

THE NAZI GERMAN ESCAPE stories are well-known. Still hidden, however, is their Soviet underside.

In fact, the Soviets learned about—and used for their own purposes—what became a sort of postwar Nazi underground. That the KGB did so, and exactly how, remains largely unrecognized by history. Fragments of the story have leaked, some from reliable sources, but Moscow has managed to discredit them as "unfounded speculation." The full truth would, even today, be hugely embarrassing to the Russian regime.

That is why Aleksandr Korotkov would not say more to his trusted associate Sergey Kondrashev. And it is why, more than fifty years later, Kondrashev only inadvertently mentioned it to me and then was reluctant to say more.

The ugly fact is that without telling their wartime allies, the KGB secretly infiltrated that Nazi exodus from Germany, took control of one or more Nazi exile organizations, and manipulated them in a classic "false flag" operation[4] as unwitting tools in its Cold War against the West.

This operation was run by Aleksandr Korotkov, no doubt helped by a few others in his Illegals Directorate.

• • •

THE RED ARMY'S 1945 sweep into Germany brought along Stalin's all-powerful military security force, SMERSH.[5] Under the command of Viktor Abakumov, it apprehended Nazi officials, scientists, and weapons specialists and shipped them to Moscow for interrogation—and varying fates. Some war criminals were executed. Others were hired for future weapons research. Still others were taken on by Abakumov's SMERSH and Korotkov's German Department to serve the Soviets' developing struggle against the capitalist West. So successfully did the KGB hide this activity within its own ranks that even after Abakumov's arrest in mid-1951 it was only whispered about vaguely within the KGB's German Department as "Abakumov's legacy."[6]

High among these hidden "weapons" was the Gestapo chief himself, Heinrich Müller. It did not matter that he had instigated some of Nazi Germany's most terrible crimes. He signed off on the "final solution of the Jewish question" as the immediate boss of its executor Adolf Eichmann. Nor did it matter that he issued under his name instructions for the round-up of Jews in many countries. Making the KGB's later use of the man even more astonishing, in the Nazi-occupied parts of the Soviet Union itself, "Gestapo" Müller had overseen mass murder, torture, and cruelty on a scale still hardly imaginable. He was arguably the least forgivable of all the war criminals, and he was also the most sought: He and Martin Bormann stood at the top of a postwar list of the Allies' "most wanted."

The top Soviets did not care. They not only hid Gestapo Müller's survival from their wartime allies, but they also used him for years against them.

Now, it is true that Westerners also used some Nazis beyond routine postwar interrogations. For two and a half years, the American Army Counterintelligence Corps used the Gestapo "butcher of Lyon" Klaus Barbie as a source of information on Communists in France and helped him escape in 1951 to South America to evade French arrest.[7] (However, the Americans had no further contact with him or ever dreamed of using him to enlist other Nazis in the interests of American Intelligence, and eventually he was extradited to France for trial and imprisonment.) The American-sponsored Gehlen Organization that became West Germany's BND (Federal Intelligence Service) added to their staff some former Nazi SS and SD security men with questionable, even reprehensible, wartime records.[8]

But the KGB's operation was on a different plane altogether. It used the highest-level and most wanted war criminals to

Heinrich "Gestapo" Müeller

enlist others of their ilk in a long-range pro-Nazi operation that made the KGB, in effect, their collaborators in preparing for a "Fourth Reich."

• • •

WHILE OTHER NAZI LEADERS committed suicide or fled Berlin on April 29–30, 1945, in the last days of the war, Heinrich "Gestapo" Müller walked out of Hitler's bunker a day earlier after indicating to the wonderment of some of his colleagues that he was not going to try to flee the city. He intended to stay—and wait.[9]

The Gestapo chief had reason to consider the incoming KGB as old friends. He had established good relations with them as early as 1937, had passed along valuable bits of information during secret talks preparing the Molotov-Ribbentrop Pact of August 1939, and had conducted joint actions with them in 1940 and 1941 to suppress resistance in their respective areas of occupied Poland.[10] He had long-standing pro-Communist convictions, which he disclosed in 1943 to Nazi intelligence (SD) chief Walter Schellenberg, who moreover had reason to believe that Müller had established radio contact with the Soviets by 1943.[11]

And indeed Abakumov's incoming counterintelligence forces picked up Müller and interrogated him in Moscow, but instead of punishing him as the worst of war criminals, took him in for clandestine work and moved him to South America.[12]

By 1952, Müller was back in Russia, in jail and under KGB interrogation. This was the time of the "Abakumov affair,"[13] when the security service was aggressively investigating all of Abakumov's activities. After Stalin's death in March 1953, most of the arrestees, although not Abakumov himself, were freed and returned to work. Apparently Müller was, too.

. . .

ALTHOUGH SERGEY KONDRASHEV WAS reluctant to reveal to me the KGB's postwar use of Müller, I had heard of it in my CIA capacity as early as 1954 from KGB Major Pyotr Deryabin, and again in 1958 via anonymous letters that I handled from the high-ranking Polish state security officer Michal Goleniewski. On my own, I had learned more after the Cold War.

Goleniewski had been uniquely placed to learn what few knew. He learned that Abakumov recruited the Gestapo chief in Danzig, Jakob Löllgen, who became involved in the early phases of the organization. To take charge of it, Abakumov enlisted other Nazi officials captured during the Red Army's advance to Berlin. Through Löllgen, Abakumov had gotten in touch with Gestapo Müller as early as 1943. Goleniewski reported further that Müller, along with Nazi Party Chief Martin Bormann,[14] working under the Soviet hand, became the chief inspirations of the organization.[15]

By manipulating this organization, Abakumov foresaw—and Korotkov pursued—a wide range of objectives. Influential members in West Germany, for instance, would secretly help fellow right-wing conspirators obtain government positions where they would unwittingly act as KGB spies. Others would unwittingly advance Soviet aims by unsettling West German politics and sowing distrust within the Western alliance through their far-right political organizations or provocative actions, like painting swastikas and desecrating Jewish tombs. And by enlisting exiled Germans abroad to this extreme right-wing cause, the KGB sought to gain access to geographical areas and to parts of society otherwise outside the reach of its spying.

Such was "Abakumov's legacy" that Korotkov managed in great secrecy, unbeknownst to the working level of the KGB.

• • •

I HAD ALSO LEARNED about Korotkov's super-secret work from the former head of communist Czechoslovakia state security, Minister of Internal Affairs Rudolf Barak.

He had been brought into the picture by the chairman of the KGB himself, Ivan Serov.[16] Serov told Barak in 1955 that Müller was living and working for the KGB in the Cordoba region of northern Argentina, not far from the Paraguay border. The former Gestapo chief had become unresponsive to KGB direction, failing to appear at scheduled meetings with his KGB Illegal handling officer and not responding to messages. Now Serov wanted to get him back to shake him up and restore discipline. Because Czechoslovakia had more trade and industrial interests with better possibilities for cover and moving people and supplies in that part of Argentina than the Soviets did, Serov asked Barak to do the job for him.

The two services jointly planned the abduction, the Soviet side represented by Serov and Aleksandr Korotkov, the Czechoslovak by four senior officers.[17] Barak dispatched Czechoslovak operatives to supplement those in Argentina and Paraguay, finally involving more than a hundred people in the operation.[18] For nearly a year, they studied Müller's environment, contacts, and movements, finally infiltrating his circle. When the opportunity arose, they drugged his drink, bundled him unconscious into a car, and loaded him boxed as cargo onto a Czechoslovak plane ostensibly returning machine parts for repair.

Müller was flown to Prague where, as Serov had arranged with Barak, the KGB would take custody and return him to the Soviet Union. He was taken to Ruzyne prison where he arrogantly resisted Barak's questioning.[19] But the senior KGB Advisor to Czechoslovak state security, Fotiy V. Peshekhonov, reassured Barak. "Don't worry about it. Müller has been ours for a long time, and he'll certainly be working for us again."

KGB representatives flew in to Prague to take him over and Müller was brought to the minister's office. A side door opened and in walked the senior KGB visitor. It was Aleksandr Korotkov.

Müller's eyes lit up with recognition and relief.[20] He sprang from his chair as if to embrace Korotkov, who shrank back with embarrassment and harshly ordered him to sit down. After only a few words from Barak and no conversation with Müller, Korotkov escorted the former Gestapo chief in handcuffs out into the hall where two other KGB officials were waiting. They were driven directly to the airport where their plane was waiting to take off for Moscow.[21]

• • •

IN LIGHT OF THESE facts, we can understand Korotkov's reluctance to confide in Kondrashev, and Kondrashev's to confide in me. And we can also understand why these contacts were "known and coordinated only at the highest levels" of the KGB. The KGB was running an immense political risk even by hiding such prominent war criminals, not to speak of using them against wartime allies.

To hide this deception, the Soviets made persistent and some-times counterproductive efforts. First, they spread stories that

Müller had been killed at the end of the war, and even marked a grave or two with his name. Then as the West became increasingly aware that Müller might still be alive, for example by finding other bones in what was labelled as Müller's grave, the Soviets planted stories in the press to deflect attention toward Western use of Nazi war criminals. A Soviet-connected freelance journalist using the pen name Peter Stahl began peddling articles in Germany in 1963 showing that Müller was hiding in various countries. One or two were published a year later in a wide-circulated magazine.

But that was not enough. In the 1980s, Stahl lent his name, or rather another of his pseudonyms, "Gregory Douglas," to a fabricated and detailed biography of Müller. Finally published only after the collapse of the Soviet Union, its four elaborate volumes by their very existence testify to the depth of Soviet concern to obfuscate the fact that they had protected and used the most wanted of war criminals. Purportedly based on a 1948 CIA interrogation of Müller in Switzerland—which could never have happened— the book "revealed" that the American CIA took Müller to Washington to help American Intelligence in the Cold War, giving him the status of brigadier general in the US Army.[22]

• • •

THE MAN WHO MET Aleksandr Korotkov at that meeting in the Vienna Woods was a key player in the KGB's on-going false-flag Nazi underground operation.

Kondrashev left me in no doubt that he thought it had been Müller. I confronted him. "For years now, Sergey, whenever we've talked about that day in the Vienna Woods, you have brought up the name of Gestapo Müller. Every time we happen to mention Müller in any context, your mind turns to that outing with Korotkov. You're practically telling me it was Müller he was meeting."

Sergey did not deny it. [23]

Even a half century after the event, the subject was still too explosive to find any place in his memoirs. His outing with Aleksandr Korotkov—this brush with Korotkov's Nazi underground—came out spontaneously in our conversation, but it deserved a place in his life story as a memorable moment in his professional life. That day in the Vienna Woods had brought him close to one of the great scandals and enduring mysteries of the Cold War.

Eleven:
Richard Sorge Redux

T IS RARE and perhaps unique that a single spy could be said to have saved his country from defeat in war. It is barely thinkable, then, that the country's leader might vilify that spy as an enemy provocateur, leave him to hang, and also to punish—even kill—the intelligence officers who had made that spy's work possible. Yet all these are realities of Soviet history.

It is also part of history that—decades later—this spy finally came to be honored as a hero in the country he served. Schools and a street in Moscow were named for him, postage stamps were issued with his image; plays and movies were inspired by his story.

Richard Sorge on a Soviet postage stamp.

This remarkable rehabilitation came about thanks to the happenstance that just before taking a certain job in Moscow, Sergey Kondrashev went to the movies in Vienna one evening late in 1961.

"Look at this," said Rosa one Sunday afternoon, pointing to the newspaper's entertainment page. "There's a film about Sorge!" As the daughter of a prominent KGB officer, she knew as much as her husband did about the espionage exploits in wartime Tokyo of the famed Soviet operative Richard Sorge. Famed in the West, that is, where books and articles had recounted his story as revealed by captured Japanese files and by the Germans against whom

Sorge had spied. But not famed in the Soviet Union, where Stalin had caused his name to be remembered only as a traitor or else completely forgotten.

"Let's go see it," Rosa said, "you have nothing special to do tonight."

So Sergey and Rosa Kondrashev went to see *Wer sind Sie, Dr. Sorge?*[1] So moved was Kondrashev by this presentation of Sorge's historic contribution to Soviet victory—which may have helped to save Kondrashev's own life—that an idea occurred to him, and he went back a few days later to see the film a second time and take notes.

Not long afterward Sergey moved back to Moscow where, after working into his job as deputy to Ivan Agayants, head of the KGB's "active measures," he thought back to that movie and talked to Agayants. The film would make a good active measure, he told his boss: More publicity about such spy successes would stir admiration for Soviet Intelligence and enhance KGB and GRU recruitment efforts.[2]

Kondrashev next went to KGB Chairman Semichastniy. "I'd like to call your attention to a film I've seen," he said. "Agayants and I both think it can contribute to our mission." Semichastniy said that the idea was okay with him, but to have it shown in the USSR, Kondrashev would need the approval of the Minister of Culture, Yekaterina Furtseva.

Kondrashev phoned the minister, saying, "I have a proposal that would be better discussed face-to-face." She was pleased to invite him to her office, but there, having listened to him, she stiffened. "I've seen that picture!" Furtseva exclaimed. "It's a slander on our country and the classics of Marxism-Leninism![3] I won't let it be shown here!"[4]

Kondrashev went back to Semichastniy, commenting that Furt-seva's opposition presumably had less to do with "Marxist classics" than with the black image of Sorge that Stalin had imprinted.

"Okay, let's do something about it," the KGB chairman said. He called his friend and former KGB deputy Pyotr Ivashutin, who had just taken over command of Soviet military intelligence (GRU) where Sorge had worked.[5] They agreed that Kondrashev should meet with GRU Colonel Igor Chistyakov[6] to review the entire record in both KGB and GRU files to assess Sorge's achievements. If justified, they should then make a proposal that might overcome Furtseva's opposition.

"First of all," Semichastniy said, hanging up the phone, "write me a summary of the film to help me get Khrushchev's backing."

Kondrashev thus became the first person to see Moscow files that had been sequestered for nearly twenty years and that remain top secret to this day: The inside story of a spy hero whose phenomenal performance was rewarded by rejection and consignment to death. Here is a fresh look at this classic episode of espionage history.

• • •

ANSWERS TO THE MOVIE's title question, "Who are you, Dr. Sorge?" would have varied. To the outside world, he was German born and bred, a First World War soldier decorated for bravery and invalided out of the army after being badly wounded. Still young, he worked as a coal miner, wrote newspaper articles, and studied successfully for a doctorate in a German university.

Less well-known, he had joined the Communist Party of Germany (KPD). And although his father was indeed German, Richard had been born in Baku, then in Russia, of a Russian mother.

Sorge's secret path to Tokyo began in Frankfurt in 1924 when the KPD made him responsible for ensuring the safety of two top Comintern (Communist International) leaders during their visit to a KPD congress. Lodged in Sorge's apartment, they came to know him and, like so many others, to admire his competence and charismatic personality. Before they returned to Moscow, they invited him there for a vacation and medical attention to the after-effects of his war wounds. He went, and they persuaded him to stay on as a functionary in Comintern headquarters.

Sorge's charismatic personality made him so prominent in Moscow's German community that he was easily elected to the board of the Club of German Communists, far surpassing the runner-up, future East German President Walter Ulbricht.

Though he stuck to the Comintern job for five years, it bored him except for occasional trips to coordinate and counsel the Communist parties in Great Britain and Scandinavia. Therefore, he was pleased in October 1929 when the chief of GRU negotiated his transfer from the Comintern to the GRU. After a few weeks of training, Sorge was dispatched to China in early 1930 to establish an illegal residency. He set up his own cover by passing through Germany to get a new passport showing no Russia travel and to arrange with some German newspapers to accept his freelance contributions.

Once in Shanghai, this new "foreign correspondent" quickly established close relations with fellow German war veterans now acting as military advisors to the Chinese army. He set up intelligence networks in several cities and transmitted to Moscow information on the economy, Western influence in China, the 1931 Japanese move into Manchuria, and the fighting in Shanghai in 1932. The files Kondrashev saw revealed that of Sorge's 597 reports from China, the GRU headquarters deemed no fewer than 235 important enough to pass to Soviet Party and government leaders, an extraordinary percentage for any overseas residency. But then in January 1933 Sorge was recalled to Moscow after the Shanghai police came to suspect that he might be a Comintern agent.

At that very time, the GRU needed his talents elsewhere. Moscow felt an acute need for intelligence from Japan. The Japanese army had invaded Manchuria, and conflicts were growing between Japanese and Soviet interests along their newly shared border. Hardly had Sorge returned to Moscow than he was sent out again in May 1933 to establish an illegal residency in Tokyo with a few of his Shanghai helpers.

He again first travelled to Germany and arranged to represent and submit articles to several newspapers and magazines, and got another new passport free of any stamps showing he had been in the Soviet Union. He then went to Shanghai, turned over his residency to his successor, and went on to Japan.

Arriving in Tokyo, Sorge became active and prominent in the German community and joined the Nazi Party. He renewed old acquaintances, including a former girlfriend named Helma, now the wife of Colonel Eugen Ott, the German Embassy Military Attaché. Sorge became a close friend of Ott and of Ambassador Herbert von Dirksen and supplied them with valuable information on Japanese politics and planning. The information so enhanced their reputations in Berlin that when Dirksen left in 1938, Ott was appointed his successor.

Ott and the deputy military attaché (a veteran of the same army unit as Sorge during the war) even used Sorge to write the text of telegrams sent to Berlin in cipher. By 1939, he was preparing the Embassy's daily press review and had become, in effect, its press attaché.

It was not only from his insider status with the German Embassy that Sorge was able to get priceless information for Moscow. His secret collaborator from Shanghai days, Hotsumi Ozaki, now had a good source inside the cabinet of Prime Minister Prince Konoye. And through another member of his group, Yotoku Miyagi, Sorge received inside details from military circles in Japan and Manchuria.

Kondrashev's review of Sorge's reports showed how consistently and powerfully they bore on Soviet interests in that part of the world. Of Sorge's 805 messages radioed from Japan from early 1936 to October 1941, nearly half were passed up to Soviet government and Party officials and to the chief of the General Staff. He kept Moscow up to date on Japan's secret negotiations to join Germany in an Anti-Comintern Pact and traced the increasingly aggressive nature of the Japanese Army and its rising influence over foreign policy. He informed the GRU about provocations by the Japanese Army along the Manchurian border and how it was deploying while preparing its aggression against China in 1937.

He learned from his high German Embassy contacts about German preparations for attacking Poland in 1939 and France in 1940. In the spring of 1941, he warned that the Germans would attack the Soviet Union and told when. Stalin rejected and ignored this precise warning—among the first of many—of Hitler's impending attack, though it was confirmed by many other sources.[7]

But it was Sorge's discovery of Japanese war plans that was most critical to eventual Soviet victory. He got details of meetings of the Japanese High Command in July and August 1941 that firmly directed strategy towards Southeast Asia and the Pacific. This time Stalin did not dismiss his report as Nazi disinformation. At a moment when German forces were advancing toward Moscow, this assurance that the Japanese did not plan to attack Russia enabled the Soviet high command to transfer seventeen divisions and nine tank brigades from the Far East to bolster Moscow's defenses. These winter-hardened troops then played a crucial role in the first great defeat of the German Army.

• • •

AN ASTONISHING ASPECT OF this chronicle of spying success was that if Stalin had had his way, it would never even have begun. In 1937 and 1938, Stalin purged the intelligence and security services, on one pretext or another calling back from abroad their most experienced and productive operatives to be shot for imaginary treason.

When Sorge got his recall orders, he knew what fate awaited him. As a German, he lacked that Russian fatalism that drew so many others back knowingly to their doom, so he told Moscow that he couldn't leave his post because his development of promising sources was reaching a critical stage.[8]

While political leaders everywhere often fail to accept and act on the information they are provided, Stalin was a singular case. He actively distrusted all intelligence gatherers and killed them by the hundreds. Sorge was to be among those hundreds, all the more so because he had been reporting things Stalin did not want to hear. It took only a stroke of Stalin's pencil to write off this patriot as a Nazi provocateur, to prevent talk of his exploits, and to bury the files that recorded them. Kondrashev saw with his own eyes Stalin's blue-pencilled note in the margin of an important report from Sorge: "Please don't send me any more of this German deception!"[9]

Although Stalin missed that first opportunity to murder Sorge, he found another later, as Kondrashev discovered in the files.

• • •

IN THE YEARS SINCE Stalin's death, no one in Russia seemed to have thought of rehabilitating Sorge's memory. Kondrashev found that the files, locked away in the mid-1940s, had never been reopened or reviewed since then.

Kondrashev and Chistyakov had them brought out for the first time. The two reviewers used assistants to do the preliminary culling, Kondrashev's on KGB files, Chistyakov's on those of the GRU. They met two or three times a month to evaluate what had been found and to direct further digging. They worked this way for more than a year, which may sound like a long time for a mere "file review" but, as Kondrashev said, they could hardly have done it much faster while attending to their primary duties. The old NKVD files that Kondrashev reviewed were voluminous while Chistyakov faced dozens of GRU volumes, each of some three hundred pages.

Remembering the dire fate of Sorge's GRU superiors during Stalin's purges of 1937, Kondrashev called for the reports of the interrogations the NKVD had conducted before executing them. Asking only for those cases where GRU leaders had been punished specifically for involvement with Sorge, he was horrified to be presented with no fewer than ten.

Among these shot had been Jan Karlovich Berzin, the GRU chief who had selected, dispatched, and overseen Sorge until 1935, and his successor Artur Khristianovich Artuzov. While each had faced multiple accusations—dereliction of duty, spying for a wide variety of foreign intelligence services, and a whole catalogue of other invented misdeeds—the list of charges included one that until Stalin's intervention would have been a source of pride: assigning and promoting Sorge.

. . .

KONDRASHEV AND CHISTYAKOV SUMMARIZED their findings in a twenty-page report to the Central Committee (in effect, to the Politburo). This report confirmed Sorge's brilliant performance, pointing out his priceless role in the wartime victory, his insightful analysis, and the high professional skill that had long kept his secret work undetected.[10] They pushed their chiefs to sign it fast to get a Central Committee decision before November 7,1964, the twentieth anniversary of Sorge's execution, which Kondrashev proposed to use as the starting date of a campaign to restore Sorge's reputation and, as an "active measure," to enhance that of Soviet Intelligence. On November 2, Semichastniy and Ivashutin signed (and the Minister of Defense initialled) it. Kondrashev quickly went to the Central Committee for the signature of Aleksandr Shelepin, the secretary overseeing the security and intelligence services, and made his deadline.

● ● ●

WHILE KONDRASHEV HAD BROUGHT back the bright side of Sorge's story, his file review discovered a dark shadow: Sorge had been betrayed by his own side.

Although the prime culprit was Stalin, the GRU leaders also played a shameful role in the tragedy. Toadying to Stalin's paranoia, they had gone back to look through Sorge's reporting from Japan for signs that might support Stalin's view that Sorge was working more for the Germans than for the Soviets. GRU chief Berzin, for example, told his NKVD interrogator, "I talked with Artuzov about the possibility that German Intelligence had planted Sorge on us. We decided that they had, and that he had been disinforming us." Just to look back would have been enough to condemn Sorge, but to find such signs would not only do that, but also condemn their colleagues who had been connected to Sorge's operations.

Having thus been induced to distrust Sorge, the GRU leaders seem to have cared less for his safety. Western histories based on Japanese police files captured at the end of the war attribute the Japanese police's discovery of the Sorge spy network to their chance detection in September 1941 of a spy who happened to be a minor member of Sorge's apparatus. While it is no doubt true that this started the Japanese looking at other people with whom Sorge had secret contact, Kondrashev found in those files mistakes made by Moscow that helped the Japanese to pin him down.

At a moment in 1939 when radio communications had become difficult, the GRU ordered Sorge and his radioman Max Clausen to meet with a Soviet official. Finding this order in the old files shocked Kondrashev as a professional intelligence officer: It violated a basic principle that no Illegal should come into direct contact with colleagues working abroad undercover as diplomats, military attachés, trade representatives, or journalists, all of whom are routinely watched by local counterintelligence forces. Indeed, Japanese records confirm that this order undid Sorge. Between November 1939 and October 1941, the Japanese observed no fewer than eleven meetings of Sorge or his clandestine associates with two Soviet consular officials.[11] As soon as the Japanese got their first break into his network, these sightings lit the path to Sorge.[12]

Perhaps the darkest of the shadows Kondrashev found in the Sorge files was the GRU's refusal, under Stalin's order, to make a prisoner exchange for him. This effectively killed Sorge—and it wasn't even recorded. Of all the GRU files offered for Kondrashev's and Chistyakov's review, not one mentioned any Japanese proposal for exchange. But as Kondrashev later learned from Japanese scholars and as is well-known in the Western literature about Sorge, the Japanese had in fact offered twice[13] to exchange Sorge for a prisoner held by the Soviets. On both occasions, the first in

1943 when the GRU was headed by Filipp I. Golikov, the second in 1944 when his successor Ivan I. Ilychev was chief, the Soviet regime curtly replied, "No one by that name is known to us."

With nothing more standing in their way, the Japanese hanged Richard Sorge (and Ozaki) a few days later, on November 7, 1944—the twenty-seventh anniversary of the Soviets' October Revolution.

Kondrashev knew Ilychev well and saw him quite often in the years during and after his study of the Sorge case. By then, Ilychev was long out of the GRU. One day in the Ministry of Foreign Affairs, Kondrashev took the opportunity to get Ilychev's side of the story of the Japanese exchange offer.

He got no further than introducing the subject, saying "Ivan Ivanovich, your conduct of the Sorge case left a lot of questions." The matter evidently still smouldered bitterly in Ilychev's memory. Instead of answering, he made a dismissive motion with his hand, thus closing the subject for good.

• • •

HAVING ACCEPTED KONDRASHEV'S AND Chistyakov's report in November 1964, the Soviet Politburo and Government issued a decree declaring Richard Sorge to be a Hero of the Soviet Union.

The same decree honored Sorge's collaborators and authorized a pension to his devoted mistress Hanako Ishii, which she continued to receive for thirty-seven years until her death in 2001. The Government invited "Hanako-san" to Russia in 1965 for a vacation in Sochi on the Black Sea. While in Moscow, she saw a play about Sorge that had just been written, and she was honored at a reception attended by prominent Soviet cultural figures.

On that occasion, Kondrashev asked her about the massive gold ring she was wearing. "Oh, Mr. Kondrashev," she answered, "I had

"Hanako-san" tending Sorge's grave.

this ring made from Richard's gold teeth, which I found among his ashes." (She had had his body cremated after locating its burial place four years after the war.)

Another movie on Sorge, this time East German, premiered before an invited audience in East Berlin with Max and Anna Clausen attending. After an introduction by DDR State Security Minister Erich Mielke, Kondrashev took the stage to describe the case as he had learned of it from his perspective.

And the film that started it all, *Who Are You, Dr. Sorge?* was finally shown in Russia. Having learned that Khrushchev had approved it, Madame Furtseva changed her mind.

Twelve:
Organizing to Disinform

THE WESTERN WORLD has long been familiar with the frauds, forgeries, and deceits that the Soviet regime inflicted on it during the Cold War. The accounts by Western victims and even by a few of their Eastern perpetrators have filled bookshelves.[1] But until Sergey Kondrashev, who had directed such activities throughout the world, opened up for his memoirs, no one had exposed the Moscow heart and brain of these Soviet "active measures."

Kondrashev's accounts were especially gripping for me, for I had spent a lot of time during my CIA years trying to expose and thwart these Soviet schemes. Now I found myself getting the view from the top, seeing how they were planned and executed, discovering the problems the schemers had been facing, and learning how they themselves assessed the value of their work.

• • •

THE WARM ATMOSPHERE OF the famous old pastry shop Demel in the center of Vienna might seem an unlikely gateway to the dark world of Soviet deception and "dirty tricks," but that's what it proved to be one afternoon in the late summer of 1961.

Sergey Kondrashev, acting KGB chief in Vienna, was hosting an unusual visitor from Moscow: Ivan Agayants, the head of KGB disinformation operations, who was ending a tour of KGB residencies abroad. They had talked for hours in Kondrashev's office in the Soviet Embassy when Agayants suggested they step out for a private chat. Kondrashev proposed a stroll to Demel, the perfect place to take a man he knew to be fond of sweets.

As they sipped their tea over jam-and-cream-filled, chocolate-topped *Indianerkrapfen*, Agayants came to the point. He was focusing his work on divided Germany, a pivotal area of Soviet foreign policy and central battleground of the Cold War, and was looking for a senior colleague who had a good understanding of that region. He knew Kondrashev well; they had often worked together while Kondrashev was deputy chief of the German Department in 1955–57, and he had recently read Sergey's file. This was just the man for the job. Knowing that Sergey's tour in Vienna would soon end, Agayants invited him to Moscow as his deputy.

The offer was irresistible. Sergey was being asked to move into direct support of worldwide foreign policy and to work closely with one of the most respected officers in the history of Soviet Intelligence. He accepted with genuine pleasure.

At that time nearly fifty, tall, slender, balding, soft-spoken, distinguished in bearing, and known to all as kind and considerate, Ivan Ivanovich Agayants had long been the central figure in Soviet clandestine manipulation and deception abroad.

Agayants with Kondrashev a few years later, and in an official KGB picture.

His career began in 1930 at the knee of Artur Khristianovich Artuzov, mastermind of cunning deception operations like the false anti-Soviet resistance organizations of the 1920s "Trust" and "Sindicat 2." Stationed in France from 1937 to 1940, Agayants had operated from there into Spain during its civil war. During the Second World War, he served in Iran.[2] Using the name Avalov as he always did abroad, he was sent to Algiers late in 1943 as Moscow's first envoy to General Charles de Gaulle's Free French Committee of National Liberation. From there, he assured Moscow that de Gaulle welcomed wartime cooperation with the Soviet Union and friendly relations afterwards, so Moscow sent a permanent diplomatic representation to Algiers, laying the basis for postwar relations with France.

After the liberation of France, he followed de Gaulle to Paris where he became the KGB's first postwar rezident. In the turbulent political atmosphere of those times, he and his men won the secret cooperation of highly-placed French officials, including (as we in CIA learned much later) several intelligence and security services officers. For decades, they undermined Western efforts to cope with Soviet subversion and espionage; most were never uncovered.

So well placed in the French hierarchy were Agayants's sources that he quickly saw that better than merely revealing their government's policies, they might even help shape those policies to favor Soviet aims.

As head of the KGB's West European directorate in 1954, Agayants directed these secret sources along with Soviet-friendly French diplomats, journalists, and politicians in a massive months-long clandestine campaign to influence the impending French parliamentary vote on the proposed European Defense Community treaty. Moscow strenuously opposed the treaty because it would have integrated half of Germany into an international military structure, promoted West German rearmament, and ended Moscow's hopes that the Communist Party might come to power in France.

Agayants directed influential Frenchmen, including parliamentarians on the right as well as the left, to whip up old fears of German militarism. He arranged bribes to parliamentarians and clandestine payments to Communist and left-oriented organizations to mount large street demonstrations. His agents bombarded the press with ostensibly neutral or right-wing arguments with the message that the treaty would lead to a clerical and capitalist Europe, crush socialism and threaten democracy, and lead to German domination of France. He planted rumors and press stories to discredit individual supporters of the treaty.

The parliamentary vote rejected French ratification, effectively killing the EDC plan.

Inspired by Agayants's success, the new KGB Chairman Aleksandr Shelepin sought ways his KGB might better support Soviet foreign policy objectives everywhere. Agayants showed him how in a five-page memorandum proposing worldwide coordination of clandestine political action. As Kondrashev put it, this memo effectively told Shelepin, "Here is what has to be done. Now you'll have to create a new organization to do it."

Shelepin adopted Agayants's proposal. In 1959, the CPSU Central Committee ordered the formation of an independent KGB department to centralize this KGB work. It was designated Department (*Otdel*) D,[3] and Agayants was put in charge.

A few weeks after accepting Agayants's offer in the Vienna pastry shop, Kondrashev visited him in Moscow to talk over the job. At the end of his tour in Vienna early in the next year, Sergey returned to the Soviet Union. After turning down a tempting promotion offered by the head of Counterintelligence[4] he reported for duty as Agayants's deputy in early March of 1962.

• • •

DEPARTMENT D'S TASK WAS ambitious. It took a lot of knowledge and creative imagination to find clandestine ways to influence opinion and policy in countries with widely varying political structures and ever-changing social pressures—and ever new ways to avoid patterns that would betray the Soviet hand behind them.

Kondrashev said admiringly that Agayants was superb at the job. "Often when I would make a general proposal," he told me, "Agayants would ask perceptive questions, take a few notes, and then go off and in no time turn out a sharp plan of action."

Even after Kondrashev was shifted to head the Austro-German Department in 1964 when its chief fell ill, he and Agayants continued to work closely together. When Agayants was promoted to Deputy Head of Foreign Intelligence in the fall of 1967, Kondrashev came back to replace him. In the intervening years, Department D had grown from the forty officers when Kondrashev first joined it to more than a hundred and had been raised in status from "department" (otdel) to "service" (sluzhba) and redesignated as "A".

Kondrashev was destined soon to follow Agayants upward yet again. Only weeks after leaving "A," Agayants fell ill with lung cancer. "My old wounds are aching, my friend," he told Kondrashev in the hospital. "You'd better get ready to take on a higher position." Agayants resumed work for a couple of brief periods, but in early April 1968 entered the hospital for the last time. His last words to Kondrashev showed his devotion to their specialty: "Please give your staff my heartfelt wishes," he sighed, "You know how hard we've worked to build that service." A few days later, on May 12, he died.[5] Kondrashev moved up to fill Agayants's position as a Deputy Head of worldwide Foreign Intelligence, with the rank of general—still overseeing disinformation and active measures.

• • •

THE "A" IN SERVICE A stood for Aktivnyye Meropryatiye or Active Measures, which Kondrashev described as clandestine actions designed to affect foreign governments, groups, and influential individuals in ways that favored the objectives of Soviet policy and weakened the opposition to them.[6]

This was not identical with disinformation, Kondrashev stressed. "Disinformation" was defined, as he remembered, as "purposeful dissemination of wholly or partially distorted information with the aim of hiding our own capabilities and methods and weakening or misleading those of our adversaries." An "active measure"—for example, the public release of documents or facts embarrassing a hostile Western government or statesman—may or may not involve "disinformation"—distortion, concealment, invention, or forgery. In practice, Kondrashev found that actions based on truth had greater impact. The distinction became clear when an officer would propose such a measure and Kondrashev would ask, "How much disinfo (deza) is in it?"

Kondrashev scoffed at Western writers' tendency to describe "active measures," and even "disinformation," as a purely Soviet phenomenon. Masking one's own objectives, promoting one's own positions by underhanded means, and discrediting one's opponents or rivals are no recent arrivals on the world stage. Individuals as well as governments have practiced them since long before the departing Greeks left behind a false defector to misinform the Trojans about that wooden horse outside their gates. The Machiavellian intrigues of the Renaissance and modern forgeries like the anti-Semitic "Protocol of the Elders of Zion" joined such frauds as the so-called "Testament of Peter the Great." This famous late-eighteenth century forgery purported to show that Tsar Peter had urged his successors to expand and dominate abroad. (It succeeded at least to the extent of furnishing Napoleon with superficial justification for his invasion of Russia in 1812 by making it look a bit more "defensive".)[7] In the Cold War's lively exchange of "active measures," Kondrashev pointed out, those from the West went under names like "political action," "covert action," "black propaganda," and "dirty tricks."

· · ·

THE KGB, HOWEVER, TOLD lies with a freedom denied to its democratic adversaries, and it had longer and deeper experience in clandestine trickery. By the time Lenin's men took power in 1917, they had enough experience to begin immediately launching sophisticated deception operations—and quickly turned this practice into policy. As early as 1923, an order of the Central Committee formally established a bureau within the KGB (then the OGPU) with the mission of "upsetting the counterrevolutionary plans and activities of the opposition" by:

- determining how much our adversaries know about us and see what kinds of information they are seeking;
- creating and passing to them false information and documents that project the desired image of the internal situation in our country and the work of the Soviet leadership, its foreign policy, and the Red Army; and
- disseminating such disinformation in the press of various countries.

From the beginning of the 1920s, Artur Artuzov guided such now-famous KGB operations as the "Trust" and "Sindikat-2" that devised and took control of "resistance organizations" with the goal of identifying and crippling internal opponents and of misleading foreigners. When Stalin began his giant purges that were all based on fabricated charges, he needed even more lies to justify himself, and, in new orders of 1934, his Central Committee called for more disinformation. Disinformation had now become systemic. As Kondrashev reminded me, hardly an agency of Soviet government or party failed to disseminate misleading facts and statistics.

· · ·

UP TO 1959, THESE measures had been conducted by a number of different organizations, only tenuously related.

After the Second World War, the Committee of Information (or KI), formed in 1947 under Foreign Minister Molotov to join together State-Security Foreign-Intelligence with the GRU (military intelligence), was given the high-priority task of influencing policies of foreign governments and compromising their anti-Soviet public figures. Its unit for this purpose was designated "D."[8]

After the KI's dissolution in 1951, this function remained under the Ministry of Foreign Affairs (MID) in a unit of about ten officers, of whom the leader and a couple of others were from the KGB,[9] and which was known within the KGB as the "Department of Gogol Boulevard" (*Otdel na Gogolevskom*) because of its location. In addition, a group on the twenty-second floor of MID called "Special Office No. 2" also developed action plans and rough drafts for articles that KGB residencies abroad planted in Western publications.[10] And people in each geographical department of the KGB's foreign intelligence directorate (FCD) continued to propose active measures (some foolishly ill-conceived, Kondrashev remarked) while KGB residencies abroad, too, were independently thinking up and carrying out ploys to serve their local purposes.

It was to concentrate these activities in a coordinated world-wide program with clear focus, and to better exploit the "influence" potential of the KGB's secret sources inside Western governments, that Shelepin and Agayants set up the new Department D in 1959.

• • •

AGAYANTS DIVIDED HIS ORGANIZATION into five basic fields: political, economic, scientific/technical, military, and counterintelligence. There was a section (and later, a department) for each plus a separate section to supply them all with necessary documentation including forgeries.[11]

The largest by far was the political department with officers specializing in one or another geographical area. The other departments were smaller (counterintelligence, for example, normally counted about twelve members), but their numbers were flexible. Whenever more were needed to handle a particularly urgent issue, such as opposing a proposal before a parliament vote, people from other elements of Service A or even from geographic departments of the FCD would be moved in to help. (Some of their work is described in the next chapter.)

Service A had no officers of its own stationed abroad, but each of the FCD's geographic departments and each important residency made one or two officers responsible for developing relationships with local people who were willing to accept and propagate ideas or plant articles and other items of information. Each department and rezidentura kept Service A informed of such "assets" (as the locals were known) at its disposal.

Kondrashev stressed that these assets abroad were often mere sympathizers and not necessarily recruited agents. In fact, Service

A tried to avoid using agents to plant articles for fear of exposing their pro-Soviet leanings.

• • •

AGAYANTS AND KONDRASHEV HUGELY expanded their capabilities in early 1964 by building active-measures units parallel to the KGB's inside the state-security services of Eastern Europe. Kondrashev personally travelled to East Berlin and Prague in the process.[12]

These satellite services also conceived their own measures and carried them out through their own assets, sometimes coordinating with or at least informing the KGB liaison staff in the country—but not always. Kondrashev had seen Western exposures of "Soviet" disinformation actions that Service A had little or nothing to do with and that it might not have approved. One such was the Hungarians' publication of a counterfeit issue of *Newsweek* with John F. Kennedy on the cover, its contents visibly fabricated and its message cloudy, and suffering from the terrible coincidence that it was printed just before the president's assassination and dated December 18, 1963, three weeks after the event. Kondrashev indicated that the Czechoslovaks' distribution of a distorted version of the American Declaration of Independence was similarly counterproductive.

• • •

CHOOSING STAFF PERSONNEL FOR this kind of work posed a special problem. It called for different talents than those for which foreign-intelligence officers were normally selected and judged. This work did not require a talent for recruiting and handling agents so much as an inventive mind with good knowledge of the target countries' histories and internal situations, along with skill in formulating plans and expressing ideas. The FCD's geographic departments sometimes tried to use Service A as a dumping ground for officers who had not measured up, so Agayants and Kondrashev took special care when studying the files of and interviewing such candidates, then closely watching them during a test period.

But some such "rejects" had just the talents Service A needed. Kondrashev remembered one man whose department chief was saying privately (as Kondrashev learned by some judicious nosing about) that "he can't do *anything* right." But his file reflected political insight and writing ability so Kondrashev decided, on a hunch, to accept him. He did a fine job for Service A and then moved out to a successful journalistic career, later giving Kondrashev fulsome credit for setting him on the right career path.

. . .

SERGEY KONDRASHEV STRESSED HOW many different channels he used to pump out disinformation.

The most obvious route toward the broad Western public was, of course, newspapers and magazines—planting articles in cooperative papers (of the many, Kondrashev remembered *Paese Sera* in Italy, *Blitz* in New Delhi, and *Die Furche* in Vienna) and replaying them in other target areas. But that was not as simple as it might sound. It was easy to compose an article in Moscow that seemed to get over the desired point, but then it had to be planted in a paper with its own well-established line and style. And the journalist being used might not agree with the details or even the theme.

Inside the Soviet Union, Service A could use any outlet it chose to begin this process, but one in particular, the Press Agency Novosti, was in effect an integral part of the KGB. It even had a department with a double designation, simultaneously part of

Novosti and part of Service A, with its people paid on Novosti's budget but given bonuses by Service A. Although about half of this department of some two dozen were (cleared) Novosti journalists, the KGB assigned officers to it just as it did to any other part of the FCD. Agayants and Kondrashev sent to head it some of the KGB's most effective officers, like Norman Borodin, Boris Mikhailov, and Vitaly Chernyavsky. Service A handed journalists in this department subjects and themes, the writers researched and drafted the articles and sent them to Kondrashev or his deputy who would add editorial comments like "develop this point in more detail" or "add x or y item." Once approved, an article would either be issued by Novosti or sent to a geographic department to be dispatched to residencies abroad known to have the potential for planting it.

But such periodicals were just one sort of channel. Soviet diplomats abroad served as outlets, too, in ways that had become familiar to me during my CIA service. I would read a report of some surprising, offbeat opinion expressed by a Soviet diplomat and then remember that I had read the same opinion or insight—sometimes word for word—from a different area. I would shake my head and think, "There's Agayants at work!" I mentioned to Kondrashev one of these recurrent themes I had noticed, so-called differences of opinion between Politburo "hardliners" and "liberals," "hawks" and "doves." Kondrashev confirmed that his people had pushed this misconception, so beloved of Western commentators and analysts, to cause confusion about Soviet policy-making options.

A promising channel—going directly into Western intelligence services—lay in microphones that American or British Intelligence had planted in Soviet Bloc officials' apartments or offices, or taps on their phones. When they were discovered, Kondrashev was more interested in using them for deception—staging "revealing" conversations—than in ripping them out. On his recommendation, FCD chief Aleksandr Sakharovsky instructed KGB residencies throughout the world to leave any discovered devices undisturbed without Moscow's permission. (We in CIA got an echo of these instructions at the time, reported by a KGB defector.)

Then, too, there were KGB-controlled double agents and supposed KGB sources whom the KGB knew to be under Western control. Like discovered microphones, such channels could be especially efficient because intelligence services are prone to believe what they learn through their own secret operations and because the message would go directly to national leaderships.

• • •

THE NUMBER OF ACTIVE measures that the KGB carried out was immense. During Kondrashev's years in "D" and "A," he might have reviewed three or four new proposals a day. When I showed him Western publications exposing scores of specific Soviet forgeries and disinformation operations,[13] he confirmed that they correctly represented Service A's techniques, and he even recognized some of them as his own. Though he had launched far too many active measures to recount them all—surely hundreds every year—the next chapter contains his recollections of some of the more notable ones.

Thirteen:
Active Measures

"WHO THOUGHT UP all those active measures?" I asked Sergey Kondrashev, "and where did the ideas come from?"

"First of all from policy itself," Sergey replied. "Within a day of every meeting of the leadership (collegium) of MID [the Ministry of Foreign Affairs], its Spetsburo 2 would send us in Service A any policy positions that had been adopted there with regard to any region or country of the world."

He paused here, to correct what he considered a widespread Western misapprehension. The KGB's "disinformation" actions were not, he insisted, part of Communist Party propaganda campaigns. The International Department (ID) of the Party's Central Committee was constantly using Western Communist parties and international front organizations like those of lawyers, peace lovers, and students, to sow dissension in the West, weaken NATO, burnish the image of the Soviet Union, and promote any Soviet propaganda campaign of the moment. While Service A shared such goals, it worked entirely independently, its active measures were in no way subordinated to any ID program and seldom inspired by them.

Of course, Kondrashev added, we in Service A were in touch with the ID. They were aware in general what the Service A was doing and could do. "We even provided officers for their staffs."

And KGB officers abroad routinely delivered funds for them, carrying the black bag to front organizations abroad. Kondrashev would frequently walk over to the Central Committee building on nearby Staraya Ploshchad [Old Square] to talk with leading ID figures, whom he knew well—but not to get ideas or approval for planned measures.

Service A conceived and carried out its own measures according to its own periodic general plan based on the requirements of Soviet foreign policy at the time. Advance "clearance" would rarely be needed—only if a proposed measure were likely to shake the scene heavily—and then only from the top level. (A few of the measures described here did have Khrushchev's or Brezhnev's personal go-ahead.)

So, beyond those policy positions, where did Service A get its ideas?

"Often they sprang from our own officers," Kondrashev said. All were required to keep up to date on current events. They also read specialized publications. (He mentioned as examples the quarterly *Foreign Affairs* and the US State Department's *Foreign Service Journal*.) They whipped up ideas when talking to each other or chiefs of geographic departments and visiting heads of stations abroad.

And from what spies were telling abroad. Service A was the only element of the KGB (outside of the Information Analysis Directorate) to be routinely given copies of reports coming in from secret sources throughout the world. In fact, Agayants and Kondrashev—on a strictly personal basis—were even given (by hand) information gleaned from the most sensitive of these sources: deciphered foreign communications, moles inside Western governments, and microphones in Western installations (although in a format concealing the identity and often even the general nature of the source).

Guy Burgess, the 1951 defector from Britain, bubbled with suggestions for active measures. Kondrashev would bring him plans that were being worked out in the Service, and Burgess would make constructive and thoughtful comments. He took drafts of articles the Service was preparing to float in the English-language press abroad and edited them into native English. He helped them to counterfeit British or American official documents. And he helped forge letters ostensibly from private citizens to British MPs and to British and American newspapers and hate letters to be sent to religious organizations with the aim of stirring discord.

Kondrashev enjoyed contact with Burgess and was impressed by his grasp of foreign and domestic affairs, his lively imagination, and his intuition about people. He considered Burgess's death in August 1963 a big loss to the KGB.

When I mentioned Burgess's well-known habits and character, Kondrashev admitted that it had taken a lot of patience and forbearance to work with him. "Guy was very demanding." From the very beginning, he "couldn't live" without his daily *Times* of London, and "absolutely needed" the KGB to recuperate from England his porcelain desk lamp with its huge shade, a lot of reference books, and even his own favourite clavichord. (The KGB had duly transported all this from England.) Often when arriving at Burgess's apartment, Kondrashev would find him in the company of some young man whom he would introduce without embarrassment as his "girlfriend." He was moody and could be wilful and petulant. He would get utterly absorbed in playing his clavichord while Kondrashev stood by waiting for him to settle down to work. Or he would insist on first having a drink—or several.

But Kondrashev treasured Burgess as a unique asset. He was far more useful than the other defectors from the British establishment who were then living in Moscow. Kim Philby occasionally sent an idea through Yuri Modin, by then in Service A and previously Philby's handler in England (and Kondrashev's predecessor there). Sergey could not remember any help at all coming from Donald Maclean, the former British diplomat who was then working in IMEMO, the Institute of International Economy and Foreign Relations.

● ● ●

AT THE TOP OF Service A's priority targets was, of course, the United States, "the main enemy." Agayants and Kondrashev grasped at any chance to reduce American influence, to cause distrust and rifts between the United States and its NATO allies, to expel the American military presence from Europe, to discredit American actions—like its intervention in Vietnam—and to stir discord in American society. Practically every evil and misdeed in the world was attributed to the Americans, even imagined ones like developing and spreading AIDS (a disinformation measure taken long after Kondrashev's time and one which he deplored).

Kondrashev recalled vividly his campaign to portray the people of the US Strategic Air Command as irresponsible and insanely ready to blow up the world. (He remarked that the British film *Dr. Strangelove* had been helpful to this campaign, though in no way a part of it.) Service A forged and "leaked" a letter ostensibly from the US Assistant Secretary of Defense to his boss reporting that two thirds of flight crews had become psychotic, irrational, and depressive after flying with atomic and hydrogen weapons.

Sergey and I discussed Service A's well-known attempts to discredit Westerners who were actively opposing Soviet aims. "A" exposed publicly things it learned about their hidden misdemeanors or embarrassing behavior—or invented them. Kondrashev remembered several of his service's targets.

To weaken the influence of the outspoken NATO Secretary General Joseph Luns, for example, Service A circulated (through non-attributable channels) allegations that he had misused official funds. Luns denied it and remained in office, but after he retired about a year later, Kondrashev heard through agent sources that these allegations, though false, had indeed played a role in his departure.

The Turkish Cypriot leader Rauf Denktash was opposing Soviet clandestine efforts to move more friendly politicians into power in Cyprus. So Service A leaked forged allegations, based on Denktash's genuinely close ties with the British, that portrayed him as a secret British agent working against Cypriot interests.

Active opponents of Soviet aims in Germany came in for special attention. The KGB had a rich trove of German documents captured during and immediately after the Second World War. Kondrashev's service found evidence (and often tampered with it to heighten its effect) that now-prominent anti-Soviets had collaborated or passively participated in reprehensible Nazi activity.

Among Service A's most widely publicized targets were the General Inspector of the Federal Armed Forces Adolf Heusinger, State Secretary in the Federal Chancellery Hans Globke, and Minister of All-German Affairs Theodor Oberlaender. When I mentioned to Sergey the most famous and most obviously Soviet-inspired of these campaigns, the one directed against Defense Minister and Bavarian leader Franz-Josef Strauss, Kondrashev conceded his role. He even complained that the Western press had given too much "credit" to Markus Wolf's East German HVA for this campaign. Although the Stasi had played a substantial role, he said, Service A had handled the major part of it.

Kondrashev worked extensively with Wolf's service and (as I observed in my contacts with them together after the Cold War) they became good friends. In 1967, at about the time Kondrashev returned to the leadership of Service A from his post as head of the German Department, he arranged with Wolf and his Disinformation Chief Rolf Wagenbreth a whole series of joint actions to be played out over the following two years. To sow mistrust between West Germany and the United States they exposed some spying by each against the other; they discredited German scientists who were working on American rocket projects, like Wernher von Braun, by stressing their work for the Nazis. Service A instigated right-wing hate sessions against Jews and arranged that Jewish tombs be desecrated and swastikas painted. They planned forgeries to undermine West German relations with India, Pakistan, and the Arab countries, and to influence those countries to grant diplomatic recognition to East Germany.

Such attacks on selected opponents were not limited to Europe. To support the position of Prime Minister Indira Gandhi in India (whom the Soviets favored), Service A used KGB intelligence about an Indian Army general who opposed her and was a particular friend of the West. To destroy his influence, Yuri Modin of Service A (who had served in India and had already planted forgeries to smear Indira Gandhi's opponent) travelled to New Delhi to brief the KGB resident on what was wanted. Through plausible sources, their Indian friends leaked to influential politicians—and, eventually, the press—allegations (supported by forged "proof") that the general was maintaining suspicious contacts with British and Pakistani military circles.

And they smeared electoral opponents of their own favorites. So routinely, in fact, that Kondrashev had trouble citing specific examples. "Almost every day, somewhere" Service A forged letters "exposing" their rumored misdeeds or illicit connections. Sergey recalled such actions in several countries of Latin America as well as India and Pakistan.

• • •

WHEN THE SOVIETS THEMSELVES were about to launch actions abroad, Active Measures rallied to their support.

Shortly before Soviet leader Nikita Khrushchev took off for London in April 1956 to discuss the Suez Canal crisis, he asked KGB Chairman Serov to give him something to strengthen his bargaining position. Serov referred this to Foreign Intelligence Chief Sakharovskiy who asked Kondrashev, then in the German Department, to come up with a suggestion.

Kondrashev did. Still on his mind was the Berlin Tunnel that his agent George Blake had uncovered to him but which had been allowed to go on leaking secrets (by now for more than a year) to protect Blake. Now, Sergey thought, enough time had passed that the Tunnel might safely be exposed (Blake agreed when consulted). So he proposed to Foreign Intelligence Chief Sakharovskiy that the Tunnel be "discovered" and blasted in public—in time to permit Khrushchev to express outrage and embarrass his British interlocutors. Khrushchev and Serov agreed.

This is why the Berlin Tunnel came to its end—and to public view—when it did.

It was on the night of 21–22 April 1956, just when Khrushchev was talking with the British in London, that the KGB staged an "accidental discovery" in Berlin, during an ostensibly routine check of communications lines after some heavy rainfall. An "outraged" propaganda blast followed; a press conference was called and the Tunnel revealed for all to see.[1] It was the work of Service A.

Another such call for hurry-up active measures came with the building of the Berlin Wall. In 1961, hundreds and finally thousands of Eastern citizens were pouring out daily across the sector border in Berlin. The German Democratic Republic was losing its population and its credibility as a state and the military posture of the Soviet Union was threatened. East German leader Walter Ulbricht came up with the idea of building a wall to stop this outflow, but this would raise a hostile roar of world opinion. Agayants's Service A (then still Department D) was called to the rescue.

Agayants recognized that the wall must be presented as a defensive move against Western "aggression." Because he was privy to some of the most secret Soviet spies abroad, he was aware that a valuable agent had recently supplied the KGB with the secret wartime contingency plans of the so-called Baghdad Pact— CENTO, the regional security arrangement for the Middle East. If doctored up a bit, these plans could be made to look aggressive, so Agayants asked Aleksandr Sakharovskiy, the Foreign Intelligence chief, to release the documents for publication. So severe was the East German crisis that Sakharovsky overcame his initial fear for the security of the valuable secret source and agreed.

Thus on 12 August 1961, only hours before Soviet soldiers laid the first barbed wire in Berlin, the Soviet news agency TASS revealed "shocking" secret war plans of CENTO that envisaged dropping atomic bombs on Iran, Pakistan, and Afghanistan as well as the USSR and China. The Central Committee instantly confirmed the validity of the CENTO documents and ordered TASS to pass them to Western press correspondents, ordered Soviet embassies to transmit copies to those Middle Eastern governments, and ordered the Foreign Ministry and KGB to spread the word far and wide.

Left unspoken was the true reason for this loud splash: to mitigate the roar that would follow the construction of the Wall that very night.

It was rare indeed for the KGB thus to risk such a valuable[2] and active agent by publicly exploiting his secret revelations.

But, Kondrashev said, it felt little compunction if the source was no longer active or valuable. An American Army sergeant had been removing top secret war plans for Europe from an American courier center near Paris for KGB operatives to photograph overnight. When he lost his access to the center and to other secrets, he became expendable.[3]

Thus in a replay of the CENTO operation three years earlier, Service A sent to Western newspapers NATO war plans that foresaw an eventual need to organize partisan warfare in Western Europe and even to take over political power or drop atomic weapons on the territory of America's allies. Nevermind that these were merely wartime contingency plans and nevermind that any bombing would be directed at enemy forces: Their exposure had the desired effect. Western media expressed outrage against the Americans' seeming arrogance and unconcern for friendly allies, questions were raised in parliaments, and citizens wrote angry letters (some forged by Kondrashev's service).

· · ·

NOT ALL DOCUMENTS SERVICE A exposed publicly were genuine and some genuine ones were not entirely genuine.

Within Kondrashev's section for "documentation" *(Otdeleniye po dokumentatsiya)* was a subgroup *(sektor)* devoted to forgery.

It compiled and stored samples of official documents of foreign governments and institutions along with the paper, letterheads, logos, inks, typescripts, and anything else that might lend authenticity to a forgery. The chief of this group had chalked up great successes for more than twenty years.

Another KGB foreign intelligence unit, outside of Service A, helped it forge documents. This was the section that backstopped the false life histories ("legends") of Illegals—operatives sent to work abroad under Western identities. Kondrashev was full of praise for the skillful imitation of signatures, logos, passport entries, and the like by that section's chief forger Pavel Grigoryevich Gromoshkin. (Sergey also admired this artist's "marvelous" sketches of prominent KGB personalities like Yuri Andropov and Willy Fisher, the Illegal operative better known as Rudolf Ivanovich Abel. Gromoshkin later published thirty or forty of them in a book that was offered for sale inside the KGB.)[4]

Service A did not have to forge entire documents and letters. Sometimes they just inserted phrases or names into otherwise genuine Western documents to heighten their propaganda effect or to exacerbate some particular rivalry or internal dissension abroad.

Though the Western press properly identified a lot of these KGB-planted letters and documents as Soviet forgeries, Kondrashev stressed that these forgeries were usually based on genuine materials and some of them shifted a part of public opinion in the desired direction.

• • •

"ACTIVE MEASURES" COULD BE very active indeed, like the radio transmitters the KGB planted and quickly shifted from point to point along the Chinese border, emitting broadcasts ostensibly from Chinese nationalists calling for independence for Sinkiang from Beijing's rule.[5]

Kondrashev took mitigated satisfaction from this political work. It had sometimes influenced Western political organizations and it had weakened some of the most potent adversaries of Soviet policy. It had drawn headlines in the Western press, it may even have shifted some parts of public opinion and shaken Western solidarity. But Sergey saw its effect as temporary and never decisive. These actions had less impact on the course of events in the Cold War than some Western publications credited them with, Kondrashev thought. But he was a bit more upbeat about the effect of some of his economic, military, scientific, and counterintelligence works.

· · ·

THOSE "POLITICAL" MEASURES WERE only one aspect of Service A's work. It also had departments for economic measures, military deception, scientific and technological measures, and counterintelligence.

Economic measures included—but went far beyond—slipping false statistics and estimates into the public domain. When the Soviet government was preparing to sell twenty-five tons of gold in London, they delayed until the KGB could jack up the price. To US and African gold-producing governments, Service A slipped data that overestimated difficulties and underestimated production. The Ministry of Finance and the president of the State Bank participated in this active measure and the operational plan was signed by the Chairman of the KGB, the Minister of Finance, and either the Prime Minister or his deputy.

· · ·

MILITARY MEASURES BEGAN AFTER Kondrashev arrived in Department D in 1962. Agayants said, "We've got to expand our active measures into the military field" and together they turned to the task.

The General Staff of the Soviet Armed Forces had a section devoted to misleading NATO about Soviet military capabilities. Agayants and Kondrashev set up their own small military-deception section under KGB Colonel Poryvayev, to establish regular and systematic cooperation with the colonel heading the General Staff section. It proved fruitful: The General Staff colonel came to the KGB offices and absorbed some of Service A's techniques while they, in turn, found his knowledge of high-level military procedures a great help in devising actions of their own. Proposals stemmed from within Service A or from the deputy chief of the KGB's Third Chief Directorate (armed forces security), while the General Staff cleared and supplied the factual material. Together the two sections would work out deception plans that Agayants and Kondrashev would sign as initiators, with the countersignatures of the chairman of the KGB and the chief of the General Staff.

So close and frequent did this collaboration become that both Agayants and Kondrashev were given special identity cards affording them a high level of access in the Ministry of Defense. One or the other would go there to keep abreast of objectives and problems and to discuss what the KGB might do to help. They usually talked with General Staff Chief Marshal Zakharov or with his deputies General Lobov and the future Marshal Akhromeyev.[6]

The General Staff was trying, among other things, to deflect the West from the true location of Soviet intercontinental ballistic missile launch sites and to mislead the West about Soviet capabilities of launching such missiles from trains. Together with Department D, Soviet military engineers planned and built dummy missiles, train platforms, and even railway lines to be placed a certain distance from the genuine sites (though not too far, because the West was aware of the general locations). Kondrashev's service also produced (and arranged the sale of) maps that contained a deviation from actual coordinates, hoping to mislead the targeting of NATO missiles. Kondrashev noted that such actions were possible only in those early days, because satellite photography later became far too precise.

Kondrashev remembered one time when, through a double agent, they drew Western attention toward one factory that was producing ten missiles per month to divert attention from another producing many more and sending out its products in special wagons designed to hide from spy satellites the nature of their cargo.[7]

• • •

IN THE FIELD OF scientific and technological deception, Kondrashev's service learned a lot from the Americans, he said. Through secret sources, the KGB got information on American research and development in the nuclear energy field—for one thing, that lithium was being favored in certain manufacturing processes. They passed this information to the Kurchatov Institute and got a surprising response: The Institute told them that this was false information and if Soviet science were to accept it and pursue that line in its own research and development, it would cause a vast waste of time, money, and resources.

All right then, Kondrashev thought, let's do the same to them. His service then initiated projects to convince the Americans, through secretly-controlled channels (including some of the same that had supplied the KGB with that false information), that Soviet researchers were succeeding in certain other lines of development. And Kondrashev thought this worked: Secret sources confirmed to the KGB that the Americans had swallowed the bait.

• • •

THE OTHER LINE OF activity was counterintelligence.

Service A's little section was but one of countless KGB units attacking and thwarting Western intelligence services and it was one of the smallest, counting a dozen or so officers, sometimes fewer. But it worked with the foreign-counterintelligence directorate ("K") of its own directorate (FCD) and Department 14 of Counterintelligence (SCD) in operational "games" against Western intelligence services.

This section cleared with other governmental agencies the information that double agents might pass to hostile intelligence, to ensure that what was passed out through one channel would not contradict others. From files on what earlier defectors had exposed to the West, it provided genuine "secrets" that KGB provocateurs sent to the West as false defectors could re-use to make themselves seem genuine and well-informed.

One way this section weakened and discredited Western intelligence services (notably CIA) was by exposing their (real or invented) activity and the names of their officers. As a by-product, they discredited anti-Soviet political activists by falsely "exposing" them as CIA tools. It produced (jointly with Rolf Wagenbreth's East German unit) a book titled *Who's Who in the CIA*,[8] listing some three thousand names—of whom (as I remember from the time) the vast majority had no connection with CIA.

In a one-time publication in 1978 of a magazine ostensibly originated in Switzerland called *CIA Insider*, Service A similarly smeared opponents—western publications disliked for their anti-Soviet slant. It listed mass media ostensibly being "used as cover, subsidized or otherwise influenced by CIA" (none were) and invented a list of "paid CIA agents [and helpers] in the world mass media" in sixty-two countries.[9]

Service A's counterintelligence unit was always seeking new ways to confound Western intelligence services. For example, Kondrashev recalled proposals to give them real or ostensible Soviet intelligence officers as ostensible traitors, who would actually mislead and entrap them. We stumbled upon one such KGB operation—not run by Service A—in which both Kondrashev and I had been involved. It remains one of the great unresolved mysteries of the Cold War.

Fourteen: "How Could CIA Ever Have Believed in That Man?"

DIGGING INTO HIS past for his autobiography, Sergey Kondra-shev and I came across one KGB operation that we had nearly shared—as adversaries. In the KGB he had turned down the offer to run it, whereas in the CIA I had had no such choice.

It popped up while Sergey was recounting ways the counterintel-ligence section of his Department D/Service A had been thwarting Western espionage against the Soviet Union. A favorite KGB method, he said, was to send an agent of their own into the eager hands of the enemy (say, CIA), pretending to defect or to spy for him. Winning the enemy's trust, the agent could not only feed him false information and identify some of his secret operatives, but more importantly could lead him into deeper waters by pointing him toward the wrong targets, entangling him in useless activity, and diverting his attention from things the KGB was really hiding.

This was nothing new, as Sergey reminded me. The KGB had been routinely using this provocative[1] technique long before he arrived on the scene. When his father-in-law Vasily Roshchin had been called into this sort of activity by its maestro Artur Artuzov in the 1920s, Artuzov and OGPU Chief Felix Dzerzhinsky had already been using it for years to expose and ensnare the regime's opponents inside and outside the country. Two of their successful provocations, codenamed "Trust" and "Sindikat 2," were celebrated in Soviet history, novels, and films. After the Second World War, Roshchin had redirected these techniques against American and British intelligence services.

But during Sergey's time as deputy and later Chief of Department D/Service A, his group had not planted any false defectors. His chief, Ivan Agayants, favored the technique, but would turn skeptical whenever faced with a specific proposal. Agayants was acutely aware that any such operation could boomerang against its perpetrator. If the would-be dupe (say, the CIA) should recognize that one of his spies had been handed to him by the enemy, he could look behind the ploy and spot the very things the ruse was designed to hide. Agayants queried each project critically. Did it take contingencies into account? Was the proposed cover story credible? Was the candidate-provocateur really up to the job? (It took exceptional motivation, resourcefulness, and acting skill to successfully play such a tricky role.) Kondrashev heard Agayants questioning several FCD unit chiefs making such proposals. "Would you really trust this particular guy to do this job?" he asked one. Another he confronted: "Are you really ready to sign off on this operation—and take personal responsibility if it fails?" Again and again Sergey saw them back off and withdraw their proposals.

But other KGB elements not subject to Agayants's rigor launched many such operations. In fact, Sergey said, he himself had been asked to manage one.

"How's that again?" I asked.

"Yes, Gribanov asked me to help him run one he was about to launch against your service."

He meant General Oleg Mikhailovich Gribanov, overall head of Soviet internal counterintelligence and security, whose formal title was Chief of the KGB's Second Chief Directorate (SCD)—the equivalent, and more, of the American FBI Director. "Gribanov was a ball of fire," Sergey recalled, "always out to beat the FCD at its own game." No sooner had Ivan Agayants set up his disinformation department ("D") in the FCD had Gribanov set up his own deception unit in the SCD, which he designated as Department 14. As the KGB itself later defined that department, it would "penetrate foreign intelligence services" by way of "mounting complicated counterintelligence operations and operational games[2] against them."[3] So closely did Gribanov wield that department as his personal weapon that even its definition specified that Department 14 worked "under the immediate direction of the SCD chief."

That SCD chief was the man who invited Sergey Kondrashev

Oleg M. Gribanov

to his office in early February 1962. He had long known Kondrashev from his nine years' successful work in the SCD, his handling of a mole inside British Intelligence, and from their work together in the mid-1950s against West Germany. And he knew that Sergey was now headed toward high-level deception work as Ivan Agayants's deputy.

Kondrashev had no idea what to expect, but Gribanov came right to the point. He was in the process, he said, of launching a complex deception operation against the CIA which he wanted Kondrashev to help him run. If Sergey would come back to the SCD for this purpose, Gribanov would make him his deputy, a post carrying with it the rank of a one-star general.

Kondrashev admitted to me that he had been attracted to Gribanov's proposal. When he went to Agayants to discuss the possibility, he sensed that Agayants knew Gribanov would make this offer and was also aware of the operation Gribanov was preparing. "I understand that you're tempted," Agayants said. "But relax. You'll get general's rank soon enough in the FCD. And in this particular case, you wouldn't be doing yourself any good in the long run. Gribanov is going to screw it up. He's rash, doesn't have time for the detailed preparations that these things need."

True, Sergey might be able to prevent some of the slip-ups and shortcuts that Agayants foresaw, "but not all of them." If Gribanov's ploy failed as Agayants evidently thought it might, Sergey would share the blame, of which there would be plenty if the CIA saw through the deception.

Kondrashev took Agayants's counsel, turned down Gribanov's offer, and as originally planned became Agayants's deputy.

• • •

BUT GRIBANOV WENT AHEAD with his grand deception, as Kondrashev found out by chance a few months later. He even learned whom Gribanov was sending out to the CIA and who was managing the operation in the field.

It happened in a corridor of KGB Headquarters in May 1962, when Sergey bumped into Yuri Ivanovich Guk, an old friend he had worked with ten years earlier in the SCD against the American Embassy in Moscow. Knowing Guk was stationed in Switzerland, Sergey was taken aback. "Hey, Yura! What brings you to Moscow?"

"Just in to discuss an operation," Guk replied cheerily, "I'm still in Geneva." And he began extolling the pleasures of life in that city and talking about colleagues. Right now, in fact, he was having a lot of fun carousing there with Yuri Nosenko.

Sergey knew that name only as a minor SCD headquarters officer. "What in the world is Nosenko doing in Geneva?"

Guk stiffened at the realization that he had committed an indiscretion. ("He must have suddenly remembered that I was no longer in the SCD," Sergey said to me.) He passed his finger near his lip, shook his head, and said, "Sorry. I can't talk about it. Forget I mentioned it."

It was clear to Sergey that Guk and Nosenko were doing Gribanov's business. Why else would Guk clam up to his friend Sergey, whom he knew to be high in FCD deception work? And Sergey knew Guk, a long-time practitioner of counterintelligence deception,[4] to be still working for Gribanov's SCD.[5]

$$\bullet \quad \bullet \quad \bullet$$

As SERGEY TOLD ME this anecdote forty years later, I thought, "Ha! I was right!" I had long suspected the real purpose of Guk's trip from Geneva to Moscow.

At the end of May 1962, a little more than three months after Gribanov told Kondrashev he was launching a provocation against CIA, Yuri Nosenko—an SCD Moscow officer temporarily acting as watchdog of a Soviet conference delegation in Geneva—volunteered to spy for CIA. As it happened, it was I who received him. During the week remaining before he was to return to Moscow, he continued living it up with his old friend and KGB colleague Yuri Guk, sometimes before and sometimes just after his secret meetings with me. And by "coincidence" his pal Guk had made a short trip to Moscow and returned to Geneva bringing a letter and pictures from Nosenko's wife—just before Nosenko first came to CIA.

Later that same year, I came across reasons to suspect that my shiny new spy inside the KGB was in reality a plant sent to us by Gribanov. That made me take a fresh look at Guk's constant presence near Nosenko, and his Moscow trip came to look like part of last-minute KGB preparations to put Nosenko into our hands.

Now many years later, Kondrashev had confirmed my old suspicions. Nosenko had to be the provocateur whom Gribanov had wanted Sergey to help him launch against the CIA. The dates and circumstances matched perfectly, and no other such thing had come CIA's way in 1962. Moreover, Gribanov's presence had been evident from the start of Nosenko's tales to us: Gribanov was Nosenko's special friend and career help, Gribanov told Nosenko things that he was passing on to us, Gribanov had figured personally in events that Nosenko recounted.

The Nosenko operation has been well publicized and richly documented, and its details offer a classic example of how the KGB played the deception game.

It began for the CIA when Yuri Nosenko walked in to us in Geneva. His Moscow job, he told us, was supervising SCD work against foreigners in the USSR and, until a couple of months earlier, against the American Embassy in Moscow. We met several times in the few days before he was to return to Moscow. A year and a half later, at the end of January 1964, he emerged again as a delegation watchdog in Geneva, but this time defected outright. He was taken to the United States where he lived until his death in 2008.

As I mentioned above, soon after Nosenko's first contact with CIA in 1962, signs began to suggest that the KGB had sent Nosenko to us as a provocateur. Then when we debriefed him after his defection in 1964, such indications multiplied in number. When interrogated under conditions he could not evade, he proved unable to explain away any of the doubtful circumstances and contradictions in his story. He admitted lying, but refused to confess that the KGB had sent him.[6] But ultimately CIA came to believe in Nosenko.

• • •

"HOW COULD CIA EVER HAVE BELIEVED IN THAT MAN?"

BECAUSE KONDRASHEV AND I had seen this Nosenko case from both sides, it served particularly well to illustrate things that Sergey wanted to describe in his autobiography: why the KGB might mount such deception operations, for example, and how they went about it. And Nosenko's clumsy performance of his delicate mission—his self-contradictions, blundering improvisations, and blatant indifference to truth—showed why Agayants was so skeptical about whom the KGB selected for such jobs and why Agayants criticised Gribanov's carelessness about details. Our (temporary) detection of Nosenko's fraud confirmed Ivan Agayants's foresight in warning Sergey to stay away from this case.

Why did SCD chief Gribanov launch this provocation against CIA? On a personal level Gribanov was eager to emulate heroes of the KGB's history and, intramurally, to outdo the FCD in thwarting the CIA and MI6. But, Sergey reflected, Gribanov surely had more specific reasons to turn to this time-honored method at this particular moment. As we can see in retrospect, it offered him a way to cope with two problems that rose before him in 1961.

The first had come to light in the spring. To its dismay, the KGB learned from a secret source abroad that a Soviet Military Intelligence (GRU) colonel named Oleg Penkovsky had just made secret contact with British and American intelligence during a trip to London. That traitor was now back in Moscow continuing to pass military secrets.

It would have been Gribanov's job to arrest him immediately and end the treason, but his hands were tied. Were he to arrest Penkovsky now, at the very beginning, Penkovsky's CIA and MI6 handlers would have wondered what had happened so soon to their new source. Inevitably they would suspect that Penkovsky had been betrayed from inside, and even worse, they could identify the KGB's secret source, because only a tiny few inside British or

American intelligence could have learned of such an affair at this early stage. So Gribanov had to wait—and let Penkovsky go on spying. Before he could arrest the traitor, he would have to provide the West with another more innocuous but plausible explanation for the KGB's discovery.

Oleg Penkovsky at his trial in 1963.

That took more than a year, and a costly year it was. While delaying the arrest, Kondrashev said, the KGB even had to let Penkovskiy go ahead with one or two more scheduled trips to the West— letting him continue to spill secrets at his leisure in London or Paris and perhaps even stay in the West and avoid the dire punishment hanging over his head.

I could hardly believe that Soviet leaders would permit such a sacrifice and told Kondrashev so. He just shrugged. "The value of the source outweighed the value of the secrets," he said. "It was the same with Blake." He reminded me that the MI6 traitor George Blake had given to the KGB (to Kondrashev personally) timely news of the CIA-MI6 plan to dig the Berlin Tunnel, but the KGB had let the tunnel be dug and tap into Soviet military secrets for more than a year, a sacrifice to protect Blake.[7]

While developing the plausible, innocuous excuse to arrest Penkovsky, the KGB organized tight surveillance to collect evidence that could be used in an eventual trial. As Sergey described the KGB's watch, whenever possible they bugged even the most routine of Penkovsky's meetings with foreigners. They peered into his apartment from neighboring space in the building. They observed his apartment windows through long-range telescopes, keeping a special eye on one particular window that, according to Penkovskiy's secret communications plan—which the KGB knew—

he would keep lit unusually late at night to signal an important message in his dead drop.

On one or another pretext, the KGB in autumn put a stop to Penkovsky's further travel abroad, so by late 1961 they had him "cornered like a bear in its den" (as the Soviet prosecutor later put it[8]). Henceforth Penkovsky would have to make any spy contacts in Moscow itself. As the KGB expected and hoped, they spotted him doing it. Now the KGB not only had evidence for an eventual trial but, just as important, they also had their "innocuous explanation" for the arrest.

From that time on, the KGB took great pains to make the West believe that they had tumbled to Penkovskiy's treason by sheer luck during routine surveillance of Western diplomats. They even told this tale to their own personnel in an official briefing paper after the arrest. It is true, Kondrashev said, that the KGB "stompers" had spotted Penkovsky contacting British intelligence operatives, but they had known exactly whom to follow where. Knowing his contact plan, they even prepared one of his meeting sites in advance to capture the meeting on film. The surveillance was "a mere technicality" (as another former deputy chief of the FCD put it[9]) because Penkovsky's treasonous activity had already been uncovered by an FCD source.

By the spring of 1962, the surveillance had become obvious even to Penkovsky and his Western contacts. On one occasion, they saw what was obviously a surveillance car behind them make a U-turn on a one-way street, unthinkable for skilled professionals who knew Moscow's streets as well as the backs of their own hands. To me, this clumsy work suggested that the KGB was purposely exposing their surveillance to support the cover story they planned to use.[10]

In the spring of that year, by which time Penkovsky's Western contacts had begun to notice surveillance, Yuri Nosenko walked in to the CIA. Claiming long experience with Moscow's surveillance of foreigners, he took pains to impress us with its powerful and cunning technical support. Tailing an American diplomat a couple of years earlier, Nosenko said, those footpads had uncovered the CIA's great spy in the GRU, Pyotr Popov, and thus hoped to "catch another Popov." And when Nosenko next came out to the West after Penkovsky's arrest, he certified with authority that it had been that powerful and cunning Moscow surveillance—of British diplomats, this time—that had detected Penkovskiy's treason.[11]

• • •

THE OTHER 1961 EVENT that evidently shaped Gribanov's deception plan, the one he invited Kondrashev to handle, occurred in mid-December. KGB Major Anatoly Golitsyn stepped into the living room of the Helsinki CIA station chief, defected, was flown with his family to the West, and unloaded before startled American eyes an unprecedented cornucopia of KGB secrets. Unlike other defectors, all of whom had jumped on short notice, Golitsyn had been preparing his flight ever since Khrushchev's "secret speech" of 1956, exposing Stalin's crimes, had shown him the true nature of the regime he served. For years he systematically stored in his

Anatoly Golitsyn

memory what he learned in his KGB duties and conversations with colleagues, secrets that would ensure him and his family a warm welcome by the CIA. And a treasure trove it was indeed: the identities of or hints leading to dozens of KGB spies, double agents, influential supporters in Western governments, and clandestine procedures.[12]

"HOW COULD CIA EVER HAVE BELIEVED IN THAT MAN?"

The KGB leaders quickly found out how much they had lost. Only hours after learning that Golitsyn had fled, the KGB Chairman set up a three-man commission, consisting of himself and the chiefs of his foreign intelligence and personnel directorates. They set their subordinates to work examining all files Golitsyn had ever handled and ordered interviews of his former colleagues to find out what they might have inadvertently exposed to him.

Kondrashev, who was acting KGB chief in Vienna, got a cable from Moscow within a few days after Golitsyn's defection, instructing him to query all his officers. Three weeks later, Moscow informed him which of them Golitsyn had actually exposed—including Kondrashev himself—and warned them to be ready for Western "provocations."

Through the wreckage shone a weak ray of hope. Yes, Golitsyn knew a lot of important KGB spies, but not all the identifying details. The Americans and their allies would have to mount painstaking investigations to identify some of them and might never succeed. For example, about Kondrashev's code-clerk agent "Jack" Golitsyn had heard only that the KGB had recruited and given this code name to some American code clerk sometime in the early postwar years.

The commission's "hugely important" damage assessment was passed to SCD Chief Oleg Gribanov. He was shocked to learn that among the compromised KGB spies were important ones his own SCD had recruited: Western code clerks, intelligence officers, and diplomats. It galvanized him into action to protect and preserve them insofar as might still be possible. His provocateur Nosenko would provide a channel, but if he were to divert these Golitsyn betrayals, he would need a fresh briefing and change of legend. Because Nosenko was already on the point of leaving for Geneva, Gribanov saw this would have to be done there, on the scene. A

Department 14 officer by the name or pseudonym of Aleksandr Kislov would accompany Nosenko and along with Gribanov's officer in Geneva, Yuri Guk, would train and brief Nosenko for his revised mission.[13]

To give Nosenko authority to convincingly divert certain of Golitsyn's leads, Gribanov tacked onto Nosenko's career legend the claim to have overseen the SCD's operations against the American Embassy's code clerks and security officer throughout 1960 and 1961.[14] As a result, the attempted deception became blatant. For instance:

1. Golitsyn had revealed to CIA that a Moscow SCD officer named Gennady Gryaznov had come to Golitsyn's KGB office in Helsinki in 1960 to borrow one of its agents, a Finnish businessman who made frequent trips to Moscow. Better than any Russian, this Finn would be able to get into social contact with American Embassy people and specifically an unnamed American Embassy code clerk whom the KGB had targeted for recruitment. Gryaznov had later given Golitsyn reason to believe that the code clerk was successfully recruited.

   Then along came Nosenko in Geneva, six months after Golitsyn's defection, claiming to have been Gryaznov's direct supervisor and to have been personally involved in the recruitment attempt, even having befriended the Finnish businessman in the process. Thus he could certify with first-hand authority that the code clerk, an Army NCO whom he named as James Storsberg, had refused the KGB's offer.[15]

2. Golitsyn had revealed to CIA that a Moscow KGB officer named Vadim Kosolapov went to Helsinki during this period to take the train back to Moscow to chat up an American communications specialist who was arriving for duty in the American Embassy. The KGB had earlier found the man

vulnerable to recruitment and, as Kosolapov told Golitsyn, they had high hopes for success. (Sergey Kondrashev, a long-time friend of Kosolapov, confirmed to me that "Vadim made some important recruitments" that had boosted his career; he rose to general's rank.) We in the CIA identified the American and confirmed both his and Kosolapov's presence aboard the train. The American had never reported the approach.

Then along came Nosenko to CIA claiming to have been Kosolapov's direct supervisor at the time and denying any such trip and certifying that the KGB had never recruited any American communications personnel or code clerks, only the mechanic "Andrey" (see below).

3. Golitsyn revealed to CIA that an American Embassy code clerk in Moscow had been recruited in the postwar years and codenamed "Jack". Although Golitsyn did not know it, this was Kondrashev's 1949 recruitment.

   Then along came Nosenko telling the CIA that "the most important spy ever recruited in the American Embassy in Moscow" had indeed been recruited in "1949 or 1950." But the spy, according to Nosenko's version, was not a code clerk but simply a cipher machine mechanic whom the KGB code-named "Andrey." (Here came another Gribanov blunder: In 1962, Nosenko told me repeatedly that the KGB recruited "Andrey" in 1949–1950, years before Nosenko even entered the KGB, but in 1964 told that he had himself witnessed the operation while it was active in his time,1953–1955.[16])

4. Golitsyn had revealed to CIA that the KGB came to suspect Pyotr Popov, the CIA's important spy in Soviet Military Intelligence, as early as 1957.[17] The fact that Popov was not recalled from Berlin and arrested until late 1958 showed that the Soviets must have had some important reason to delay the

presumably as discussed in (5) below, to protect a mole
the CIA who had betrayed Popov.

Then along came Nosenko claiming that he had personally supervised the KGB watch over the American Embassy
security officer who had replaced Popov's CIA contact man
in Moscow. Thus Nosenko knew "for sure" that the KGB
did not uncover Popov until early 1959 and then only by
happening to see another Embassy officer, George Winters,
mailing a letter to him.[18]

5. Golitsyn revealed to the CIA that the head of the KGB's
operations against the American Embassy in Moscow,
Vladislav Kovshuk, had secretly travelled to Washington (CIA
confirmed that he had indeed come in 1957 and stayed ten
months, operating in the company of Yuri Guk and Aleksandr
Kislov[19]) and that his trip was related to the KGB's discovery
of CIA's spy Pyotr Popov. (Indeed, Sergey Kondrashev knew
that Kovshuk, his long-time colleague and friend, had gone to
Washington to meet with a spy "who was never uncovered.")
Then Nosenko in 1962 reported with the authority of having
recently been Kovshuk's deputy that Kovshuk's only purpose
in Washington had been to restore contact with Sergeant
"Andrey" (see 3, previous page).[20]

6. In the autumn of 1956, Kovshuk compromised in a sex trap
Edward Ellis Smith, the man the CIA had sent to Moscow
as the Embassy's security officer to support the Popov case,
and offered him the chance to get out of trouble. Somehow
Smith didn't report this deal until days later. He was recalled
for questioning and the Agency, dissatisfied with his expla-
nations, fired him and did not let him return to Moscow.
(Forty years later, after the Cold War, the Soviets themselves
admitted in a book about Soviet intelligence[21] that they had

successfully recruited Ed Smith. Kondrashev knew this to be true and was surprised that it had been published.)

In 1962, Nosenko claimed to have personally participated in Kovshuk's pitch to Smith, even giving the KGB's code name for this target, "Ryzhy" [Redhead]. He could thus certify that Smith had refused to cooperate with the KGB. This was another blunder: By early 1964, when he returned to Geneva, Nosenko had already forgotten what he had told me eighteen months earlier. He now denied ever having heard of the name of Smith or of the episode. Moreover, by Nosenko's own account of his career, he had not even been in Kovshuk's section when Smith was pitched.

Although Ivan Agayants had forewarned Kondrashev about Gribanov's rashness and indifference to detail, Sergey was still amazed at how sloppily Gribanov had prepared Nosenko for this delicate mission. He shook his head in disgust as he and I looked over published accounts of things Nosenko had told the CIA:

- Having himself held that post a few years earlier, Kondrashev knew for sure that Nosenko had never been deputy chief of the SCD's American-Embassy section.[22]

Yuri Nosenko

- No KGB officer with the level of responsibility that Nosenko claimed could conceivably have been sent away to perform miscellaneous tasks unrelated to that responsibility—like watchdogging travelling groups—much less as often or as long as Nosenko had been.

- Kondrashev could not imagine a KGB officer failing, as Nosenko did, to remember the year he entered service, and especially whether that was before or after Stalin's death.
- "Shouldn't this alone have made it clear that Nosenko was not honest?" Kondrashev asked me when he learned that Nosenko had been unable to describe how to send a KGB cable. Whereupon Kondrashev described the procedure, demonstrating that it was unforgettable.[23]
- He chuckled at several of Nosenko's claims: that he had been brought into the KGB, and moreover into its SCD American Department, without a security clearance; that he had instructed Castro's Cuban counterintelligence how to operate against Americans; and that while heading operations against the American Embassy in Moscow, he had recruited a homosexual American tourist in Bulgaria.
- It was, Kondrashev asserted, impossible that a Soviet delegation security officer would be housed apart from his delegation, as Nosenko was in Geneva. That, Sergey said, could only have been to facilitate his movements for other purposes. (It is surely no coincidence that Aleksandr Kislov had roomed with Nosenko in a little hotel far from the flock of delegates whom Nosenko was supposed to be protecting in Geneva.)

Kondrashev looked pityingly at me and asked, "How could your service ever have believed in that man?"

• • •

Just as Agayants had foreseen, Gribanov's blunders exposed to the CIA the fraud and thus the very things the fraud was designed to hide. Seeing Nosenko covering up how the KGB had uncovered

Oleg Penkovsky had pushed us to look for their real source. Seeing Nosenko divert us from Golitsyn's leads to successful KGB recruitments of American code clerks put us halfway to uncovering really important KGB assets.

But Agayants had often said to Kondrashev that in order to succeed, these deceptions had to tell the dupe what he wanted to believe. And with this Nosenko ploy, Gribanov—along with his blunders—had done just that. As a result, his Nosenko operation ultimately succeeded.

You see, the CIA badly wanted to believe Nosenko's messages. To disbelieve them and look behind them might bring to light ugly things no one wanted to see: undiscovered moles inside the agency or breaks of American ciphers that had enabled the Soviet Union to read America's secret communications at critical periods of the Cold War. Three years after Nosenko's defection (and a year after I had been assigned abroad), other CIA people found ways to rationalize, overlook, or dismiss the signs that Nosenko had been sent to us. I have since recalled no fewer than forty questions that had troubled us at the time, any one or two of which would have cast doubt on the genuineness of any defector, and not one of which CIA ever answered.

Ignoring all that, our CIA made an act of faith, denied there had ever been any real reason to doubt Nosenko, officially accepted him as genuine, and took him in to counsel their work against the KGB. To this day, as far as I (or the public) know, the agency officially believes that both Popov and Penkovskiy were caught by routine KGB security measures via surveillance of Moscow diplomats and that no code clerk or CIA officer of that early Cold War period was ever recruited by the KGB. And so Gribanov's operation ultimately succeeded.

. . .

SERGEY KONDRASHEV WAS INDEED glad that he had declined to participate. Gribanov was dropped from his high post and from the KGB in 1964 or early 1965 (Sergey remembered the date only vaguely). Stories floated from Moscow in 1964 and after to the effect that Gribanov had been fired because he had sponsored the career of the "genuine" defector Nosenko and had participated in sex and drinking parties that Nosenko had organized. Kondrashev, who knew this "orgies" story to have been a pretext, thought it quite possible that Gribanov was really dropped because of the CIA's initial suspicions and confinement of Nosenko.

Nevertheless, Agayants be thanked! Kondrashev could have shared Gribanov's fate.

Fifteen:
The Top Hat Paradox

SERGEY KONDRASHEV AND I were ambling around a large pond one evening, idly commenting on things we had been talking about earlier in the day. These relaxed, off-duty times were, by our tacit understanding, off the record. I shook my head with admiration at how securely his service handled his recruitment of the American code clerk described in Chapter 1, holding his identity to only six or seven people.

"Oh, that was not so rare in 'valuable' cases," Sergey said. "When I went to London as acting rezident, they didn't tell me the identity of a certain agent being run by one of my own officers. And while I was handling George Blake there, not even the rezident himself knew who my source was, and hardly more than three in Moscow."

After a pause he added, "And in one SCD case, I was the only person in the whole FCD who even knew its existence."

I asked, "How was something like that managed?"

Sergey explained. An officer from the SCD, he said, would bring Kondrashev a stiff leather portfolio that held a report of developments in the operation. He would stay there in the office while Kondrashev read it, signed for having done so, and handed it back in its portfolio. The courier would then turn and depart without leaving any written word and no chance for anyone else to see the report.

"Why you?" I asked.

Sergey reminded me that he had been FCD deputy chief at the time, specifically overseeing disinformation operations abroad.[1]

"Oh, I see," I said. "This must have been about some deception operation the SCD was running abroad—FCD territory."

"Yes." And remembering that I would have been acquainted with the case, he added, "It was Polyakov."

"What?" I exclaimed. Suddenly our idle chat had turned sensational.

For forty years I had been convinced that Dmitry Polyakov, a Soviet Military Intelligence (GRU) officer spying for the FBI and then the CIA in my time, must have been a KGB plant. But my successors in CIA had evidently found good reasons to trust him, because after his arrest and execution, they publicly praised him as their greatest source of the Cold War.

I added, "But they announced he was executed for treason!"

"He was."

"But you just said—"

"Yes, that the SCD sent him out."

"But why in the world would they execute him for doing what he was sent out to do?"

"They found out that he was giving you much more than he was supposed to."

"Found out? How?"

"Through some source inside American Intelligence."

I thought that over for a moment. "Maybe that source was Aldrich Ames?"

Kondrashev brushed off the question. "Maybe. I don't remember, if I ever knew." He was clearly not going to say more.

"But executed? For that, he must have told a whole lot more than he was supposed to! I've read in the newspapers that CIA people considered him their best source ever—and that's saying a lot if they remembered Popov and Penkovsky. Are you sure you mean Polyakov? Sure, I know they announced they had shot him, but I've always doubted it. Maybe you were thinking of some other execution, Penkovsky for example?"

Kondrashev, habitually precise in what he remembered and said, shot me an irritated frown and snapped, "It was Polyakov." After a moment he added, more gently, "But you are right; of course, it had to have been a lot more."

As we walked on in the growing dusk, I thought out loud, "It's odd that they would give a planted source access to secrets beyond what he was supposed to tell the adversary."

"They had no choice, using a person like this," Sergey commented.

I went on. "But wouldn't it be the Third [Chief Directorate of the KGB, responsible for military security] to put an army officer into enemy hands?"

Again Kondrashev answered with a trace of irritation. "I told you. It was the Second." Sensing his growing discomfort at having raised the subject at all, I did not press further. He knew: He had been officially briefed.

Sergey later told a bit more. "It was one earlier contact of Polyakov's that caused [SCD chief] Gribanov to choose him for this assignment," he said.[2] Also, Gribanov had made the choice after a "thorough analysis" by one of his officers, whom Kondrashev chose not to name.

However, at another time and in a different context, Kondrashev identified Valentin V. Zvezdenkov as the first chief of Oleg Gribanov's new (in 1959) Department 14 for operational deception. Just before then, Zvezdenkov had assisted Gribanov in investigating Pyotr Popov, the CIA's spy inside the GRU, and then had interrogated him. Popov confessed having made the GRU an open book for the CIA by identifying more than 650 of its officers, giving leads to hundreds of GRU agents, and describing its secret procedures.[3] Now Gribanov could re-use all this information by sending a GRU officer into the hands of American Intelligence to tie them up, lead them astray, and expose their work.

I remarked to Kondrashev that this sequence of events did not look like coincidence: 1) Zvezdenkov under Gribanov investigates Popov in 1957–59; 2) Popov confesses to Zvezdenkov in late 1958–early 1959; 3) Zvezdenkov knows Popov worked with Polyakov; 4) Gribanov appoints Zvezdenkov in 1959 to head his new operational-deception department; and a few months later 5) that department sends Polyakov out to New York to become a (false) American spy.

"No," Sergey smiled, "It was not coincidence."

• • •

INSCRUTABLE, DEFINED AS "THAT which cannot be understood," aptly describes the espionage affair of GRU General Dmitry Fyodorovich Polyakov Even insiders in the CIA, for whom Polyakov spied so long and brilliantly, may not realize just how much of the story remains inscrutable. Even insiders in the KGB who finally caught and interrogated and executed him may not realize it. Perhaps no one alive today can say exactly how and when and why things happened as they did. But Sergey Kondrashev had just given me an exclusive insight that seemed to resolve some of the puzzling questions hanging over this case:

- How could serious CIA insiders on the one hand call Polyakov their "jewel in the crown" and America's "most productive spy of the Cold War,"[4] speak movingly about his personality and the nobility of his motivation, and point to thousands of pages ("twenty seven file drawers") of authentic Soviet military secrets he disclosed—while on the other hand different CIA insiders, also with serious reason, could say confidently that Polyakov must have been sent by the KGB to mislead the United States?

- How could this one senior GRU officer have managed to go on spying for twenty-four years, whereas another senior GRU officer (Oleg Penkovskiy) who volunteered to spy in the same year 1961 was uncovered by a KGB penetration agent within weeks after taking up his treasonous contact with the same CIA?

- Why, after learning from a mole inside the FBI (Robert Hanssen) that Polyakov was betraying the Soviet Union, would the KGB wait as long as five years before arresting him?

- Why was Polyakov tried in secret, in contrast to the very public trial of CIA's other GRU spy of the time, Oleg Penkovskiy?

- Why then, long after the secret trial, did the Soviet government publicize this case in unprecedented detail, even exaggerating the number of spies he betrayed to the Americans?

Even with the answer to such questions that Kondrashev had now provided, there remains a drama still largely hidden, of daring risk and multiple betrayals, crafty deception, and the poignant tragedy of a brave man caught in a terrible web of intrigue. Although it is worth an entire book, all I can do here is add Kondrashev's input to the raw material of that story.

• • •

AT THE BEGINNING OF the 1950s, the GRU assigned then Lieutenant Colonel Dmitry Polyakov, who had served with distinction in World War II, to a tour of intelligence duty in New York. Undercover as a member of the Soviet delegation to the United Nations, he fulfilled his assignment without attracting any unusual attention from the Americans. After years back in Russia and now a colonel, he was again assigned to New York in October 1959. After a first two-year tour, he went back to Moscow on leave, and on his return to New York in November 1961, began seeking a secret meeting with the CIA, with the aim of spying for the Americans.

Made aware of his feelers, the FBI contacted Polyakov early in 1962 and began secret meetings with him. They gave him the code name "Tophat" and in their liaison with CIA, he was dubbed "Bourbon."[5]

Polyakov's FBI handler John Mabey described him as tall, husky, and of ruddy complexion, of high moral character, exuding self-confidence and an aura of leadership, a family man devoted to his wife and two sons, not a heavy drinker, and forthright in his manner of answering and not answering questions. By cooperating with American Intelligence, he considered himself to be fighting for the oppressed Soviet people against evil rulers and helping to prevent a disastrous war. Whatever happened, he told the FBI that he would never abandon his country to live in the United States.

Dmitry Polakov

He felt sure he could get away with it.

As Polyakov's New York assignment came to an end in 1962, the FBI arranged methods for future contact. However, he made no further communication from Moscow and contact was only re-established in January 1966, after the GRU had sent him as military attaché to Burma. His FBI case officer John Mabey met him for three months and then introduced a CIA officer. CIA remained in contact with Polyakov until he returned to Moscow in August 1969.

In 1974, after occasional messages and long silences, Polyakov emerged again, this time as military attaché and GRU chief in New Delhi, where he met with CIA representatives until his tour ended in August 1976. Back in Moscow, he continued to communicate many and valuable military secrets, some via a small CIA-supplied short-range transmitter by which he sent encoded bursts of only 2.6 seconds—say, from a bus passing close to the American Embassy or another designated place. In 1978, he returned to New Delhi in the same capacity as before and again in direct contact with CIA representatives. Then unexpectedly he was recalled to Moscow in May 1980, ostensibly for a meeting of military attachés. He did not return and nothing further was heard from him, although until about 1985 articles appeared under his name in a hunting magazine for which he had written in the past. Around 1985, these articles ended, and that year his son was recalled from a diplomatic assignment abroad.[6]

It was only years later, in 1990, that the Soviets publicly announced that they had arrested Polyakov in 1986, tried him in secret, and executed him in March 1988.

New oddities added to this strange delay in arresting Polyakov. Instead of hiding or belittling the gravity of their loss as they had done after discovering other spies in their ranks, the Soviets stressed it, even exaggerated it. They labelled Polyakov "superspy" and gave exaggeration numbers of GRU spies he had betrayed to the Americans. As never before in other cases, they published a close-up film of his face at the moment of a carefully staged indoor arrest and film and still pictures of him being marched into prison just afterwards. The KGB even planned a documentary film about his treason, to be titled *Agent Number One of the CIA*.

History, as now told in Russia and the West, counts Polyakov as a traitor to Russia and as a genuine spy of the Americans. But from what I knew about the case in its early years in the early and mid-1960s, I could not believe he had genuinely volunteered to spy for us. It seemed unthinkable that the GRU would have innocently assigned Polyakov to New York in 1959, for that was the moment when they were pulling back from abroad their operatives who, like Polyakov, had been exposed by our GRU spy Pyotr Popov. The GRU knew that in 1957 Polyakov had personally escorted to Popov in East Berlin an Illegal named Margarita Tairova whom Popov sent onward to New York. The GRU was fully aware that in the United States the FBI looked hard for Soviet Illegals, who might be handling the most important spies, and therefore focused special attention on any Soviet official they knew to be supporting Illegals. No GRU supervisor in his right mind would have dared approve the assignment abroad of this identified Illegal-support officer at that time (much less to New York, Tairova's destination), and thereby assume responsibility for anything that might later go wrong. Then, of all the hundreds of Soviet Intelligence officers in the United States, it was this unlikely assignee who volunteered to be an American spy. No wonder I was convinced that Moscow must have sent Polyakov there to be recruited by the Americans.[7]

The FBI itself later came to doubt that Polyakov had really been their agent. By 1977 they had found grounds to suspect that he might have been deceiving them during his years in New York, and they went back over their records of their relations with him. Ultimately they could not decide one way or the other, but by leaving the possibility open, the FBI showed that in New York Polyakov must never have supplied them with any information truly harmful to Soviet interests beyond what Popov had earlier betrayed.

During his first contacts with Polyakov in Burma, the CIA case officer Jim F. felt strongly that Polyakov was a plant, but soon noticed such a dramatic improvement in the value of his reporting that he reversed his earlier view and became convinced that Polyakov was genuinely cooperating.

Then, long after Polyakov's arrest, the CIA and FBI learned that both GRU and KGB had long known of Polyakov's treason; Soviet moles had betrayed him in 1979 (Robert Hanssen from inside the FBI) and again in 1985 (Aldrich Ames from inside the CIA). But the KGB did not arrest him until much later.[8]

Kondrashev's revelations resolved these contradictions. In this new light we can see why the KGB failed to arrest Polyakov as soon as Hanssen betrayed him. Hanssen would only have known of the first, New York phase of Polyakov's spying, no surprise if the KGB had sent him there.[9]

• • •

THEREFORE, BOTH OF CIA's apparently conflicting views of Polyakov were right. He was a KGB plant—and yet he was CIA's "jewel in the crown."

What a story remains to be told! Exactly at what point, and why, did this brave man really come over to the American side? Did he ever drop even a hint to the Americans that the KGB had sent him? How did he get the forbidden secrets he then passed to CIA, and how did he hide this from his KGB handlers? What must his relations have been with those handlers? Who was the American traitor who told the KGB how much Polyakov was really passing to the CIA?[10] And when the KGB came to recognize the truth of Polyakov's triple game, what happened to those who had conceived and managed this grandiose provocation that had so disastrously backfired?

It was an epic affair—but it continues to remain inscrutable.

Sixteen:
Prague Spring at the Politburo

ON THE CROWDED beach along the Moskva River that hot summer day Sergey and his wife Rosa were among the families picnicking and sunning peacefully in the grass when the clatter of a descending helicopter grew to a deafening roar. The voice from a loudspeaker boomed down: "We are looking for Comrade Kondrashev! Where is Comrade Kondrashev?" again and again. Sergey shrugged at his wife, stood and waved, and the helicopter rose and flew off.

A few moments later another loudspeaker, this one on a car, summoned Sergey to the nearby road. Its driver told him that Yuri Andropov was calling on the car phone. "Get dressed!" said the KGB Chairman. "The driver will bring you to the office. The *pyatërka* [group of five] is coming together unexpectedly, and I need you."

Such was the urgency of the Kremlin climate that early summer of 1968. Czechoslovakia was sliding away from Soviet-style Communism and Moscow was struggling to cap this imminent threat to its rule over East-Central Europe. And such was the importance of the role Sergey Kondrashev was playing inside the highest body of Kremlin decision-making.

• • •

KONDRASHEV'S ACCOUNT IS NO doubt the only personal view of events at that top level. Because it contradicts details recorded in Central Committee documents accessed by scholars after the Cold War, it deserves the attention of historians and indeed of everyone who is interested in this period of world history. Therefore I have left this narrative in Kondrashev's own words, as he wanted them in his autobiography—the manuscript that the KGB refused to clear for publication because it revealed too much of the truth.

Kondrashev writes:

• • •

BY THE SECOND HALF of May 1968 new Czechoslovak leaders under Alexander Dubcek, whom the Kremlin itself had just elevated to top position, were making changes that challenged Moscow's control over the world Communist movement.

The crisis had developed gradually. Public discontent in Czechoslovakia had been growing through the 1960s; Antonin Novotny, simultaneously head of both the Party as First Secretary and of the government as President, brought only old solutions to changing economic and social problems. Even Party voices were being raised in favor of reform, including that of Alexander Dubcek.

Moscow considered Dubcek a special friend and supporter. He had been schooled and worked in Russia and made friends in the Soviet leadership. And so it was with serious attention that in December, 1967, S. V. Chervonenko, the Soviet Ambassador in Prague, listened to Dubcek's views on the growing problems.

Dubcek proposed that the Czechoslovak party leadership be separated from that of the government. If he were to become First Secretary of the Party, he assured Chervonenko, he would loyally support Novotny as president: "I will firmly defend the Prague Kremlin."

Chervonenko so cabled Moscow, and Dubcek's proposal was handed to Politburo members and Party secretaries for consideration. Because it seemed to offer a way out of a dilemma, a wave of support quickly built up. The Politburo member and Ukrainian leader Pyotr Shelest gave his early, strong endorsement.[1] Central Committee members chimed in with letters and phone calls about what a fine fellow Dubcek was, pretending to know him better than they really did in order, I thought, to gain greater influence in future relations with Czechoslovakia.

That the Politburo decided to support Dubcek's proposal came as no surprise to Novotny, for Chervonenko had broken the news to him in advance. On January 5th, 1968, the Czechoslovak Central Committee duly accepted President Novotny's resignation as party First Secretary and elected Dubcek in his place. And on that winter day began the "Prague Spring" that lasted through most of the summer.

No sooner had Dubcek stepped up to the top of the party than to Moscow's dismay he began placing his people—reformers all—in key governmental positions. Although they adopted the slogan "Socialism with a human face," their actions seemed to threaten a slip from Socialism itself. Right at the beginning, Dubcek appointed Josef Pavel as Minister of Internal Affairs, a dedicated reformist to head the police and security services. Also boding ill for Soviet interests and influence were other cabinet appointments, particularly those of Otto Sik and Frantisek Kriegel, whose Western connections the KGB had long noted with concern. Sik was especially close to Austrian, Italian, and German politicians and was definitely no friend of the Soviet Union. As a leader of the Jewish community in Czechoslovakia, Kriegel had wide connections abroad that we feared might draw the country away from the Warsaw pact. We also distrusted Josef Smrkovsky who, while ingratiating himself with Soviet representatives, was in fact urging Dubcek to oppose our policies.

After first favoring Czechoslovak reforms, Politburo leaders soon became deeply concerned about the pace and the form they were taking. There may indeed have been, as reported, differences of opinion about how to resolve this problem, for how could it be otherwise? No one had a firm idea of how to cope. The government was in real danger of collapsing and fatally infecting other Socialist countries. In everyone's mind loomed the awful experience of our military intervention in Hungary in 1956, perhaps most of all in the memories of Andropov, Suslov, and Mikoyan, all of whom had played key roles there. They had to keep all options open while trying to prevent the slide and counter what Dubcek was doing.

• • •

Moscow leadership was quick to manage the crisis.

In May of 1968 the Central Committee of the Communist Party of the Soviet Union established a pyatërka, a "group of five" Politburo members, and gave it decision-making powers.[2] Presided over by First Secretary Leonid Brezhnev, it included KGB Chairman Yuri Andropov, Minister of Foreign Affairs Andrey Gromyko, Minister of Defense Dmitry Ustinov, and Mikhail Suslov representing the Party leadership.[3]

The pyatërka set up a working group of four senior officials, one each from the KGB, Ministry of Foreign Affairs, Ministry of Defense, and the Central Committee of the Party.[4] They kept members up to speed on developments in Czechoslovakia and elsewhere, drafted their orders to various agencies, and coordinated intelligence gathered and actions to be taken by any government or party element.

I was the KGB member, supporting Andropov. Though I had only just been appointed Deputy Chief of Foreign Intelligence, Andropov doubtless saw me as the closest to Czechoslovak affairs. I had for years as head of the German Department informed Soviet leadership on the growing unrest in the Socialist countries neighboring East Germany. And having resumed my former post atop "active measures" in late 1967, I had already been doing whatever I could to actively counter the unfavorable Czech developments.[5]

The pyatërka routinely assembled twice a week for two or three hours, altering this arrangement if and when circumstances demanded. In the early months of the crisis, two meetings a week usually sufficed, but in the accelerating developments of July and August, the pyatërka met almost daily whenever a member received information, usually through one of us on the Working Group, that required their urgent attention and decision. They met in the Great Hall of the Politburo next to Brezhnev's office on the fifth floor of the Central Committee building on Staraya Ploshchad (Old Square).[6]

We members of the Working Group stayed in our respective offices during these sessions, ready to receive and take to the pyatërka any new, relevant message. Whenever they needed one or more of us to explain some paper or to draft a message or issue an instruction to Prague, we were summoned by phone. We had access to the CC building at any hour. Our names were put on a special list there, but in practice that was hardly necessary: The guards came to know us well and passed us through without a formal document check.

If any of us in the working group received new information during these meetings, he would carry it over to the CC building and take it directly into the conference room. I would come in and lay a cable or transcript of a phone message in front of Andropov.

He would scan it quickly and either pass it to Brezhnev or ask that I quickly have five copies typed. Or sometimes he would say, "This is important, Sergey Aleksandrovich. Please read it to the others." So I would stand there and read it aloud. Either way, they would usually discuss the matter while I waited and often take a quick decision then and there. Then Brezhnev would assign tasks. He would say, for instance, "This part is for KGB action and MID will take care of the rest." If the pyatërka chose immediately to compose an outgoing cable or statement, I would sit farther down the long table and write on my pad as they dictated.

A large room two doors down from the Politburo secretariat was reserved for our use, with a desk for each of us and a little round table where, if we had to miss a meal, the serving staff put delicious sandwiches and tea and coffee. Our hours were so irregular that we could call at any time for meals or snacks or drinks. Two Politburo stenographers were assigned specifically to us, but if we had too much work for them, we could always count on getting as many and as soon as needed.

Andropov was a stickler for keeping abreast of developments no matter how fast-moving. Even on the way to his office (to arrive punctually at 9:00 a.m.), he phoned from his car to key people involved in the most pressing matters of the moment so that on arrival he could instantly attend to priorities. Hardly a day passed during the Prague Spring without my receiving one of these morning calls, though I might have been twice in his office the day before or even have phoned him at home during late evening hours, as I often did.

Whenever the pyatërka met unexpectedly, Andropov made sure to be briefed in advance, which is why I got that noisy call by the river that bright summer Sunday. Leaving Rosa with our car at the beach, I was driven home to change and then to KGB headquarters. Andropov had already left for the Central Committee, but had left a note telling me the subject of this unexpected meeting. I checked with the duty officer for any new information that might have come in and dashed off to brief him.

Evidently this delay in finding me inspired Andropov to improve our communications. The very next day, technicians installed a new phone line at my apartment for direct contact with him. I was also given a new service car, this one with a telephone.

Telephones played a big role in our work. To pass the pyatër-ka's commands to Prague or to get a clarification or update on ever-changing events and questions, our Working Group was assured the instant use of secure lines kept open for us. Incoming messages from KGB representatives in Prague came by high frequency transmissions over guarded landlines or by cable addressed to either the chief of foreign intelligence or to me as his deputy.

On the scene in Prague stood several units of our service to inform us and to pass on the pyatërka's orders to other elements. One was our group of permanent advisors to the Czechoslovak state security service, who used that service's ability to get information from factories or outlying areas of the country. However, many of our most trusted collaborators in the service were moved out as the crisis grew and were replaced with reform-minded officers who were reluctant to help us.

Our chief advisor in Prague, Ivan Vorobyev, had a permanent staff of four or five members. To help them cope with the increased pressures of this period, we sent back to Prague some former advisors who knew the people and conditions there.

And beginning in the early spring of 1968, we also sent special groups into the country. We sent Mikhail Grigoryevich Kotov as our senior representative for the crisis to oversee all our officers there including Vorobyev's advisor group. Much later, my KGB colleague Yelisei Sinitsyn was sent to help him, but he operated somewhat independently as a representative not of the KGB but of the CPSU Central Committee; that added authority to his dealings with senior Czech party and government leaders.

We brought in some Illegals, too. In their guise as sympathetic businessmen or tourists from Germany or Austria or elsewhere, they got better results talking to Czechs than did our official representatives during the latent hostility of this period. (Our representatives complained that even high Czech officials were reluctant to tell them anything useful. "While professing friendship," one told me, "they wasted our time with empty generalities.") Sent out from Moscow for this specific task, these Illegals had their own communications channels—using phone lines or intermediaries for urgent reports—so their reports reached me through the Illegals Directorate.

We alerted KGB residencies everywhere to plumb every source that might enlighten us on what their governments knew, how they assessed the situation, and what they planned to do about it. As soon as an incoming cable from a residency in, say, London or Paris was recognized to bear on the Czechoslovak situation, the geographical department forwarded it to me.

• • •

AT ONE POINT, THE Moscow leadership became willing to support an effort to oust Dubcek by what we then termed "the healthy forces," those Czechoslovak Party and government leaders opposed to Dubcek's reforms. One night at a house outside the center of Moscow, where I had accompanied Andropov to a dinner meeting with KGB leaders, a phone call came from Sinitsyn in Prague.

Sinitsyn had been dealing with Gustav Husak, whom we considered one of the "healthy forces" though he pretended to be a friend and supporter of Dubcek, who elevated him to the post of vice premier. I took the call in an adjoining room. Sinitsyn told me that Husak envisaged taking power and wanted to know whether the Soviets would support him. He promised to cooperate with the USSR and normalize the situation.

I asked Andropov to meet me in the adjoining room. When I gave him Sinitsyn's message, he frowned. "We'll have to check with Brezhnev." Then and there he phoned Brezhnev at home and turned over the phone to me. I explained what Husak was proposing. Brezhnev answered, "If Yuri Vladimirovich [Andropov] is for it, I agree. Go ahead." I immediately phoned Sinitsyn with the reply. No doubt this is why Husak became party chief in place of Dubcek.

So eager were Soviet leaders to negotiate a solution that the Politburo agreed to go en masse to meet Dubcek on Czechoslovak soil at the end of July, in the border town of Cierna nad Tisou. Never before had the Politburo met abroad (and never would again). I have some thoughts—though I cannot confirm them—about what lay behind this unprecedented action: I think the pyatërka found a pretext to bring in the other Politburo members in order to spread responsibility for the decision that by now many people in high place feared would be necessary. I base this supposition on my knowledge of Andropov's foresight and acute sensitivity to political danger.

The Party leaders of the DDR, Poland, Hungary, and Bulgaria met in Bratislava a few weeks later in yet another attempt to solve the crisis (my friend Yelisei Sinitsyn representing the CC CPSU), but as in Cierna nad Tisou, they found no way to get any clear commitment from Dubcek.

At this point, the pyatërka's reliance on the "healthy forces" caused problems and delays. Should it be necessary to intervene militarily, the pyatërka had to get a written request for "fraternal assistance," a "letter of invitation" from the Czech goverment. As head of KGB operations there, Kotov served as the main channel between the "healthy forces" and the Moscow leadership. He was getting assurances from Czech officials that they could persuade Dubcek to change his line. Failing that, they promised to write the necessary letter of invitation. Kotov, perhaps naively, took them at their word and assured me they would draft and sign the letter imminently. Day after day passed, and no letter materialized. Andropov kept pressing me to get Kotov to produce it, and I in turn urged Kotov, who kept assuring me that the letter would be forthcoming at any moment. The pressure mounted. Andropov hounded me with "Where's that letter?—you told me we'd have it by now," or "I need it now!"

Tentative "letters of invitation" came, but not what the Soviet leadership felt it needed. A first one was written to Brezhnev by Antonin Kapek, but it was useless; Kapek was no more than a candidate member of the Party presidium and his letter was signed only by himself. A few days later in early August, Vasil Bilak handed to Shelest a second letter, signed by five of the "healthy forces," asking the Soviet Communist Party to "use all means at your disposal"—but not specifically mentioning military force— to "prevent the imminent threat of counterrevolution." It was too vague to be useful.[7] Ultimately, we never did receive the letter that Andropov hounded me to get during those tense August days.

In those first two weeks of August, it gradually became clear to the pyatërka that military intervention might be the only way to brake Czechoslovakia's slide. Up to that point, I had never once heard anyone use the words "military intervention." Instead, the participants even at these high level meetings, remembering the events of Hungary in 1956 and hoping that something short of invasion might still be possible, played with euphemisms like "decisive measures." To the very end, we in this inner group thought that military intervention would be undertaken only if and when the West intervened to preserve Dubcek's power.

It is well established that the decision to intervene was made on or about August 17. But exactly who made that decision—and how? As close as I was to the discussions and to the key players, one might suppose that I could answer this question, but it was a mystery to me at the time and remains so to this day. The decision was surely not taken in a session of the pyatërka, for then I would know it. I can only assume that it was made in phone conversations among Andropov, Brezhnev, and Ustinov, and with Shelest as Czechoslovakia's Ukrainian neighbor.

The military intervention itself came as a surprise to me and even to our key operatives on the spot. I have read assertions that Party leaders of Socialist states knew of the decision for weeks and even knew the date of military intervention. That is impossible. And even if desired by the "healthy forces" in Czechoslovakia, it came as a surprise to them, too.

Late in the evening August 21, one of the "healthiest" of them, Vasil Bilak, sat in Prague with Yelisei Sinitsyn discussing the chances of the "healthy forces" taking power. Neither of them even mentioned the possibility of armed intervention, Sinitsyn told me. Both thought that it would be ordered only if "certain conditions" were met. Those conditions remained vague, but Sinitsyn and Bilak (and I, too) assumed that meant Western intervention, to which we would respond with military force.

As they talked that night, the phone rang. Bilak picked up the receiver, turned pale, hung up, and turned to Sinitsyn. "Soviet forces have entered Bratislava!" Though he had practically been proposing military intervention, Bilak was clearly shocked. And Sinitsyn, feeling that something had started that could have fatal consequences for the Soviet Union, said not a word and left the room.

The Prague Spring was over.

Seventeen:
Other Places

AFTER TWENTY-TWO YEARS in the First Chief Directorate, Sergey Kondrashev was moved out—or, more accurately, sideways. It was the result of his own success: the climbing pole had narrowed at the top.

By 1974 he had earned high regard as one of the FCD's top operators, supervisors, and linguists. Counting in his favor were his earlier years of success in counterintelligence. He was considered as one of the KGB's "intellectuals" as distinguished from mere "practitioners." He had handled a historically important mole inside British Intelligence. He had long headed the KGB's work against Germany, a prime target, and managed two of its major stations abroad. He had achieved notable success with worldwide active measures in support of Soviet foreign policy. He had worked closely and successfully with some of the KGB's most notable figures and chiefs. He had long been seen as headed to the very top.

Then one day in early 1974, Chairman Yuri Andropov called Sergey, one of three deputy FCD chiefs, into his office. "I think you should know," he said, "that Mortin will soon be leaving. I know that will not upset you unduly"—Andropov was aware that Kondrashev, like others, despised the FCD Chief Mortin—"but I am appointing [First Deputy FCD Chief Vladimir] Kryuchkov to replace him. And I don't think you will be able to work very happily under Kryuchkov."

Andropov was right: Kryuchkov saw colleagues like Kondrashev as rivals. He was jealous of any with long experience in the intelligence business into which he, a Party worker, had been inserted near the top. He had taken every opportunity to edge his fellow deputy Sergey aside, upstaging him and opposing his positions.

But why at this point had Andropov selected this Party functionary instead of a long-time professional? For some reason Andropov had long been carrying Kryuchkov along with him, as administrative assistant in the Party organization to the Embassy in Budapest and back to the Party then on into the KGB. But to start him as deputy chief of Foreign Intelligence and then to elevate him to its command seemed contrary to Andropov's clear-headed appointments. I asked Sergey, "Did Kryuchkov have something on Andropov?" Instead of denying the possibility, Sergey simply shrugged, leaving the implication that my question was relevant.

However, Andropov offered Kondrashev a way around the problem—transfer to the Chief Directorate of Border Guards as deputy chief and head of intelligence, with promotion to two-star general's rank (the same that Kryuchkov would assume as FCD chief). Andropov stressed the importance of the new job and the need there for Sergey's experience and talents to improve cross-border operations. With no real choice, Kondrashev accepted.

The new job held fascinations. Kondrashev reminisced with enthusiasm about his visits to far-flung border posts, which were handling spies across the frontiers while keeping a sharp eye on their own internal regions. He travelled as far as the

Kondrashev as a two-star general in 1974 shortly after his appointment as Deputy Chief of the Chief Directorate of Border Guards.

Chupchi Peninsula on the narrow straits of the Bering Sea across from Alaska. He toured the frontiers of Iran and Afghanistan and the thousands of miles of border with China and Mongolia. His anecdotes were redolent of exotic foods and smells, with moments of danger and suspense. One day, his border patrol boat played "chicken" with an oncoming Chinese vessel; both were plying the exact river center that each considered to be his own territory. Kondrashev readied guns for battle, but at the last minute the Chinese veered. As they brushed alongside, the Chinese captain and Kondrashev exchanged respectful salutes.

The borders he was inspecting had their bloody histories. For many years, Chinese troops had made incursions deep into Soviet territory to be met first with written warnings, then warning shots, and when the incursions continued, shooting to kill. Soviet border troops hung the corpses of an entire Chinese platoon side by side at a railway station close to the border. Sergey told of his men's days-long hunt through a wild, wooded ravine for two missing Iranian border patrollers—and finding only those body parts that had been left uneaten by wolves.

Kondrashev's forces contributed to Moscow's efforts to destabilize China. Small units would clandestinely enter western Chinese territory to plant small "tower-like" transmitters to broadcast, in the local dialect, calls for autonomy from Beijing's rule. A message or two would draw Chinese radio-location efforts, so Kondrashev's men would slip back in, take the towers and replant them at distant points to broadcast again, to convey the impression of a widespread and active internal-Chinese separatist movement. The operation lasted only about six months, however, after running out of convincing broadcast material.

Such colorful tales would have found their place in Kondrashev's autobiography but here they rate only a short summary, for much of his short four-year stint in the Border Guards was spent elsewhere. KGB Chairman Andropov kept calling him away for special assignments like the Helsinki process described in the next chapter.

• • •

SERGEY KONDRASHEV'S NEXT OFFICIAL posting again came from Andropov's personal initiative. Tiring of interrupting Kondrashev's service in the Border Guards, the KGB Chairman simply moved him closer in.

Andropov had come into the KGB at the top in 1967 and quickly recognized his need for advice from experienced subordinates. Within months he called on Kondrashev to support him during the Prague Spring crisis. So strongly did he feel that need that he turned top-level consultation into a permanent function, establishing a full-time group of "Senior Consultants to the Chairman." Starting with two highly-experienced veterans, he added others when needed, sometimes having as many as four at a time, each with a designated field of specialty based on past experience. One was designated chief.

In 1978 he told Kondrashev, "I want you as my chief senior consultant." He handed Sergey the fields that most interested him: intelligence and foreign policy, replacing the retiring chief consultant Aleksandr Sakharovskiy.

This position required Kondrashev to prepare the KGB Chairman's participation in every Politburo meeting that dealt with national security matters, drafting his statements and preparing supporting materials. Andropov assigned Sergey ever-varying tasks, from accompanying Foreign Minister Gromyko to the United Nations General Assembly in New York in November 1978, to conducting months-long international negotiations under the Helsinki Final Act.

Kondrashev willingly described those tasks, but not the spy and counterspy operations he oversaw from this position. He mentioned only one, and that only obliquely.

Chatting about something else during one of our "off-duty" walks, Kondrashev mentioned that he had been asked for any precise expressions, formats, or word-sequences used in certain American government correspondence. The KGB's cipher-breakers had evidently gained access to enciphered materials and were looking for "cribs," those routinely-repeated formulations that can offer them a first break. That Sergey was asked at this late date for such personal knowledge suggested to me that he must have dealt with a lot of intercepted or purloined American correspondence in the thirty years since he had recruited the American code clerk "Jack." But he did not tell; this would find no place in his autobiography, and I was left to wonder what US agency the KGB was targeting in that particular cipher-breaking effort.

Kondrashev continued in this extraordinary post until his retirement in 1992 after the collapse of the Soviet Union, serving three more KGB chairmen (including Kryuchkov) after Andropov moved up to become First Secretary of the Party. On the occasion of Andropov's move, he called together the entire high command of the KGB for a farewell photo session in May 1982. This is one of the pictures taken that day, as part of Sergey's contribution to the public history of the KGB.

SPYMASTER

The high command of the KGB in May 1982. Kondrashev is second from the right in the third row.
Front row, left to right: KGB Party Committee chief, Aleksandr Borisovich Suplatov; Deputy Chairman Mikhail Ivanovich Yermakov; First Deputy (later Chairman) Viktor Mikhailovich Chebrikov; just-appointed Chairman Vitaly Vasilyevich Fedorchuk; departing Chairman Yuri Vladimirovich Andropov; First Deputy Chairman Georgiy Karpovich Tsinev; Deputy Chairman Nikolai Pavlovich Yemokhonov; Deputy Chairman Vladimir Petrovich Pirozhkov.
Second row: Chief of Moscow KGB Viktor Ivanovich Alidin; Chief of Border Guards Vadim Aleksandrovich Matrosov; head of Personnel Directorate Vasiliy Yakovlevich Lezhepikov; Chief of the 5th Directorate Filipp Denisovich Bobkov; Chief of the 1st Chief Directorate Vladimir Aleksandrovich Kryuchkov; Chief of 2nd Chief Directorate Grigoriy Fedorovich Grigorenko; Chief of 15th Chief Directorate (Security of Government Installations) Sergey Nikolayevich Antonov; Chief of 4th Directorate (Transport) Geniy Yevgenyevich Ageyev; Chief of 3rd Chief Directorate (Military Counterintelligence) Nikolai Alekseevich Dushin; Chief of KGB Leningrad Daniil Pavlovich Nosyrev.
Third row: chief of 1st Department of 3rd Chief Directorate (Military Counterintelligence) Vasily Stepanovich Sergeyev; Chief of the Economic Directorate Kirill Borisovich Vostrikov; Chief of the 12th Department of Operational Technical Directorate (eavesdropping) Yuri Sergeyevich Plekhanov; Chief of 9th Directorate (government protection) Yuri Vasilyevich Storozhev; Chief of Operational Technical Directorate Viktor Pavlovich Demin; Chief of Inspectorate Sergey Vasilyevich Tolkunov; Chief of 7th Directorate (Surveillance) Yevgeniy Mikhailovich Rashchepov; chief of Investigation Department Aleksandr Fedorovich Volkov; Chief Consultant to KGB Chairman, Sergey Aleksandrovich Kondrashev; head of the KGB Secretariat Yevgeniy Dmitriyevich Karpeshchenko.
Fourth row: Consultant to KGB Chairman, Viktor Vasilyevich Sharapov; personal assistant to Chairman Andropov, Pavel Pavlovich Laptev; head of Andropov's personal protection Yevgeniy Ivanovich Kalgin; Chief of Communications Directorate Yuri Aleksandrovich Tolmachev; head of the KGB Higher School Arkady Pavlovich Ragozin; Consultant to KGB Chairman, Vladimir G. Mityayev; Chief of 16th Directorate (SIGINT Interception) Igor Vasilyevich Maslov; chief of Finance and Planning Department Boris Georgyevich Peshcherskiy.

Eighteen:
The Irony of Helsinki

BEHIND THE HELSINKI Final Act of 1975 lies a momentous irony in which Sergey Kondrashev played a central role.

The Kremlin leaders had, by the 1970s, finally persuaded the West to accept a proposal they had been making for nearly twenty years: a conference to create a "European" security system. They calculated this would reduce American influence on the continent and also put a final, formal stamp of legitimacy on the borders that their military forces had created in the war: They had taken three Baltic states, half of prewar Poland, and chunks of Czechoslovakia, Hungary, and Romania.

Now in June and early July of 1973 in Helsinki, representatives of thirty-five countries were preparing this long-sought conference. However, by this time, the Western powers were insisting that to stabilize the peace a conference would have to do more than merely certify the politico-military status quo. Other sources of international tension, economic and cultural and social, must also be addressed. And to this, if they were to achieve their underlying aims, the Soviets had to agree. So the planners in Helsinki were piling a host of such matters onto the conference agenda.

Those intervening twenty years had changed the Soviet Union, too. Beneath the surface of growing military might and aggressive diplomacy, internal pressures had been building. The decline of the already shaky Soviet economy had been accelerated by, the rising costs of a seemingly endless arms race with the West. The Soviet Union's nationalities and the populations of its satellite regimes in Eastern Europe had become restive to the point of riots and uprisings; despite harsh repressions, its dissidents kept calling for social justice and human rights.

This Conference on Security and Cooperation in Europe (CSCE), planned in Helsinki, assembled in Geneva in 1973. For two years, there the participating nations wrestled with all of these complex and disputed matters until finally on August 15, 1975, their leaders came together back in Helsinki to sign the end product.

The "Helsinki Final Act"[1] called for follow-up meetings to assess how the participating states were carrying out its provisions and, if necessary, to amend its terms. This "Helsinki process" became firmly established in the first few of these meetings—in Belgrade 1977–78, Madrid 1980–1983, and Vienna 1986–1989—and by 1995 had evolved into a permanent organization, OSCE, which by today counts a staff of thousands.

In three of the Final Act's ten "Principles," Moscow got what it had originally sought: respect for sovereignty, inviolability of existing frontiers, and the territorial integrity of states. However, Principle 7 committed the participants to "respect for human rights and fundamental freedoms, including the freedom of thought, conscience, religion or belief"—and "the Helsinki process" was going to watch them doing it.

Principle 7 struck hard at Soviet ruling practices. It obliged signatories to "facilitate freer movement and contacts . . . allowing persons to enter or leave their territory . . . in order to visit [. . . or] be reunited with members of their families"—unthinkable in the walled-off East German context. It further demanded that they "facilitate wider travel by their citizens for personal or professional reasons" and ease "the procedures for exit and entry." It called for easing the travel and contacts of foreign journalists and "freer and wider dissemination of information of all kinds" including scientific research, books, newspapers and publications, films, and broadcasts from the other participating states.

Accordingly, while granting the desired legitimacy to the postwar borders, the Helsinki Final Act carried a dangerous side effect: It put heavy pressures on Soviet rule. It spawned an international forum meeting every few years to judge whether and how governments were abiding by their commitments, and it spawned organizations for "Helsinki Watch" that heartened and coordinated dissidence.[2] To the extent that these pressures contributed to the collapse of the Soviet Union sixteen years later, that side effect was to prove fatal.

It is ironic that such a menace should have sprung from an initiative of the Soviet regime itself. But it is even more ironic that its most threatening terms—those that had been debated and shaped in "Basket Three"[3]—were negotiated by the Soviet regime's prime defender, the KGB itself, embodied by its Chairman Yuri Andropov using Sergey Kondrashev as his prime instrument.

• • •

ANDROPOV HAD COME TO know and respect Kondrashev. When the Hungarians revolted in 1956, Kondrashev was one of the special KGB group in Budapest keeping Ambassador Andropov informed on the scene. When Andropov came to head the KGB in 1967, he had frequently called in Kondrashev to discuss KGB support of Soviet foreign policy, and in the Prague crisis of 1968, Andropov took him for support within the Politburo itself.[4]

So in 1974 when Andropov felt the need to replace his representative in the Geneva "Helsinki" negotiations, he turned to Sergey

Kondrashev. The predecessor, Igor S. Rozanov, imbued with the KGB's mission of preserving Kremlin control, viewed any concessions on "human rights" as dangerously weakening it. When Rozanov heard his Geneva Delegation Chief Anatoly Kovalev talking such concessions with the American chief delegate, he denounced him to Andropov for "sacrificing the vital interests of the country." Exasperated by Rozanov's failure to understand the changed needs of the time, Andropov recalled him at the Geneva conference's summer break and called in Kondrashev to take his place.

"I trust your judgment," Andropov told Sergey. "With your experience abroad you know how to deal with Western officials. With your experience in counterintelligence you understand our problems and you know the limits, how not to rock the boat too far." Andropov added, "But you understand, too, that we must make progress in human rights—we are doomed if we don't."

"Here is how we will proceed," Andropov went on. "When a text is being proposed, you accept or oppose it as you see fit. If you think I should decide, let me know privately what you propose. If I do not respond within three or four days, you can take it for granted that I agree with your position." He was giving Sergey, in essence, *carte blanche* to go along with Western proposals, even those that might be seen to dent the Soviet control system, but also to block any that dented it too deeply.

"I understood," Sergey told me, "that I was being made personally responsible for the texts adopted, and for their compliance with the requirements of our state security." In the event he did refer some proposals to Andropov in the months that followed, either personally or through his assistant, and invariably received tacit approval.

Although the two men kept the details of their arrangement secret, it was clear to all Soviet delegates negotiating human-rights matters both in Geneva and in the later follow-up conferences that Kondrashev had the last word. While the Geneva Delegation Chief Anatoly Kovalev found Kondrashev's direct line to Andropov helpful,[5] others in the delegation were irritated by it and a few even took occasions to humiliate him in the presence of foreign delegates. However, no one could challenge his authority. As Sergey pointed out to me, "They knew that my agreement for every text—or better said, the agreement of the KGB—was indispensable."

Andropov was rightly confident that Kondrashev supported his views of what concessions the Soviets could and could not bear. No one was more aware than Andropov of the pitfalls underlying the human-rights provisions; he had dealt with the crises in Hungary and Prague. But at the same time no one knew better than Andropov how badly Soviet society needed reform: His KGB was the only Soviet institution that systematically studied the true state of public opinion. Soviet society needed the Helsinki-related reforms that Kondrashev was negotiating,[6] and Andropov also thought these reforms could be adopted without undermining Soviet rule.

When Kondrashev was in Moscow between Geneva negotiating sessions, Andropov called him in to compliment him ("you are working well"), and after the Final Act was signed, he thanked Sergey for his contributions, decorated him with the "Order of the Friendship of Peoples," and assigned him to carry on the job in the follow-up conferences in Belgrade and Madrid.

The American delegation chief, Ambassador Max Kampelman, noticed Kondrashev's special role. Already when his Soviet opposite number at the 1980–83 Madrid meetings came to meet Kampelman, he "brought with him their number two man Sergey Kondrashev, who . . . ran the delegation." As the months passed in Madrid, Kampelman learned to "enjoy Kondrashev because of his impressive skill as director of the Soviet working team."[7] And to arrange "the release of a significant number of imprisoned political and religious activists from the Soviet Union," Kampelman turned first to Kondrashev who then "became the key player for the Soviets."[8]

Kondrashev was working outside of regular channels when he assisted these American human-rights initiatives. He warned Kampelman in Madrid "to keep our talks private even in Washington and to talk to nobody else in our [Soviet] delegation about our discussions, not even to my head of delegation." To Kampelman the message was clear: "the KGB was in charge and was the direct channel to Andropov" (who by this time had succeeded Brezhnev at the head of the Soviet Union). It was Andropov—and Sergey Kondrashev—who were making the process work.[9]

• • •

LOOKING BACK MANY YEARS later, although taking pride in having promoted human rights in his country, Kondrashev saw the Kremlin's agreement to the human rights provisions of the Helsinki Final Act as a "major miscalculation." He was no doubt right. The Helsinki accord called world attention to the Soviet failure to conform to international standards. It showed to all that the Soviet system was out of touch with present realities—that it had worn out. It gave impetus to demands for drastic change that led in Eastern Europe to the creation of powerful movements like Solidarity in Poland and Charter 77 in Czechoslovakia. It bestowed legitimacy on the dissidence in the Soviet Union that brought on Mikhail Gorbachev's loosening controls under "glasnost'" and "perestroika." And it was to the haste of those reforms that Kondrashev attributed the Soviet downfall. The economy was not keeping pace and the people were not yet ready for them. Had Andropov lived on, Kondrashev felt sure, he would have introduced even more freedom—but at a slower and more bearable pace.

"Helsinki" was indeed ironic—a result opposite to what was expected or intended.

Nineteen:
Watching It End

AS COMMUNIST RULE crumbled in Eastern Europe in 1989, Sergey Kondrashev carried a poignant message to the Soviet leadership in Moscow that foreshadowed its doom.

By mid-summer the Polish regime had legalized opposition, Hungary had torn down border fences, and huge demonstrations in Romania, Bulgaria, and Czechoslovakia called for change. Soviet leader Mikhail Gorbachev had renounced the Brezhnev Doctrine that had given the Kremlin the final word, leaving Warsaw Pact countries to shape their own destinies.

In East Germany, too, growing dissidence would within weeks take the form of great demonstrations. Long hemmed in by the Berlin Wall and deadly border defenses, its people had begun to use Hungary as an escape route. The DDR's Communist rulers hesitated, hoping that Moscow's huge military forces in East Germany would somehow restore order in their "Warsaw Pact." However, Kremlin leaders looked on as if paralyzed, though they sensed how tightly their own fate was linked to that of the DDR.

In August, Sergey Kondrashev, chief consultant to the KGB Chairman, was in Berlin meeting with Markus Wolf and other HVA leaders when he was called to the phone. On the line was his longtime associate, the East German Security (Stasi) Chief Erich Mielke, calling from Cottbus near the Polish border. "I have to see you urgently," Mielke said. "I'm coming back tonight and will come see you tomorrow morning. I must talk to you—and alone."

The next morning, Mielke appeared at the KGB Berlin–Karlshorst office, flustered and an hour and a half ahead of schedule. Catching his breath, he told Kondrashev, "Take notes, please, and carefully."

"I want you to tell [KGB Chairman] Kryuchkov, who then must immediately tell Gorbachev, that if you persist in your present passivity in the face of what is going on in Poland, Hungary, and Czechoslovakia, then I must tell you that the DDR is doomed. We're under gigantic pressure from the West. And make it clear that I am speaking with full authority on behalf of the entire Politburo."

Kondrashev flew back to Moscow the next morning and saw Kryuchkov immediately. He carefully quoted Mielke's statement, but Kryuchkov insisted on having it in writing. Sergey dictated to Kryuchkov's secretary who typed the transcript. "Sign it," Kryuchkov ordered, then went to see Gorbachev.

That evening, Kondrashev phoned while Kryuchkov was still in his office. "Well, what was the result?"

"Gorbachev read it," Kryuchkov replied, "but all he said was, 'Leave it with me, I'll think it over.' Since then, I've heard nothing."

In fact, as the KGB and Gorbachev knew all too well, the plea had come too late. "All our best sources," Kondrashev told me, "were telling us that it was no longer possible to keep Germany divided." World public opinion was unmistakable: The cost to the Soviet Union of any military effort to restore order in the area would far outweigh any benefits—even though those at the top sensed that the survival of the Soviet Union itself was in jeopardy.

Within weeks, huge demonstrations started in Leipzig and other East German cities. And on November 4th a great crowd assembled on the Alexanderplatz in the heart of East Berlin and wildly cheered as leading dissidents spoke. They hissed down Markus Wolf, who had taken a microphone to express sympathy with their demands.

Phone calls from KGB officers in Moscow and abroad flooded into Kondrashev's office in Moscow, all worriedly asking, "What's going on there? What's going to happen? What will our army do?"

The Army did nothing.

The East German regime dissolved, and two years later, in December 1991, so did the Soviet Union.

Epilogue

ONLY MONTHS AFTER the Soviet Union dissolved, Sergey Kondrashev retired from the now "Russian" KGB, after serving its Soviet incarnation from before the Cold War started until after it ended nearly a half-century later.

A few years later, he set out to write his story of that extraordinary era. But was that possible? How, while remaining discreet and loyal, could he recount such a secret life without revealing secrets? He tried, drafting and redrafting and typing hundreds of pages, but he could never get beneath broad generalities and never told anything that was not already widely known. Afterwards, he and I were able together to pull some stories out from behind their veil of KGB secrecy, as the previous chapters demonstrate, but in today's Russia, even that was too much. The KGB in its surviving guise as SVR and FSB blacked it all out.

Kondrashev threw up his hands, bowing before Putin's censors as he had bowed before Stalin, Khrushchev, Brezhnev, and Andropov. He was a proud patriot who despised defectors; he would not reveal undiscovered spies or compromise his status among his former colleagues by telling more than he should.

Had Sergey not died and left it to me to make his contribution to history, the matters in this book would have remained hidden.

He wanted to reveal the misdeeds of the system he had served and how it had destroyed the morals and cohesion of society. He loathed the cruelty and brutality of its leaders, who had "gained power more by bribery, backstabbing, toadyism, and favoritism than by knowledge and competence." He had known close-up some of the most infamous, like Lavrenty Tsanava and "Vasily the Dark" Ryasnoy, and he was disgusted by their ignorance, their indifference to the feelings of others, their sadism, petty wilfulness and crude blunders. He was repelled by the repressive work of the KGB's internal-security side in which he himself had participated at the start of his career.

But Sergey had evidently made internal peace with this system, taking it as a fact of life, and he served a lifetime in its central executor, the KGB. He chose to look aside from its tortures and persecutions, comforting himself with the thought that he had not personally participated in them. He regarded most of his leaders and colleagues as tools inescapably enmeshed in its doings, even as its victims. He chose to assess them in terms of their professional competence (or incompetence), their personal character, and their relationship to himself. Whereas Viktor Abakumov, wartime SMERSH chief and immediate postwar Minister of State Security, is infamous for the scale of his personal looting of just-defeated Germany, Sergey saw him as "guiltless of any misconduct." While historians chronicle Abakumov's killings and misdeeds, Sergey chose to highlight Abakumov's close concern with the details of counterintelligence operations, his efficiency, his quick grasp of situations, his personal consideration for his officers, and the "well-deserved" respect and esteem they felt for him. Sergey saw his friend and former boss Leonid Raikhman as a gracious and honest man and competent operative, not as one partly responsible for the Katyn massacre.

Sergey explained his loyalty simply: "Nobody chooses the time and country of his birth. I was born after the Communists had taken over. I was educated when Stalin was in power. If I was to work at all, I could only work in the political and social system that Stalin had created." He saw his KGB work as serving his country, Russia, not its ruling Party or ideology.

As a result of that loyalty, the events and personalities described in this book are all, and a bit more, that Sergey Kondrashev felt he could contribute to the public history of the regime he served throughout the Cold War.

Even these have been denied publication in Putin's Russia. That history is still waiting to be written.

Appendix: A Surprising Background, for a KGB Leader

ALMOST AS ASTONISHING as the rise of a scion of a titled family of Tsarist industrialists to high levels in the KGB is the rise of his forebears from serfdom to fortune.

The family saga began eight generations earlier. Its founder was a serf named Kondrat, who made silk textiles on the estates of his master, Prince Trubetskoy. Its first written record dates from 1758 when police on the outskirts of Saint Petersburg reported that they had arrested Kondrat on suspicion of theft because he was driving a cart heavily loaded with those rich materials. It is also recorded that the prince had certified the driver and goods as his own property, doing his own business, and so ordered Kondrat's release.

So distinctively had Kondrat designed and woven those fabrics and so successfully did he pass his skills on to the next generation that his two sons Fyodor and Kirill were among the first fifteen serfs known to have been freed in Russia, a full century before Tsar Alexander II decreed the end of serfdom. They took their father's name as the family name Kondrashev. (Fyodor was the direct ancestor of Sergey.)

Authorized to manufacture textiles on their own, they expanded from small-scale home weaving to take a place among the founders of the Russian textile industry. They and their descendants built factories in the towns of Friasino and Shchelkovo as well as in

Moscow itself, employing hundreds of workers and producing items whose quality came to be recognized beyond the borders of Russia. A decree of 1845 granted the family the hereditary title of "Honorable Citizen of the Russian Empire" that elevated them to the nobility of service, one of two categories in the Russian nobility (the other was nobility of land).

The family amassed a fortune from their textile manufacture and acquired landed property in their region to the northeast of Moscow around Sergiyev-Posad, Friasino, Shchelkovo, Grebnevo, and Raiky. Sergey's grandfather Sergey Fyodorovich Kondrashev lived on the estate in Raiky where Sergey's father Aleksandr was born.

Near the village of Grebnevo lay another estate belonging to the family, with vast acreage surrounding a palatial manor house. "I might have inherited it, under a different regime," Sergey once mused. "But," he added with a grin, "I would never have had the money to keep it up." In the village, his great-grandfather built an imposing church where plaques still commemorate his ancestors and where nine of them lie entombed.

Grebnevo became a place of reflection for Kondrashev after the Communist era. While it stirred his pride in the eight generations of competent and hard-working forebears who had built and created beautiful things, it also reminded him of how his parents could never admit this noble past—even to their own family.

And it stirred feelings of patriotism. As Sergey told of his ancestor Mikhail Kirillovich Kondrashev, who had gathered together a guer-

The manor of Kondrashev's ancestors near Grebnovo, and the church built in the town by his great-grandfather. Foreground: Sergey Kondrashev with family group.

rilla detachment to defend this region against Napoleon's invading army, I could sense his feeling of identification with that patriot. He chose to regard his long life in the KGB as having primarily served his native land, not the Soviet Communism that ruled it in his time.

"But I had other thoughts there when I looked at the marble staircase," Sergey added with disgust. Vandals had wrecked it and it stood to him as a symbol of how the Communist regime had taught people more to destroy than to create.

• • •

SERGEY WAS BORN ON March 1, 1923, in nearby Sergiyev-Posad. His grandfather Sergey Fyodorovich Kondrashev, who had moved there from Raiky in the last years of the nineteenth century, hired a carpenter skilled in the fine workmanship for which the area was famous to build him a house. It was in that house that Sergey was born.

In one respect, Sergiev-Posad was a typically rustic provincial city. Its streets were filled in the morning by cows being driven out to the pastures and again in the evening when they returned. In no other way, however, could it be called typical or rustic. Sergiev-Posad had stood since the fourteenth century as an important center of religion and culture. Behind walls so high and thick that they resisted even the fiercely determined Mongol invaders, rose great churches and a world-famous monastery that for centuries had made the town a major seat of Russian Orthodoxy and the residence of the Patriarch. Sergey was baptized in the Cathedral of the Trinity and St. Sergius, and it is no coincidence that like so many children of that place he bore the saint's name.

Sergiyev-Posad

Because Sergiyev-Posad lay on a rail line, goods destined for or arriving from Moscow were stored alongside the tracks in a depot that still stands today. In charge of the whole complex of the station, depot, and surrounding properties was Sergey's grandfather, who was introduced into the business by his father Fyodor Nikitich, who had headed the Moscow regional railroad administration.[1]

Young Sergey learned much of this family lore from his grandmother Yulia Ivanovna, a shining and enduring influence on his life. He described her as very religious, the embodiment of goodness, never angry, who instilled in him a sense of the value of family and friendship.

Yuliana Ivanovna Kondrasheva

From his father, too, came glimpses of this family history, but only glimpses. One day when Sergey was about ten, while walking along Gavrikov Lane in the Sokolniki district of Moscow, his father pointed to a large brick factory building. "That used to be a textile factory, Seryozha, and it was built and owned by your grandfather's family."

The remark was Sergey's first inkling of this aspect of the family background, but his father didn't go on. As he later came to understand, those were dangerous years when former property owners were killed or sent off to the camps. His father wanted his sons to know something, but not enough to risk their future by an indiscretion. When Sergey's grandmother reminisced about her married life on the estate in Raiky, his father would cut her off. It was better that children didn't know such things.[2]

Sergey's mother Anna's family had also suffered from the Bolshevik revolution. Her father Sergey Sergeyevich Bocharov managed a merchant enterprise as befitted coming from a family of rich merchants and guildsmen. As such, he was thrust after the October Revolution into the swollen ranks of the *lishentsy*, those "deprived" of property and basic civil rights. The term connotes hardship and in practice meant far worse. Bocharov's house and all his possessions were confiscated, and he was forced to earn his living by selling milk products on trains. Nevertheless, he lived to old age and died in the 1960s.

But the apprehension Sergey felt later whenever he filled out an *anketa* (questionnaire) centered not so much on these bourgeois ancestors as on his own father, Aleksandr Sergeyevich Kondrashev. Though he had every reason to be proud of his father, general knowledge of his life would have wrecked Sergey's career chances.

Aleksandr Kondrashev had been an officer. Because of his inherited title he was accepted in 1913 into the privileged and prestigious Aleksandrovskoye Military College in St. Petersburg, named for its founder, the Tsar Aleksandr I. He had trained there with the goal of fighting the war and making a career as an officer in one the Imperial Army's two guards regiments, either the Tsar's Own Lefortovo Regiment or the Grand Duke's Preobrazhenskiy Regiment.

Aleksandr graduated in the spring of 1917, a year that changed more than the young man's fate. The tsar he planned to serve had been deposed, and the young lieutenant was sent to

Sergey's father (front row, center) at graduation, one of a group of five new lieutenants proudly holding the straight swords that only the Aleksandrovsky graduates carried (other officers carried sabers).

261

remote Kazakhstan to fight guerrillas, an assignment that probably saved his life. In the turmoil following the Bolshevik October Revolution a few months later, he managed in this distant region to leave the army by routine procedures in February of 1918.

Aleksandr put his past behind him, hiding it deeper by moving with his family to Moscow. Like Sergey later, Aleksandr worried every time he had to give biographical details in personnel questionnaires. Not daring to work at any large, well-established Soviet enterprise that would check his answers, he had to be content with a less visible position as planner in a small Moscow construction firm, while his wife got employment in the State Bank. He did not dare apply for Party membership, with the job opportunities that brought; while not being a member was a handicap, it was far worse to have it on one's record that one had been turned down. His future thus circumscribed, Aleksandr thought of emigrating as some of his relatives and close friends had done, but he was unwilling to leave his father whose health was declining. Instead, Sergey's parents decided to make themselves a place in the new society. To hide the traces of their compromising past and with Sergey's future in mind, they moved away from Sergiyev-Posad just before he was to enter school—better for him to lose a year of schooling than all promise for the future.

• • •

MOVING TO MOSCOW IN 1930, the Kondrashevs began new lives. Neither their assumed status nor the size of their family merited an apartment, even if apartments had been plentiful, so they took what they could find for the four of them (Sergey's grandmother accompanied them): a single room in a three-bedroom apartment in the center of the city. Five years after their arrival, Sergey's younger brother Leonid was born, and the enlarged family finally got a small two-room apartment of their own in the Sokolniki district.

By 1939, Sergey's year's delay in starting school began to cause worries. War was brewing, and he might not have time to finish the ten years of the pre-university school system. However, he used all his free time preparing for a double load of examinations, and managed to finish the last two school years in one, graduating at age seventeen in 1940.

That autumn, with the help of his mother Anna who had by then become an influential employee of the Ministry of Aviation Production, Kondrashev was accepted in the Moscow Aviation Institute, one of the two top engineering institutions in the country.

Sergey Kondrashev had completed one year of study when, in June of 1941, the Germans attacked the Soviet Union, and so was not called to arms because MAI students were exempted from military service. His father, however, had no choice. Not only was it in the family tradition to defend Russia, but the recruitment office learned (in files happily never checked by Sergey's later employers) that he had military experience from the First World War and so in his late forties he joined the Moscow volunteer division (*Narodnogo Opolcheniya*), a ragtag militia without enough rifles to go around, whose soldiers wore thin black coats ill suited for Russia's notorious winter cold and, instead of military boots, low civilian shoes with puttees. Off he went to the trenches west of Moscow, ill clad and constantly exposed to the terrible winter. His lungs had been weakened by tuberculosis in his youth, and in that harsh winter of 1941–1942 Aleksandr fell ill and died of pneumonia on June 26.

Life in Moscow was hard. German planes were bombing almost daily during the first months of the war. By autumn the city was short of heating fuel, and the Kondrashevs' apartment building had none. Water froze even inside the apartment even though there was still gas in the kitchen stove and the electric lights worked albeit with interruptions. Food was scarce, and the Kondrashevs were never free of gnawing hunger.

Soon after her husband's death Sergey's mother was offered an assignment to head the financial department of an aircraft plant the Russians were building for the Chinese in Sinkiang. Although "temporary" separations in this wartime turbulence often became final, Sergey urged her to go. Anna agreed, taking his little brother Leonid and their grandmother with her. Sergey stayed alone in the Moscow apartment.

Three months after the German attacks began, MAI students were transferred to practical work in an aircraft engine factory that, luckily for Sergey, was not far from the apartment. They worked in twelve-hour shifts, one week at night, the next in daytime, with only an occasional Sunday free. The work with machine tools was laborious and dangerous because of the lack of safety precautions. Inside the building the temperatures usually rose to 104 degrees Fahrenheit near the foundry. Sergey would emerge from this heat and trudge home in the winter cold, exhausted and filthy because the plant had no facilities for washing, and boil water for tea to get some warmth back into his body.

To make the world seem even colder, there was never enough to eat. As a factory worker Sergey was rationed twenty-eight (soon to be reduced to twenty-one) ounces of bread a day, mostly low quality black rye bread filled out with bulk additives of no nutritional value, and this was often his only food. In October, all supplies of foodstuffs into the capital were cut off, and everyone was told to go pick up one pood (an old Russian measure of weight amounting to about thirty-five pounds) of wheat grain. After work Sergey would cook his grain into porridge.

"I remember still, sharply, the wonderful days when I could really eat," Sergey said. About once a month on Sundays, he hopped on a train going northward to visit his mother's sister Katya and her husband Valentin Galitskiy at a railroad stop called Iksha. Because Uncle Valentin was doing strategically important work, heading an enterprise supplying Moscow with lumber for building and firewood for heating, he was getting more food. Fifty years later, by then in his mid-nineties, he and Sergey were still reminiscing about those Sunday visits when simple sausages and potatoes and soup had seemed to Sergey like manna from the gods.

Conditions further deteriorated as the German armies neared. Government offices and main industries were evacuated to the east. When MAI was moved to Alma-Ata in Kazakhstan, Sergey chose to stay in Moscow in his factory job, studying part-time at the Stankin Institute for Machine Tools and Instruments while keeping a line of communication open to his mother and little brother in China.

"In those days," Sergey remembered, "I resented Stalin. So did everyone around me." The Russians had seen him senselessly destroying churchmen, farmers, military officers, intellectuals, and even his fellow Party leaders. "I thought a German occupation could hardly be worse."

But by the time the German armies reached the outskirts of Moscow this mood had changed, largely due to the Germans themselves. Again and again Sergey heard of their atrocities against peaceful people in the areas they occupied. Now popular resistance was stirred by a Pravda article by Ilya Ehrenburg entitled "Kill Germans!" They are not human beings, it claimed, not one of them is innocent; everyone must kill every German he comes upon, even women. This bloodthirsty message rang in Russian ears like an echo of Prince Aleksandr Nevsky's historic call to resist the Teutonic

Knights, "Rise, Russians, rise and fight the enemy!" then fresh in everyone's mind from Sergey Eisenstein's recent movie. This shift in attitude caught the Germans by surprise, Sergey thought, just when they had begun to think the Russians were finished.

As Moscow prepared for the worst, help came in the form of large, winter-ready military forces from the Far East. "This vital reinforcement was the direct result of an intelligence operation," Sergey reminded me, "although of course I didn't know it at the time." The Soviet high command had been able to shift huge numbers of winter-trained Siberian troops because a secret operative named Richard Sorge in Tokyo had given assurance that the Japanese would not attack the Russian Far East. As we have seen, Kondrashev was later able to restore Sorge to his rightful place in Soviet history after decades of neglect and discredit.[3] "I thought of it as thanking Sorge posthumously for saving my life in 1941–1942."

Soviet forces assembled north of Moscow for a counter-attack, and in months of great battles pushed the German forces back from the immediate surroundings of Moscow. Conditions improved: studies resumed in schools and in some higher institutes. Kondrashev began receiving food parcels from his mother in China carried by travellers to Moscow. And in 1944, his mother, brother, and grandmother returned from China laden with butter, honey and other foodstuffs. The worst was over—the worst of war in Moscow, at least.

It was at this point that a family friend suggested that Sergey's languages be put to work. Thus began his move toward the KGB.

Notes

Preface

[1] This enthusiastic chef was then writing a book about *The Secrets of Russian Cooking*. Markus Wolf, *Geheimnisse der Russischen Küche* (Hamburg: Rotbuch Verlag, 1995).

[2] *War of the Wolves* [the French version *La Guerre des Loups*], film by Maurice Najman and Jean-Michel Meurisse, shown on French television channel FR-3 in three parts in September 1994.

[3] *Bons Baisers de Berlin* (From Berlin with love), shown on the Franco-German TV channel Arte on 14 December 1995.

[4] David E. Murphy, Sergei A. Kondrashev, and George Bailey, *Battleground Berlin. CIA vs. KGB in the Cold War* (New Haven and London: Yale University Press, 1997). Other titles included Allen Weinstein and Alexander Vassiliev, *The Haunted Wood: Soviet Espionage in America—the Stalin Era* (New York: Random House, 1999); John Costello and Oleg Tsarev, *Deadly Illusions* (New York: Crown Publishers, 1993); and Timothy Naftali and Alexander Fursenko, *One Hell of a Gamble: Khrushchev, Castro, and Kennedy, 1958–1964: The Secret History of the Cuban Missile Crisis* (New York and London: W. W. Norton, 1998).

[5] My book appeared in 2007 under the title *Spy Wars: Moles, Mysteries and Deadly Games* (New Haven, Conn. and London: Yale University Press). Kondrashev did not see it before he died that year.

One: Breaking American Ciphers—And Starting A War

[1] This is a lesson in bureaucratic compartmentation. Kondrashev reported directly to the chief of the counterintelligence directorate, Yevgeniy Pitovranov, who with Abakumov was personally overseeing the work. Kondrashev personally typed or handwrote anything that needed to be put on paper, ensuring that no secretary would be in the know. No cables or dispatches were sent anywhere. By the time the file was retired, those leaders—Kondrashev's immediate boss and one other member of his section, and three officers in the super secret cipher-breaking directorate—were all who knew both sides of the story: on the one hand, the name and position of the spy together with the date and place of the recruitment, and on the other hand, how successfully the Soviet code breakers had dealt with its product.

[2] Dean Acheson Speech on the Far East, 12 January 1950.

[3] He did so obliquely, leaving the decision up to the Chinese and North Korean Communist leaders, knowing what they would decide but evading the burden of responsibility.

[4] *Naruzhka* was insiders' jargon for surveillance, derived from *naruzhnoye nablyudeniye*, or external observation, usually shortened to "NN." They sometimes called the street surveillants *topolshchiki* ("stompers").

[5] Ambassador Walter Bedell Smith wrote in his 1950 memoirs of his Moscow years, "Sergeant James M. McMillin . . . became involved with a young Soviet woman of the minor-agent type formerly so active in their attentions to foreigners in Moscow, and under her influence he deserted from the Army and his post in Moscow." (Walter Bedell Smith, *My Three Years in Moscow* (New York: J. B. Lippincott, 1950), 187.) Kondrashev, however, knew that the case involved no KGB entrapment and said the Ambassador's faulty assumption cast an unnecessary shadow on what Kondrashev saw as a sort of "Cold War Romeo and Juliet."

[6] In his desire to keep the identity secret, Kondrashev first called the code clerk "D," and only long afterwards admitted that "D" stood for the first letter of the Russian-language code name. A full year passed before he finally divulged that "D" stood for the transliterated code name "*Dzhak*."

[7] Born in mid-October 1948, Igor pursued a diplomatic career and retired as a Russian ambassador.

[8] See Chapter 4.

[9] Kondrashev may not have known of "Jack's" future, but he did go back to the earlier of the two code clerks who had such an impact on his career: the defector James McMillin. While he and I were working on his memoirs, Kondrashev went to see how the intervening fifty years had treated this family that he had helped create. He arranged a lunch meeting through the FSB, formerly the KGB Second Chief Directorate, where he had been working at the time.

He and "Mac" recognized and greeted each other cordially. Mac had developed into a gray-haired, "self-confident and thoughtful" man, but his Valya had died six months earlier. He showed Sergey her picture, sighing, "Valya is gone and I am lonely and desolate."

He had worked as a translator for two scientific institutes and was materially comfortable with a good apartment. Their son, their only child, had married a Russian woman and had moved with her and their two children to the United States. There, he was successful in business and phoned and visited his father often.

Interestingly, an FSB man was still controlling this defector even after fifty years and insisted on attending the lunch and that any future contact be arranged through him. Sergey was unsure whether it was himself or Mac the FSB didn't trust, and lamented this crudeness and pettiness he considered "typical" of FSB ways.

Two: Two Views of Culture

[1] See Appendix, which recounts this unusual family saga.

[2] The third bedroom offered Kondrashev his first indirect exposure to Stalinist terror. There lived an NKVD truck driver who was often out working at night. What he was doing, Sergey overheard from whispers, was carting off the bodies of people executed by the regime to some dumping ground. When home, he was drowning his nerves in vodka. Sergey felt the strain of the grownups suppressing their repugnance for the man.

[3] The initials stood for *Vsesoyuznoye Obshchestvo Kulturnoy Svyazi s Zagranitsey*, All-Union Society for Cultural Contacts Abroad.

[4] Kondrashev particularly remembered the writers Ilya Ehrenburg, Leonid Leonov, Konstantin Simonov, and Samuel Marshak, the gifted translator of Robert Burns. The composers Sergey Prokofiev, Tikhon Khrennikov, and Dmitri Kabalevsky were there in Kondrashev's time in VOKS, along with the film direc-

tors Sergey Eisenstein and Grigory Aleksandrov, the Socialist-realist painter Aleksandr Gerassimov, and scientists of world prominence like the physicists Peter Kapitza and Abram Joffe and the shipbuilding innovator Aleksey Krylov.

⁵ Roosevelt, Elliott, *As He Saw It* (New York: Duell, Sloan and Pearce, 1946). The book was translated and published two months later by the publishing house Mezhdunarodnaya Kniga (International Book).

⁶ Rosa had attended Austrian schools while her father was KGB chief in Vienna, and after returning to Moscow in 1938–39 attended the school for foreign communists to continue speaking German. She later taught English in MGIMO, the Moscow State Institute of Foreign Relations.

⁷ Roshchin had played a part in revolutionary activity in the Far East at the beginning of the 1920s and then joined Intelligence and obtained for Moscow its first copy of what was later called the Tanaka Memorandum, the (real or fabricated) Japanese plan for domination of Asia by military aggression. (Moscow's decision to expose it publicly abroad, where it became infamous, is an early example of "active measures.") Soon thereafter the then Chief of Soviet Foreign Intelligence Artur Artuzov called Roshchin back to Moscow to help manage deception operations against the West. Such as the now-famous "Trust." In the 1930s, Roshchin served in Germany and Austria (using the name Tumanov) and during the war headed the State Security residencies in Stockholm and Helsinki (using the name Razin). In 1949 he became head of the huge Apparat in East Berlin. Born Yakov Tishchenko, he had officially adopted his pseudonym Vasily Petrovich Roshchin.

⁸ See Raoul Wallenberg, *Report of the Swedish-Russian Working Group* (Stockholm: Ministry for Foreign Affairs, 2000), 86, 140, 144.

Another inside-KGB view of the Wallenberg affair is contained in the memoirs of Kondrashev's friend Yelisei Sinitsyn, *Rezident Svidetel'stvuyet* [The station chief reports] (Moscow: Geya, 1996), 255–64. In a chapter called "Attempt to Free Raoul Wallenberg," Sinitsyn tells how he and Foreign Intelligence Chief Pavel Fitin unsuccessfully plotted to free Wallenberg from Soviet Military Counterintelligence (SMERSH), which had arrested him in Budapest and accused him of being an anti-Soviet American agent. Sinitsyn and Fitin had the idea of persuading SMERSH Chief Viktor Abakumov to turn Wallenberg over to Foreign Intelligence, which would send him home as a recruited agent against the West. Unconvinced, Abakumov had Wallenberg shot.

⁹ See Chapter 18.

Three: Target: The American Embassy

[1] The "2" referred to Second Chief Directorate (SCD), the (arbitrary) "b" to its American Department (Otdel) countering American intelligence activity inside the USSR, comparable to the arbitrary "z" that designated the same directorate's Department 2z for cultural matters. The "1" designated its first section (Otdeleniye). These designations later changed, but the American Department always remained "First" among the SCD's departments and its section working against the Embassy remained "First" section.

[2] To find such local help (as against bringing in their own staff), foreign diplomats depended on the Soviet agency UPDK, the Directorate for the Support of the Diplomatic Corps. The UPDK was so thoroughly controlled by the KGB that it was, in effect, a KGB employment agency. All its functionaries were cleared by the KGB and one or more KGB officers were permanently stationed in its leading positions.

[3] One of the scandalous aspects of KGB history, this laboratory—established as far back as the 1920s—focused its scientific research on delivering death by poison that would appear to have been natural, even to an autopsy. The laboratory served as executioner of thousands, using prisoners in cruel and usually fatal tests. The most substantive recent accounts of this "scientific" work are those of Vadim J. Birstein, *The Perversion of Knowledge* (Cambridge: Westview Press, 2001) and Boris Volodarsky, *The KGB's Poison Factory* (Minneapolis: Zenith Press, 2009).

[4] Western officials expected to take their wives home at the end of their tours of duty, but Soviet regulations at the time forbade citizens to emigrate, marriage or no marriage. This became a problem between governments and finally, after years of pressure from abroad (and Stalin's death), the wives were all let go. The American correspondent Eddy Gilmore was even permitted to get his wife out of a camp in the faraway area of Kazan where she had been interned. (Kondrashev knew them both personally.)

[5] Moscow: Literaturnaya Gazeta Publishers, January 1949.

[6] See George F. Hofmann, *Cold War Casualty: The Court-Martial of Major General Robert W. Grow*, (Kent, Ohio, and London: Kent State University Press, 1993), which recounts what had theretofore become known about this extraordinary case.

[7] See Thomas Whitehead's account of the Wennerstrom case, *An Agent in Place* (London: Heinemann, 1967), based on the Swedish interrogation after Wennerstrom's arrest in 1963. Although Wennerstrom was working for Soviet Military Intelligence (GRU), "the man responsible for the surveillance of foreign diplomats in Moscow"—undoubtedly from Kondrashev's KGB section and presumably Roman Markov—was present at some of Wennerstrom's GRU meetings (Whitehead, pp. 45, 48).

[8] See Chapters 12 and 13 on Kondrashev's work in "active measures" promoting this same theme.

[9] Squires, Richard, *Auf dem Kriegspfad. Aufzeichnungen eines Englischen Offiziers* [On the warpath. Notes of an English officer] (East Berlin: Rutten und Loening, 1951).

[10] *Washington Post*, 6 March 1952, page 1.

[11] *Cold War Casualty*, pp. 34–35.

[12] Because the source was never uncovered, and because the KGB considered him "important," Kondrashev would not identify him further. He only commented, obscurely, that in counterintelligence work, big results often come from small observations and that this success was due to Markov's "inquisitive mind that wouldn't let the smallest detail escape."

Four: Inside a Deadly Purge

[1] My own wife became a witness to this repression in her family's house in Budapest. Billeted there at the end of the fighting were three Soviet Army officers. One was Jewish; the others a doctor and his wife for whom my wife baby-sat their little daughter. In mid-1946, they were recalled to Russia, and she wondered why they were crying at the prospect of returning home. Only later did she realize that they sensed what awaited them there.

[2] One victim of the "Aviators Case" was the Commissar of Aviation Industry Aleksey I. Shakhurin, whom Kondrashev had visited with Elliott Roosevelt less than two years before while with VOKS.

[3] As Svetlana recorded in her book, *Twenty Letters to a Friend* (New York: Harper & Row, 1967), 196. Zhenya was sentenced to ten years imprisonment and actually spent six in solitary confinement in Vladimir prison before she was released after Stalin's death. Her and Anna's relations with Stalin are well

recounted in Simon Sebag Montefiore, *Stalin. The Court of the Red Tsar* (London: Weidenfeld and Nicolson, 2003).

[4] Kondrashev's wife's parents were close friends of Mikhail Borodin. Kondrashev had worked under Norman and was friendly with him and his wife, Tanya Gilyarevskaya. Norman's elder brother Fred had served with success as an Illegal operative in Ethiopia before he died under murky circumstances in Germany soon after the beginning of World War II.

[5] See Chapter 12.

[6] A first such court had already struck the foreign intelligence directorate (FCD) with its inevitably "cosmopolitan" nature (its foreign contacts were its very reason to exist). One of its top officers, General Leonid A. Malinin, head of the KGB apparat in Berlin-Karlshorst, had dined with American diplomats in Berlin and this was used as a pretext to accuse him of giving away secrets and undoing the work of the Apparat. He was demoted and dropped from the KGB. (He was replaced by Kondrashev's father-in-law Vasily Roshchin.)

[7] The so called "Leningrad Affair" was Stalin's fabrication of a non-existent plot of top Party leaders in 1948–50 to establish a counterweight to the power of the Soviet Communist Party. Stalin's purpose was to rid himself of potential competitors for power, and in this period he ordered the execution of not only the principal Party leaders of Leningrad, but also some two thousand others.

[8] Kondrashev during his days in VOKS had met Zhdanov twice, once in Helsinki and later in Moscow when escorting the American politician Harold Stassen on a visit to him.

[9] The most recent and informative description of the events, based on files opened after the collapse of the Soviet Union, is in Jonathan Brent and Vladimir Naumov's *Stalin's Last Crime* (New York: Harper Collins, 2003).

[10] After Beria's arrest and execution, a long list of these women was passed around within the KGB. Among them, Kondrashev noted, were several officers of the KGB, including one from the FCD's British Department.

[11] Pitovranov was arrested on 27 October 1951, Shubnyakov and Utekhin on 2 November. All three of them, like many of the others, were restored later to full and prominent careers in State Security. This purge, thanks largely to Stalin's death and Beria's fall in 1953, ended with far less bloodshed than that of 1937–1938.

[12] Tsanava talked too long but even so, he left out a lot—including his 1948 murder, on Stalin's order, of the famous actor and director of the Jewish theater

Solomon Mikhoels. As revealed after the Cold War, Tsanava (acting on Stalin's orders transmitted through Abakumov, Ogoltsov, and Shubnyakov) sent a team of operatives of his Byelorussia MGB to snatch Mikhoels and the theater critic Golubov-Potapov off the street in Minsk and bring them to Tsanava's *dacha* outside the city. There, with their hands tied, they were laid on a road and run over by a truck. Their bodies were loaded onto the truck and thrown out at a distant site. (Confession of Abakumov after his arrest in 1951, reported by Beria, as described by several researchers of KGB files including G. V. Kostyrchenko's *Taynaya Politika Stalina* [Stalin's secret policy] (Moscow: Russian Academy of Sciences, Institute of Russian History, Mezhdunarodnoye Otnosheniye, 2003), pp. 390–92; and Michael Parrish's *The Lesser Terror: Soviet State Security 1939–1953* (Westport, Connecticut: Praeger, 1996), 203.

[13] After the death of Stalin, Beria had Ogoltsov arrested for his involvement in the murder of Mikhoels and alleged misdeeds. After Beria's fall Ogoltsov was freed, soon retired, and held other posts outside of State Security.

[14] The estimation of the total numbers varies from just under 20,000 to 26,000.

Five: Into Foreign Intelligence—and London

[1] Gorskiy continued to work, however, as a KGB "resident," recruiting diplomats and other prominent foreigners inside the Soviet Union. In these operations, he commonly posed as "Professor Nikitin of the Academy of Sciences" and gained the cooperation of, among others, the Canadian Ambassador John Watkins. See Watkins' own account, *Moscow Dispatches* (Toronto: John Lorimer & Co., 1987).

[2] The West uncovered Houghton thanks to anonymous letters (that I was handling for CIA) from Polish Intelligence officer Michal Goleniewski. The case of Houghton and his companion (in life and treason) Ethel Gee has been much publicized in Russia and the West. While Houghton was a functionary of the British Naval Attaché's office in Warsaw, he volunteered to spy for Polish state security (hence Goleniewski's knowledge), which later transferred him to KGB control (though for a time his KGB handlers pretended to be Poles). The KGB cleared some of its file information on this case, including Deryabkin's role, for

the book *The Crown Jewels* by KGB veteran Oleg Tsarev and the British writer Nigel West (London, HarperCollins, 1998).

[3] It was KGB practice at that time, Kondrashev pointed out, to assign the handling of important agents to officers in lower Embassy positions. It was thought that security services would be less likely to focus surveillance on such as an administrator going around town buying provisions and performing other low-level tasks.

[4] The award at this moment appeared natural, because (coincidentally) the Center had just compiled a list of what "Shah" had supplied—thousands of secret documents on anti-submarine warfare and other military technology. (Kondrashev believed, even decades later, that no one beside himself, Serov, and Deryabkin ever knew the story of "the wrong box" that had triggered this award.)

[5] Kondrashev and his wife had met British officials before, but seeing them in their homeland, they came to admire their "equable and reserved character, strength and self-respect, and the ease and simplicity of their personal relations." So different was this from the character and conduct of his own people that Kondrashev was reminded of an old saying about Russian rulers, "Out of mud are princes made."

[6] Already the day after their arrival, as Khrushchev and Bulganin (and Serov and Kondrashev) attended an opera in Covent Garden, British security men spotted a suspicious group trying to enter and took them away in a bus. Apparently they were Russian emigrés ignoring the British injunction to stay away from the visitors, but Kondrashev never learned what, if anything, they had intended.

[7] The KGB already knew that the British naval intelligence was interested in the maneuvering capabilities of this new cruiser, having observed the first of the class, the Sverdlovsk, moving about a harbor and docking with surprising agility.

[8] Kondrashev did not mention what the ship's crew had done after the sighting and implied that they had simply reported it, nothing more.

[9] There is persuasive evidence that the then chief of British MI5, Roger Hollis, was a Soviet mole. Hollis was one of the handful of people in the world aware in advance of this operation (and that of the betrayed spy Oleg Penkovsky as noted in Chapter 14). See Chapman Pincher's *Treachery: Betrayals, Blunders, and Cover-Ups: Six Decades of Espionage* (Edinburgh: Mainstream Publishing, 2011).

Six: A Mole and a Tunnel

[1] The location of some of these British bugs has been reported, including ones in the Soviet Commerical Attache's office in Copenhagen, the Polish Trade Delegation in Brussels, the home of a Bulgarian diplomat in London, and others in Cairo. *H. Montgomery Hyde, George Blake, Superspy* (London: Futura, 1987, p. 43).

[2] See Chapter 12.

[3] The value of the Tunnel to Western intelligence can be fully grasped only if one realizes how little it had previously known about the matters that these phone taps were revealing. The conversations provided information nowhere else available about Soviet military and atomic policy, personnel strengths and weaknesses, military intelligence activity and personnel, and East German–Soviet relations at this time when the Soviets were trying to force the West out of Berlin. For more on this vast intelligence production, see Appendix 5 of *Battleground Berlin*, op. cit., and *CIA Clandestine Services Historical Paper No. 150, The Berlin Tunnel Operation 1952–1956*, pp. 25–26 and Appendix B, declassified and available on the Internet (www.fas.org/irp/cia/product/tunnel-200702.pdf).

[4] See Chapter 14.

[5] A Russian book full of official data from KGB files reported, "Thanks to Blake's revelations more than 200 British and American agents [spies] were uncovered and neutralized just on the territory of the Federal Republic of Germany alone." A. Kolpakidi and D. Prokhorov, *Vneshnyaya Razvedka Rossii* [Russian Foreign Intelligence] (Moscow: Olma Press, 2001), p. 416.

[6] In a rare public appearance in Moscow that demonstrated his affection for his friend, Blake attended Kondrashev's funeral in September 2007 (as I learned from a member of Kondrashev's family). Interestingly—this more than a half century after his defection—Blake was accompanied there by a security officer.

[7] I am not including details here because Blake gave the same account to others and it has been published elsewhere. See, for example, Sean Bourke, *The Springing of George Blake* (N.Y.: Vintage, 1970, pp. 214–221) and Montgomery Hyde, pp. 94–96, 99.

Seven: "Why Do You Need All These People Here?"

[1] This 4th Department of the First Chief Directorate (foreign intelligence) was called, at the time, the Austro-German Department, sometimes abbreviated

to "German Department," but never changing its area of responsibility: Austria, Germany (East and West), and Luxembourg.

[2] It was in connection with an operation known within the KGB as "Pavlovsky's Trap" for Col. Ivan G. Pavlovsky, its instigator. Counterintelligence had set up a mansion in East Berlin that would be presented as being in the Western sector of the city. There, KGB Counterintelligence officers, posing as Americans, could debrief—and compromise—potential traitors and defectors who had been led there thinking they were reaching Western safety.

[3] He worked on this project with Germany expert Vadim Kuchin. They did not find many promising prospects, and of those who were subsequently contacted, as Kondrashev later learned, only a fraction even pretended to be willing to help after release.

[4] Kondrashev described the complex structural changes in the KGB representation in Germany in his book with David Murphy and George Bailey, *Battleground Berlin*, op. cit., especially pp. 30–50, 160–162, 286–88, and 291.

[5] Previously, the FCD's Illegals Directorate had controlled the operations of its Illegals in foreign countries, but by Kondrashev's time at the head of the German Department, their control had been shifted to the geographic department responsible for the Illegal's area of operations.

[6] Kondrashev described the KGB side of the Runge case, and David Murphy the CIA side, in their book *Battleground Berlin*, pp. 441–46.

[7] (see Chapter 12).

[8] Up to this time, Kondrashev had shared the common view of Adenauer as a stiff and reserved remnant of an older generation, so he was surprised by his informality and openness. Kondrashev's group was celebrating the birthday of one of Adenauer's assistants one evening in the hotel's downstairs bar when Adenauer, needing his assistant's help, dropped in on the party. He cheerfully greeted Kondrashev and the other Soviet hosts, drank a tiny vodka toast to his assistant's birthday, and with smiling apologies took him off to work.

[9] Kondrashev's department would give to the Information Directorate its own assessment of the source—annotating, for example, "This comes from a very reliable source based on his personal knowledge [or direct access]" or "from an authentic document naturally accessible to him."

[10] Directive of the KGB Collegium dated 19 July 1951, soon after the establishment of the HVA.

[11] As revealed in a document of the MfS now in the files of the Gauck Authority, as reported in Hubertus Knabe, *Westarbeit des MfS* (Berlin: Ch. Links Verlag, 1999).

[12] The extent of the HVA's "West work" is summarized in the compilation by Georg Herbstritt and Helmut Müller-Enbergs, *Das Gesicht dem Westen zu . . .* [Looking Westward] (Bremen: Edition Temmen, 2nd edition, 2003). These statistics come from page 380 in the chapter by Hubertus Knabe on the Green Party (which focuses on environmental issues).

[13] Both Kevorkov and Bahr have publicly described their roles in this back channel. W. Keworkow, *Der geheime Kanal. Moskau, der KGB, und die Bonner Ostpolitik* (1995) and Egon Bahr, *Zu Meiner Zeit* (1996). See also Rangmar Staffe, Egon *Bahr, der geheime Diener* [Egon Bahr, the secret servant] (1970); M. E. Sarotte, *Dealing with the Devil: East Germany, Détente and Ostpolitik 1969–1973* (Chapel Hill: U. of North Carolina Press, 2001); and Josef Hufelschulte, "Bahr's Geheimpakt mit dem KGB" and "Bund mit dem Teufel" ("Bahr's secret pact with the KGB" and "Alliance with the devil") in *Focus* magazine nos. 6 and 7, 1995.

Eight: A Unique Look at the Hungarian Revolution

[1] Yelisei Sinitsyn, *Rezident Svidetel'stvuyet* [A station chief reports] (Moscow: Geya, 1996).

[2] It was not the first time. As mentioned in Chapter 5, Serov had suddenly picked Kondrashev as his companion for London to prepare the visit of Khrushchev and Bulganin there in the spring of this same year 1956. In their two weeks together, Serov had developed confidence in Sergey's abilities and a liking for him personally.

[3] Korotkov was the only one of the group who had or wore his uniform during this time.

Nine: Spy Center Vienna

[1] As reported by former KGB Major Pyotr Deryabin, who himself had that culling task in Vienna before he defected there to CIA in mid-February 1954. (The author escorted him out of Vienna, through the Soviet Zone of Austria, and then to the United States.)

[2] Pyotr Deryabin was deputy chief of that new SK section. Most of the police sources he culled had been taken on by Gorkov's former counterintelligence residency.

[3] The talks at this Vienna Summit are vividly described by Frederick Kempe in *Berlin 1961* (New York: G. P. Putnam's Sons, 2011).

[4] The others were Foreign Minister Andrey Gromyko; his deputy Fyodor Molotchkov; CC CPSU representative Leonid Zamyatin; Soviet Ambassador to Washington Anatoly Dobrynin; and Khrushchev's interpreter Viktor Sukhodrev.

Ten: The KGB's Nazi Underground

[1] Teodor Gladkov, *Lift v Razvedku. 'Korol Nelegalov' Aleksandr Korotkov* [Elevator to intelligence. 'King of the Illegals' Aleksandr Korotkov] (Moscow: Olma Press, 2002), pp. 354, 387.

[2] It was not an Illegal whom Korotkov was meeting. Had it been, he would have told Kondrashev because geographic department chiefs (like Kondrashev atop the German Department) were then taking over the management of Illegals in their geographical region (previously managed by Korotkov's Illegals Directorate).

[3] The exodus to Argentina and the organization there are well documented in Uki Goni, *The Real Odessa* (London: Granta Books, 2002).

[4] A classic technique used by both East and West, not unlike a police "sting," by which the operatives of an intelligence service pretend to be of another nationality to recruit and manipulate secret agents who would think themselves working for a friendly service.

[5] When the tide of battle turned after Stalingrad, Stalin had taken military security and counterintelligence from its usual place in the KGB (then NKVD) and brought it under his direct military command (the State Defense Committee, *Gosudarstvenyy Komitet Oborony*—GKO) as the Chief Directorate of Counterintelligence (*Glavnoye Upravleniye po Kontrrazvedki*—GUKR, adding the title of SMERSH, acronym for *Smert' Shpionam*—"Death to Spies!"). In 1946 it was returned to State Security (by then called MGB) as its Third Directorate.

[6] As I first heard in the 1950s from Pyotr Deryabin, who had served in the Austro-German Department in 1952–53. The "legacy" was operational, not material, although Abakumov had swept up more than people in conquered

Germany: His phenomenal hoard of personal loot—jewels, furs, luxury cars—became an issue after his arrest.

[7] See U. S. National Archives, Interagency Working Group report of 19 September 2001 (http://www.archives.gov/iwg/research-papers/barbie-irr-file.html).

[8] One such case was publicized in *Der Spiegel* in September 2011. At the end of the 1950s, the BND used Walther Rauff, a former SS officer, to gain information on the Cuba of Fidel Castro. Although he was not a war criminal and not hiding his past, Rauff was said to have headed a group that developed the mobile gas chamber (sealed trucks) that killed tens of thousands of concentration camp prisoners.

[9] Müller was never seen again by any of the survivors, so no one knew where he went. The testimony of Wilhelm Hoettl, former high officer of Schellenberg's SD (*Sicherheitsdienst*, foreign intelligence component of the Reich Security Main Office—RSHA), suggested that Müller took refuge alone in an underground bunker on the Kurfürstenstrasse that had been prepared—but not used—by his subordinate, Adolf Eichmann, with numerous tunnelled outlets. (Hoettl testimony at Nuremberg Trial, and his book, *The Secret Front* [London: Weidenfeld & Nicolson, 2nd ed. 1954], pp. 301–303.)

[10] Rudolf Barak to the author, 3 December 1993. Sergey Kondrashev, having long headed the KGB's German Department, confirmed that KGB contacts with Müller dated from "the late 1930s," although he did not specify the nature of these contacts.

[11] Schellenberg, *The Labyrinth. Memoirs of Walter Schellenberg, Hitler's Chief of Counterintelligence* (New York: HarperCollins Da Capo Press Edition, 2000), pp. 318–21. The 1943 contact with the KGB was confirmed later.

[12] Each of these steps was reported by a reliable source, all three of them in contact with me: Pyotr Deryabin, Michal Goleniewski, and Rudolf Barak.

[13] This affair was a central aspect of Stalin's 1951 purge of the security service, involving the arrest of Abakumov and scores of his officers. See Chapter 5.

[14] While Müller's survival is well testified to, there has been endless debate about that of Martin Bormann, not even stilled by the 1973 identification by DNA of his bones buried on a train overpass in Berlin, where he was said to have been killed while escaping from Hitler's bunker at the end of the war. A pathologist reportedly found the bones covered with a type of clay unknown in the area where they were found but known to be native to a region of Paraguay.

Both Goleniewski and Rudolf Barak were convinced of Bormann's postwar role in South America, so their testimony cannot be easily dismissed.

[15] Some parts of this loose organization might have given themselves a name like "Die Spinne" or "Odessa" (Goleniewski referred to it all under the heading "Hacke") but it is doubtful that the postwar Nazi underground ever had one overall name.

[16] I visited Barak in his apartment in Prague 2–4 December 1993 (his son Pavel acted as interpreter), accompanying the French Intelligence veteran Pierre de Villemarest, who described our encounter with Barak in his book *Le dossier Saragosse. Bormann et Gestapo Müller après 1945* (Paris: Charles Lavauzelle, 2002), pp. 215–223. It was translated as *Untouchable: Who Protected Bormann and Gestapo Müller after 1945*, with preface by Vladimir Bukovsky (Slough, Berkshire, UK: Aquilion Ltd., 2005), pp. 358–65.

[17] Barak said that the Czechoslovak planners were Vlastimil Jenys (Barak's private secretary), Jaroslav Miller (chief of operations), Karel Komarek (personnel chief), and Miroslav Nacvalac (see next footnote).

[18] Nacvalac had been Czechoslovak state security (StB) station chief in Vienna in the first half of the 1950s and was a specialist in kidnappings. His operations when visiting Switzerland in the late 1950s were a subject of our attention during my time there in CIA (we informally nicknamed him "Hose-nose"). As StB station chief in the United States, he was expelled from his UN posting in June 1961 for his attempt to recruit an American Army officer.

[19] Barak said that Müller's presence in Prague leaked to the East German, Hungarian, and Polish security services and they tried to get access to question him but were refused. (Serov in Moscow was angry about the leak.)

[20] Barak to the author, 3 December 1993.

[21] The Czech kidnapping of Müller was confirmed by the Czech state security defector Josef Frolik, although he had heard inaccurate accounts and thought the Czechs had done it on their own and kept Müller in Czechoslovakia. See *The Frolik Defection* (London: Corgi Books, 1975), pp. 35–36.

[22] *Gestapo Chief. The 1948 Interrogation of Heinrich Müller* (San Jose: R. James Bender, 1995) ostensibly composed by "Gregory Douglas" (another alias of "Peter Stahl," whose real name may be Norwood Burch). Soviet involvement in its fabrication has never been proven, as far as I know, but only the KGB—terribly compromised by their own concealment and use of Müller—would have

a reason to invest such long and painstaking efforts to produce a huge work of no historical value and no prospect of profitable sales.

[23] Would in fact Gestapo Müller have been in the West again only two years or so after being kidnapped and brought back to Moscow? Rudolf Barak's information worked both against and for this supposition. Barak had heard, on the one hand, that Müller had never afterward been released to the West, but on the other hand was assured by KGB Colonel Fotiy Peshekhonov after the kidnapping that Müller "will certainly go on" working with the KGB.

Eleven: Richard Sorge Redux

[1] *Who Are You, Dr. Sorge?* Made in 1960, the film was directed by Yves Ciampi, with Thomas Holtzmann playing Sorge and Mario Adorf playing his radio operator Max Clausen. The role of the German diplomat Hans-Otto Meissner, who knew Sorge in the German Embassy in Tokyo, was played by Meissner himself. (He wrote a book about Sorge, *The Man With Three Faces*, London: Evans Brothers Ltd., 1955.)

[2] It is no coincidence that one finds in bibliographies starting from about 1964–1965 a big jump in the number of Soviet publications about KGB and GRU operations and operatives. This reflects the "active measure" of which Kondrashev's work on Sorge was an early example.

[3] Sorge's great-uncle Friedrich Adolf Sorge (1828–1906) was an early Socialist. Kondrashev read in the Lenin Library his correspondence with Karl Marx and was impressed by Sorge's command of six languages.

[4] Madame Furtseva would have seen this movie when it was submitted, as movies made abroad regularly were, to the All-Union Committee on Cinematography which passed on whether they could be shown in the USSR. On this committee sat some fifteen to twenty people including representatives of the Cultural Department of the CC, of the Ministry of Culture, of the Ministry of Cinematography, and prominent film directors and writers—and a representative of the KGB. (Later, as head of "Active Measures," Kondrashev himself was to become that KGB representative.) Kondrashev said that the committee would meet perhaps once a month to watch a foreign movie being considered, and then discuss it and vote (usually unanimously) "yes" or "no" or "yes, but . . . " requiring the cut of objectionable parts.

[5] In Sorge's time, Military Intelligence was the 4th (Intelligence) Directorate (*Razvedupr*) of the General Staff of the Red Army (RKKA) but for clarity I'll here use the more recent and familiar designation: Chief Intelligence Directorate or GRU.

[6] Chistyakov, as Chief of the GRU's General Department (*Obshchy Otdel*), served practically as a close assistant to the GRU chief.

[7] The dozens of timely warnings Stalin was given—and rejected or ignored—are described in David E. Murphy, *What Stalin Knew* (New Haven and London: Yale University Press, 2008).

[8] Aino Kuusinen (first wife of the prominent Comintern functionary Otto Kuusinen) was a Soviet Intelligence operative who was recalled to Moscow from China in that same period. She asked Sorge's advice on what to do. He told her she would be going to her death. But she went anyway—and spent nearly twenty years in the Gulag. She later published her memoirs.

[9] *Proshu mne bolshe ne prislat' etoy nemetskoi desinformatsiya!*

[10] One copy of that report remains in the KGB archives and Kondrashev was given it tell this part of Sorge's story at a Russian-Japanese symposium in September 2000. In November 1964, a second copy was received by the chief of GRU and Kondrashev believed that it is still there.

[11] Tomiya Watanabe, a distinguished researcher on the Sorge case, sent Kondrashev this police file information in October 2001. The Soviet consular officials were G. L. Budkevich and V. S. Zaitsev.

[12] Already the Gestapo liaison officer in the German Embassy, Josef Meisinger, had stimulated the curiosity of his Japanese police liaison by indiscreetly mentioning that Berlin had asked for Meisinger's view of Sorge (as Meisinger told American interrogators after the war). Though Meisinger had responded with a favorable assessment, the very fact that Berlin had questions about Sorge piqued Japanese interest in a man they already viewed as more knowledgeable and better connected than could be expected of a mere newspaperman.

[13] Or possibly three times. After the war, the GRU Illegal Leopold Trepper met General Kyoji Tominaga, Chief of Staff of the Japanese Army in Manchuria, who had been Vice-Minister of Defense when the Sorge affair broke out. Trepper asked, "Why was Sorge sentenced to death at the end of 1941 and not executed until November 7, 1944? Why didn't you propose that he be exchanged? Japan and the USSR were not at war [until August 1945]." Tominaga cut Trepper off energetically. "Three times we proposed to the Soviet Embassy in Tokyo that

Sorge be exchanged for a Japanese prisoner. Three times we got the same answer: The man called Richard Sorge is unknown to us." [Trepper, *The Great Game* (London: Sphere Books, 1977) pp. 374–75.]

Twelve: Organizing to Disinform

[1] The two best insiders' descriptions of Soviet Bloc disinformation work include that by the former deputy head of Communist Czechoslovakia's "active measures" department, Ladislav Bittman, *The KGB and Soviet Disinformation. An Insider's View* (Washington, D.C.: Pergamon Brassey's, 1985). Kondrashev remembered Bittman (acidly for having defected but favorably as a professional in this specialized field) and confirmed from his own memory many of the active measures Bittman's book described. The book by Günter Bohnsack (of the East German HVA's Active Measures Department) and Herbert Brehmer, *Auftrag: Irreführung* [Mission: Deception] (Hamburg: Carlsen Verlag, 1992), describes many active measures conducted in tandem with Kondrashev and his service.

[2] In Iran, he and his group recruited sources able to warn of threats to the vital southern supply routes to the embattled USSR. Soviet sources describe Agayants's role during the Teheran Conference of 1943 (between Stalin, Roosevelt, and Churchill) quite differently from Western writers. They say that a source of Agayants's rezidentura learned of a German plot to assassinate President Roosevelt and that Foreign Minister Molotov passed this information to American Ambassador Harriman with a suggestion. He proposed that Roosevelt and his immediate entourage live inside the Soviet compound (where the ambassador and Agayants would give up their apartments to accommodate them) to avoid being exposed to assassins while being driven through the city to the Soviet Embassy where the meetings were to be held. Western historians see this as merely a ploy to bring Roosevelt's free hours into range of Soviet microphones. Kondrashev insisted that he had never heard anything from Agayants or anyone else to support the latter theory and personally did not believe it.

[3] Kondrashev insisted that this was an arbitrary choice and did not stand for disinformation (*dezinformatsiya*), as some in the West assumed. The letter "D," he pointed out, had designated a number of earlier departments, some with no special focus on disinformation.

[4] The offer by SCD Chief Oleg Gribanov is described in Chapter 14.

[5] Kondrashev was the main speaker at Agayants's interment and spoke so movingly that Agayants's son asked for a copy of his words. Kondrashev wanted to include these words in his autobiography, but died before getting them to me. His family searched on my behalf but could not find the text.

[6] In public usage, the term "active measures" remains vague enough that some historians have wrongly applied it to such KGB actions as assassination and kidnapping abroad. These were not functions of Service A.

[7] As late as 1836, the "testament" was actually published in France as a historical document and even after being exposed as a fraud it was still being cited seriously as late as the early twentieth century.

[8] It was headed first by Pavel Zhuravlev and then by Andrey Graur.

[9] This unit was headed from 1950 to 1953 by Kondrashev's father-in-law Vasily Roshchin and later by Vasily R. Sitnikov and Vitaly V. Korotkov.

[10] Agayants suggested to Foreign Minister Gromyko that one of Agayants's officers should, logically, head Spetsburo 2 and proposed Vasily Sitnikov. Gromyko agreed, but only if Sitnikov would leave the KGB and join MID. That was not at all what Agayants had in mind, so Gromyko put the MID officer Ivan Filipovich Filipov in charge.

[11] "Section" (*otdeleniye*) in Department D, "department" (*Otdel*) in Service A. For simplicity I will refer to the organization as Service A and to its subunits as departments, whether or not chronologically correct at any given time.

[12] All of these departments were created in 1964 and, regardless of their numerical designation, were called "Active Measures" (e.g. the Hungarian unit was *Aktiv Intéskedések Alosztalya*—Active Measures Department). Their creation in East German has been described by Bohnsack and Brehmer, op. cit.; in Czechoslovak by L. Bittman, op. cit.; and in Hungary in the testimony of Miklos Szabo in Hearing of the Internal Security Subcommittee, Committee on the Judiciary, September 24, 1957, Part 83 (Washington: U.S. Government Printing Office, 1958), p. 5348.

[13] For example, *Soviet Covert Action: The Forgery Offensive: Hearings of the Permanent Select Committee on Intelligence, House of Representatives, Ninety-Sixth Congress* (Washington: U.S. Government Printing Office, 1980) and *Soviet Active Measures: Hearings of the Permanent Select Committee on Intelligence, House of Representatives, Ninety-Seventh Congress* (Washington: U.S. Government Printing Office, 1982).

Thirteen: Active Measures

[1] Kondrashev admitted that the effects of this active measure had been double-edged, perhaps generating more admiration for British and American Intelligence daring and imagination than outrage against their violation of Soviet secrecy and sovereignty.

[2] The KGB had a category of "valuable" (*tsenniye*) agents (in high or especially sensitive portions of their governments and providing vital secret information) whose identities and very existences were known only to a few members of the KGB and whose reports were given only very limited circulation. To preserve such sources, the KGB was prepared to make extraordinary sacrifices, as it did for at least two mentioned in this book (George Blake and the betrayer, still unknown, of Oleg Penkovskiy; see next chapter).

[3] While Kondrashev did not know the name of the sergeant at the time, he later learned from Western publicity that his name was Robert Lee Johnson. For an account of this case, see for example John Barron, *KGB: The Secret Work of Soviet Secret Agents* (London, 1974), pp. 199–229. See also my book *Spy Wars*, pages 179 and 281, for another KGB exploitation of Sgt. Johnson for deceptive purposes: After he had lost his value to the KGB, they tossed him away to provide fodder for a false KGB defector.

[4] There was and still is a bookshop in the building housing Soviet Intelligence that sells Russian and Western books on intelligence, espionage, and technology.

[5] See Chapter 17.

[6] Kondrashev came to know Akhromeyev well and often chatted with him about common interests. He saw him as forceful and positive and could not accept the widely-spread story that Akhromeyev committed suicide by hanging himself in his office. While something unknown to Kondrashev may indeed have impelled him to kill himself, Sergey knew that Akhromeyev had pistols and found it unthinkable that he would have used any other method. But he drew no sinister conclusions from this anomaly.

[7] The Department D officer preparing this latter deception was the former Illegal operative Conon Molody, who had used in the West the false identity of "Gordon Lonsdale." He had returned to service after his release in a 1964 spy swap for the British agent Greville Wynne and worked in "D" and "A" until his death in 1970. A year later, as an active measure, Service A wrote his "memoirs" and caused them to be published in the West—but as Kondrashev ruefully

admitted, the book contained such crude propaganda and falsifications that it did not even begin to have the desired impact.

[8] Julius Mader, *Who's Who in the CIA* ([East] Berlin: J. Mader publisher, 1968).

[9] *Soviet Active Measures: Hearings of the Select Committee on Intelligence, House of Representatives (Washington: U.S. Government Printing Office, 1982)*, pp. 170–95.

Fourteen: "How Could CIA Ever Have Trusted That Man?"

[1] Kondrashev admitted freely that this technique was, indeed, "provocation," although in the Soviets' lexicon, provocation was a dastardly crime committed only by their adversaries. When they themselves would "take the initiative," they preferred to label it "aggressiveness" (*nastupatelnost*).

[2] "Operational game"—*operativnaya igra*—is a KGB term for an operation manipulating enemy intelligence, using such as a double agent or false defector.

[3] www.soldat.narod.ru

[4] Guk was involved in SCD work against the Americans as early as 1948. Kondrashev encountered him then in Berlin in the course of an operation informally known as "Pavlovsky's Trap." The KGB had long been setting up false border posts inside Soviet territory to lure and compromise would-be escapees from the Soviet regime. This particular "trap" was a house pretending to be inside the American Sector of four-power-occupied Berlin and was manned by American-uniformed, English-speaking KGB personnel—including the young Guk.

[5] "Yura tried repeatedly to transfer into the FCD," Kondrashev told me, "but because of his excessive drinking and other negative factors, he was never admitted." This surprised me, because I knew that the KGB defector Anatoly Golitsyn had been sure Guk was in the FCD. How, I asked him, could Guk have been stationed abroad in Washington in the mid-1950s and Geneva well into the 1960s without being in the FCD? Kondrashev answered that Gribanov had long tried to place his SCD people abroad in FCD residencies, to handle the foreign aspects of SCD operations based in or stemming from inside the USSR. Although repeatedly turned down, he had managed to obtain "a very small number" of such slots. Kondrashev was confident that Guk had been stationed in both Washington and Geneva primarily for Gribanov's SCD business.

[6] See my account of the case in *Spy Wars: Moles, Mysteries, and Deadly Games*, op. cit.

[7] See Chapter 6. In Penkovskiy's case, the KGB may have had more than one precious source to protect. There were signs that Penkovskiy was betrayed by someone inside CIA (as I pointed out in my 2007 book *Spy Wars*) and also from the British side. The Chief of British Counterintelligence (MI5), Roger Hollis, at his own insistence, was told Penkovskiy's name at the very outset of the case. There is persuasive evidence that Hollis was spying for the Soviets. See Chapman Pincher, *Treachery: Betrayals, Blunders, and Cover-ups: Six Decades of Espionage,* op. cit.

[8] After using these words in his press conference after Penkovsky's arrest, the USSR Chief Prosecutor A. G. Gorniy was asked the obvious question: Why then did the KGB delay arresting him until nine or ten months after that? Gorniy's (prepared) reply was that the security authorities "needed more proof" and moreover, needed time to determine whether Penkovskiy or his handlers had other, still unknown, spy contacts in Russia (*Izvestiya,* 29 May 1963). Kondra-shev scoffed at this blatant cover-up of the obvious reason for the delay which, he said, was source protection.

[9] Vitaly Pavlov memoirs, *Operatsiya Sneg* [Operation Snow] (Moscow: Geya 1996).

[10] Kondrashev did not share this idea; he said he knew of no instance of purposely-exposed street surveillance.

[11] Nosenko on three different occasions told three different stories of how he had learned that Penkovsky was caught by surveillance of British diplomats; one of his three sources was Gribanov himself.

[12] I had an opportunity to see what Golitsyn had reported and was impressed not only by the number of sensitive cases, but also by his precision in describing what and where and when and how he had learned of each:

- He pointed to likely KGB recruitment of no fewer than three American code clerks (one confirmed by Kondrashev's revelation of "Jack").
- He cited at least twenty separate indications that the KGB had penetrated the CIA staff, together indicating they may have recruited as many as three CIA officers. (These in addition to the CIA principal agent "Sasha," Igor Orlov.)
- He gave at least ten specific signs that the KGB had penetrated other American intelligence organizations.
- He pointed to high penetrations of the staff of British and French intelligence and counterintelligence including in Britain the "ring of five" that

became famous as the "Cambridge spies" and in France the "Sapphire" sources, some of whom were identified.

• He gave details on at least twenty agents whom the American and British intelligence services thought were genuinely reporting Soviet secrets to them but were actually KGB double agents.

• Having had the job of handling intelligence reports coming from KGB spies inside NATO, Golitsyn knew of several inside other Western governments and intelligence services.

[13] Nosenko's companion, using the name Aleksandr Konstantinovich Kislov, was posing as a TASS (Soviet telegraphic news agency) correspondent with the delegation. (Five years earlier, under the same name and same cover, he had worked with Yuri Guk and Vladislav Kovshuk in Washington, pursuing a recent SCD recruit from the American Embassy in Moscow.) In Geneva, he roomed with Nosenko in a little hotel far distant from the one that housed the delegation that Nosenko was ostensibly watchdogging. Kondrashev was aware of Kislov's role and knew him to be a Department 14 officer, but not having heard the name Kislov, he assumed it was a pseudonym. He mentioned two possible identities but because of age differences neither of them fit "Kislov."

[14] While Gribanov may simply have taken this risk, it is also possible that he *knew* CIA had no means to check Nosenko's career story. This would suggest that the KGB had a mole in a key position in CIA's Soviet Division. If so, that mole was never uncovered.

[15] Storsberg (who never reported any KGB approach) was named in this context on page 4 of an FBI document of 26 February 1964, released for publication per PI-102-526 (JFK Act), NARA, 2 April 2009, with CIA certification dated 19 March 1998, "no objection to declassification." Storsberg and the Finn, whose name was Preisfreund, are thus the people referred to in paragraph 8 of CIA's "interim report on progress in the Nosenko case" dated 24 October 1966, released for publication by NARA on 17 November 2008 under the same JFK Act.

[16] This change of dates permitted CIA to identify "Andrey" (as revealed in CIA documents declassified after the Cold War) as Sergeant Dayle W. Smith, who confessed to having been recruited while in Moscow 1953–1955. But the American authorities saw no reason to prosecute him because he had had no access to sensitive information and never passed any to the Soviets. For the KGB, he was a free "give-away."

[17] Major (later Lieutenant Colonel) Popov volunteered to spy for CIA in Vienna at the end of 1952 and produced military intelligence of immense value (in an operation of which I was one of the four most closely involved) for years before returning to the USSR at the end of the military occupation of Austria in 1955. From 1956 he was again in contact with CIA after being reassigned to East Germany and then East Berlin. Recalled to the USSR in November 1958 (and no doubt arrested then), he had several contacts with CIA in Moscow (under KGB control) before he and his CIA contact were openly arrested in December 1959. He was later shot. See my book *Spy Wars*, pp. 71–75.

[18] See *Spy Wars,* pages 11–12 and 70–71.

[19] For Kislov, see footnote 13, on previous page.

[20] But Nosenko thought that Kovshuk's "trip" lasted no more than a few weeks. He was unaware that Kovshuk had gone on permanent assignment and stayed ten months and that he had not contacted "Andrey" until after nine of those months.

[21] A. Kolpakidi and D. Prokhorov, *Vneshnyaya Razvedka Rossii* [Russian foreign intelligence] (Moscow: Olma Press, 2001), p. 70.

[22] So incredible did Kondrashev find Nosenko's claim that he began to question his own memory; perhaps he had missed something by being away in Vienna during the years 1960–61 that Nosenko claimed to have held that post. On his return to Moscow from that talk with me in Brussels, he checked it with a surviving colleague from the SCD's American Embassy section, Roman Markov, who confirmed to Sergey that Nosenko had served in the section for about a year, shortly after Kondrashev had left in 1952, but had proved troublesome and was moved out to a less demanding post—and had never returned to the American Department, much less as its deputy chief.

[23] The text to be enciphered was handwritten on a pad kept by the cipher personnel, with numbered pages torn off a permanent strip at the top with corresponding numbers and signed by the sender.

Fifteen: The Tophat Paradox

[1] Kondrashev was Deputy Chief of Foreign Intelligence (FCD) from 1968 to 1974.

[2] While Kondrashev did not remember (or would not say) more, that earlier contact of Polyakov's might have been the GRU Illegal Margarita Tairova whom

Polyakov had turned over to Pyotr Popov in Berlin in 1957 for onward dispatch to New York. On another occasion, when I mentioned her name, Kondrashev quickly reacted: "Tairova, hmm. That was a very unusual affair"—but he would not amplify.

[3] *Battleground Berlin*, op. cit., p. 281.

[4] The first from former Director of Central Intelligence James Wolsey, the second from an insider in CIA's operations against the USSR.

[5] Within weeks after this, a KGB officer in New York, Aleksey I. Kulak, walked into the FBI and began a long secret relationship that became as mysterious as that of Polyakov. Following the new procedure of codenaming such sources, the FBI called him "Fedora" and his CIA-liaison cryptonym was "Scotch." I refer to the Kulak case in *Spy Wars*, op. cit., pointing out similarities to that of Polyakov.

[6] I have drawn the dates and other details of this case from authoritative sources in published accounts: Polyakov's New York FBI case officer John Mabey in an interview dated 2 January 1998; David Wise, *Nightmover* (New York: HarperCollins, 1995) 59–6, 105–6; *ANF Razbor Internet* Moscow, No. 23–24, 14 December 2000; and CIA desk officers on the case, S. Grimes and J. Vertefeuille, *Circle of Treason* (Annapolis, MD: Naval Institute Press, 2012), 26–54.

[7] I was so sure of this that I even wagered on it. In 1959 the FBI had caught and doubled against the GRU an Illegal named Kaarlo Tuomi. In 1964 I was told that shortly after the arrest, the FBI had shown Tuomi photos of Soviet officials and had identified Polyakov among his GRU trainers in Moscow in 1957–58. I didn't believe it. I made a bet that Tuomi had *not* identified Polyakov with the others when originally shown the photos in 1959, and moreover that Tuomi had never done so prior to Polyakov's walking in to the Americans in late 1961. A check with the FBI won me my wager. In September 1962 (by which time, as he later admitted, Tuomi had secretly turned back under Soviet control) Tuomi told his FBI handlers that he was suffering a crisis of conscience for having omitted to identify a certain one of his GRU trainers, and asked his FBI handler to show him the pictures again. That was when, for the first time, he identified Polyakov.

[8] *Spy Wars*, op, cit., 171–72. In 1980, the year after Hanssen betrayed Polyakov (and long before Ames betrayed him again), the Soviets cut short Polyakov's tour in India and brought him back to Moscow, ending his contact with CIA. But he was not arrested, they said, until 1986.

[9] Groping for some innocent explanation for this delay, some have speculated that the GRU—to whom Hanssen betrayed Polyakov in 1979—might not have informed the KGB. But the GRU would not hide such a threat to Soviet security, and even if they tried they would be unlikely to succeed. Like all units of the Soviet armed forces, the GRU was staffed by Party members and riddled with informants reporting to the KGB's Third Chief Directorate (military counterintelligence) whose 1st Department covered the General Staff, of which GRU was a part.

[10] The American traitor who told the KGB how much Polyakov was really giving CIA could not be either Hanssen in the FBI or Ames in the CIA. Hanssen could not have known anything of the case after Polyakov's departure from New York, much less details of his later reporting to CIA, and Ames did not begin betraying until 1985, five years after Polyakov's abrupt recall from New Delhi. Who might that traitor have been? Only a tiny few even within CIA knew the details of what Polyakov was reporting.

Sixteen: Prague Spring at the Politburo

[1] Attacks on Dubcek later in the year in newspapers of the Ukrainian SSR were particularly virulent, Kondrashev said. He thought this the fruit of Shelest's disappointment and his effort to compensate for, or efface the memory of, his earlier support for Dubcek becoming Party chief.

[2] I called Kondrashev's attention to a Politburo document stating that Brezhnev on 23 May 1968, in order to ensure "tight control" over Soviet policy at this time, set up "a high-level commission on the Czechoslovak question" of nine members (only six of them Politburo members). Keeping a daily watch on events, it regularly brought its findings and recommendations before the full Politburo for consideration. (*Rabochaya zapis' zasedaniya Politbykuro TsK KPSS 23 maya 1968*, [Working record of Politburo meeting of 23 May 1968, quoted by Mark Kramer in Chapter 4 of *1968: The World Transformed.* New York: Cambridge University Press, 1998). This was Kondrashev's reply: "I never heard of any such commission (which could not have escaped my attention) and I cannot conceive what it might do or why, since Brezhnev 'tightly controlled' the group of five Politburo members which I served. Nor can I even imagine what many of the nine named members of this 'commission' might have had to do or say in these affairs—or why Ustinov, the Minister of

Defense and Politburo member, was not among them. Perhaps, unknown to me, Brezhnev first conceived of a commission of nine and then changed his mind and created the tighter and more efficient group of five in its place before the 'nine' ever met."

³ Suslov was occasionally represented by CC Secretary and International Department Chief Boris Ponomarev, but the others were never represented by subordinates. If any of them could not be present, there was no meeting.

⁴ The other three beside Kondrashev were Vice Admiral Leonid Konstantinovich Bekrenev, deputy head of the GRU, supporting Ustinov; Anatoly Ivanovich Blatov from the leadership of the Ministry of Foreign Affairs, supporting Gromyko; and Nikolay Konstantinovich Shishlin from the so-called "Department of the Central Committee," which oversaw relations with the ruling parties of the People's Democracies, supporting Suslov.

⁵ In early 1968, a supposed Western arms cache was "accidentally discovered" in northern Czechoslovakia and quickly recognized as a fraud designed to give "evidence" that the reformers were counterrevolutionaries supported by Western capitalist governments. As the head of KGB active measures at this time, Kondrashev stated with certainty that his "disinformation" service had nothing to do with the planting and he did not know to this day who did it—though they exploited the opportunity by spreading the story widely.

⁶ That room (*Bolshoi Zal Politburo*) was filled by a long table that could seat twenty-five or thirty people, with additional chairs lining the side walls. At the far end of the room was a large window overlooking the boulevard, but the five would sit at the other end, with Brezhnev at the end of the table. From the beginning Suslov—who always considered himself as *primus inter pares*—took the first seat at Brezhnev's right. For the others it was a matter of chance when they came in, though Ustinov usually took the place next to Suslov. During a few unusual sessions, guests were invited such as the Chief of the Armed Forces General Staff or a CC Secretary. Suslov and Ponomarev contributed almost nothing of substance to the discussions, contenting themselves with making petty changes in the wording or punctuation of a draft message. (For Ponomarev, said Kondrashev, "We felt something close to disgust.")

⁷ Shelest, as Party head in the Ukraine neighboring Czechoslovakia, tried again and again to play an important role, to increase his own stature in the Politburo, but neither he nor this letter was taken seriously by the pyatërka, Kondrashev said.

Eighteen: The Irony of Helsinki

[1] The origin of this name was described by the later head of the American delegation, Ambassador Max Kampelman: "The agreements were adopted as part of a package that was to be called, at the suggestion of some anonymous State Department officer, the 'Helsinki Final Act' although no one knew what that meant. It was not a legally binding treaty or executive agreement. It was not an act or a statute and was certainly not a 'final act,' there being no such thing under international law. . . . It stood by itself as a unique international agreement, presumably without teeth." (Max Kampelman, *Entering New Worlds* [New York: HarperCollins, 1991], pp. 217–19.)

[2] The cost of agreeing may not have seemed exorbitant to the Soviet leaders, thanks to Principle 6, "non-intervention in the internal affairs" of the signatory States. No doubt they thought they could ignore or violate with impunity Principle 7 as they had ignored earlier toothless international accords on human rights, like the 1966 United Nations' International Covenant on Civil and Political Rights and the 1948 Universal Declaration of Human Rights. Indeed they tried: The American chief delegate said of the Soviets as late as 1982, "The only work I know they are doing on the act is flagrantly to undermine it" (Kampelman, p. 263). In the event, they did not get away with it. Western delegations and international human-rights organizations publicly called them to task for specific violations, with names and dates.

[3] The negotiations were separated into three categories, referred to as "baskets." The first covered military-political principles while the second dealt with economic and scientific cooperation. In Moscow, different Politburo members oversaw these baskets, but the Third Basket (essentially, the human rights provisions) was overseen by Andropov. In Geneva, Foreign Ministry representative Yuri Dubinin formally directed Basket Three negotiations, but he was aware that Kondrashev was representing Andropov (and the Politburo, including Foreign Minister Andrey Gromyko); he chafed at Kondrashev's authority but could do nothing about it.

[4] See Chapters 8 and 16.

[5] A military delegate had a similar direct line to Politburo member (and Defense Minister) Dmitry Ustinov on military-political matters, dealt with under "Basket One."

[6] Andropov was already taking slow, measured steps to loosen Soviet controls, Kondrashev said. One he cited was Andropov's oft-vilified creation of the 5th Chief Directorate against "ideological sabotage" soon after taking command of the KGB in 1967. Although still treating dissidents cruelly, Andropov was, as Kondrashev saw him, moving toward reform by warning, exiling, even treating with psychiatric drugs, dealing with them as "other-thinkers" rather than as deadly "enemies of the people."

[7] Kampelman, pp. 238, 251.

[8] Together they arranged help for the families of Nathan Sharansky and the Pentecostal Christians who had taken refuge in the American Embassy in Moscow. President Ronald Reagan asked Kampleman to make Kondrashev aware of his personal interest—and together they arranged satisfactory solutions. (The Soviets permitted the refugees and their families to leave the country—for Israel, though none were Jews.) Kampelman, pp. 269–272.

[9] Kampelman, p. 269. In 1981, after weeks of impasse in Madrid, due largely to Soviet delegation chief Dubinin's opposition to monitoring compliance with the terms of the Final Act, Moscow removed Dubinin and replaced him with Deputy Foreign Minister Leonid Ilyichev, who was immediately more forthcoming. (Kampelman, pp. 243, 258) Had Dubinin continued as delegation chief, Kondrashev thought, the whole Madrid meeting (and perhaps the Helsinki process) would have collapsed. Yuri Andropov, alerted by Kondrashev, presumably caused this change.

Appendix

[1] Sergey's grandfather survived the revolution unharmed, Sergey thought because he had such good relations with the railway workers at his station. But he had never been in robust health even in childhood, and now he suffered from insecurity, the disruption of family ties, the emigration of relatives, and worries about his son and daughter-in-law, Sergey's parents. He died at the age of sixty-three, just a year after Sergey's birth.

[2] As long as his parents lived, Sergey learned only scraps of his family background. After the Soviet period, he was contacted by historian Georgy Vasili-yevich Rovensky who had been writing the history of the region around Friasino. He had learned about the founding and development of the textile enterprises

there and in the eastern districts of Moscow. He had dug out from the historical archives of Moscow Oblast more than a hundred files on the Kondrashev family, with details down to the numbers of workers employed in each of their many factories. Rovensky had also been drawing on the most reliable of Russian historical records, the church registrations of people who came for confession. Unlike other documents of recent Russian history that were altered or destroyed to suit the needs and whims of successive Communist leaders, these church texts, some ancient, were preserved intact through those early years when Bolsheviks were smashing churches and murdering priests. The cathedral priests had taken written note of the social and material status of their visitors, so these "confession books" bore witness to the gradual expansion of the Kondrashev family's textile manufacturing.

[3] See Chapter 11.

Index

INDEX

Bourbon (code name) 218
Brandt, Willy 110, 111
Braun, Werner von 184
Bremer, Herbert 284n1
Brezhnev, Leonid 111, 225–33, 292n2, 293n6
Britzke, Viktor V. 19
Bucar, Annabelle 42
Budkevich, G. L. 283n11
Bulganin, Nikolay 81–82, 94
Burch, Norwood (pseudonym) 281n22
Burdin, Vladimir P. 120
Burgess, Guy 72–73, 181–82

C

Cairncross, John 72
Chebrikov, V. M. 240
Chernyavsky, Vitaly 176
Chervonenko, S. V. 224–25
Chiang Kai-Shek 53
Chistyakov, Igor 155, 160–63, 282n6
Clausen, Max 162, 164, 282n1
Crabbe, Lionel 82–83
Curiel, Henri 88

D

De Gaulle, Charles 167
Demin, V. P. 240
Denktash, Rauf 183
Deryabin, Pyotr (Peter Deriabin) 148, 278ni, 278n2, 279n6
Deryabkin, Nikita 74, 77–79, 274n2, 274n4
Dirksen, Herbert von 157
Douglas, Gregory (pseudonym) 151, 281n22
Dozhdalev, Vasily A. 87, 89
Dubcek, Aleksander 224–33
Dubinin, Yuri 295n3, 296n9
Dushin, N. A. 240
Dzerzhinsky, Feliks 195

E

Eden, Anthony 80

Ehrenburg, Ilya 28, 33, 265
Eichmann, Adolf 144, 280n9
Emerson, Faye 27–28
Erdberg, Aleksandr (see Korotkov, Aleksandr M.)
Erlich, Henrykh 68
European Defense Community project 167–68

F

Fadeyev, Aleksandr A. 31
Fedora (code name) 291n5
Fedorchuk, V. V. 240
Fedotov, Pavel V. 131
Feklisov, Aleksandr S. 71
Felfe, Heinz 109
Filippov, Ivan F. 285n11
Fisher, Willy ("Rudolf Abel") 188
Fitin, Pavel 270n8
French Intelligence, KGB penetration of 167
Frolik, Josef 281n21
Furtseva, Yekaterina 154–55, 164, 282n4

G

Gandhi, Indira 184
Gee, Ethel 274n2
Gerö, Ernö 124
Globke, Hans 183
Goebbels, Joseph 113
Goleniewski, Michal 97–98, 148, 274n2, 280n14, 280n15
Golikov, Filipp I. 163
Golitsyn, Anatoly 3–4, 204–11, 284n3, 287n5 282n12
Gorbachev, Mikhail 65, 246, 250
Gorkov, KGB Colonel 131–32
Gorny, A. G. 288n8
Gorshkov, Nikolay M. 284n3
Gorsky, Anatoly 69, 71, 72, 86, 274n1
Graur, Andrey 131–32, 285n5
Gribanov, Oleg M. 196–212, 215–16, 287n5, 289n14

INDEX

INDEX